Throat Chakra 101: Truth, Voice, Self-Expression
Copyright © 2025 by Dr. Constance Santego.

Copy Editor & Interior Design: Constance Santego
Book Layout: ©2017 BookDesignTemplates.com

Ordering Information:
Quantity sales. Special discounts are available on quantity purchases by corporations, associations, and others. For details, contact the "Special Sales Department" at the address above.

Trade Paperback ISBN: 978-1-997907-00-8
Ebook ISBN 978-1-997907-01-5
Created and published In Canada. Printed and bound in the United States of America

First Edition
Published by Maximillian Enterprises
Kelowna, BC Canada
www.constancesantego.ca

Throat Chakra 101: Truth, Voice, Self-Expression

"The power to express, the courage to be authentic, the peace to simply be."

(Vol V)

Dr. Constance Santego

Maximillian Enterprises
Kelowna, BC

Dedication

To every soul who has ever silenced their truth.
May this book remind you that your voice is sacred, your words
are power, and your silence holds wisdom.

— Dr. Constance Santego

ALSO BY DR. CONSTANCE SANTEGO

NOVELS
Illegitimate Grace
Ashcroft Hollow

Okanagan Trilogy:
Beneath the Vineyards
Under the Okanagan Sun
Guardian of the Lake

The Nine Spiritual Gifts Series:
Journey of a Soul – (Vol 1 Michael)
Language of a Soul – (Vol 2 Gabriel)
Prophecy of a Soul – (Vol 3 Bath Kol)
Healing of a Soul – (Vol 4 Raphael)
Miracles of a Soul – (Vol 5 Hamied)
Knowledge of a Soul – (Vol 6 Raziel)
Wisdom of a Soul – (Vol 7 Uriel)
Faith of a Soul – (Vol 8 Pistis Sophia)

NONFICTION
The Intuitive Life, The Gift Of Prophecy, Third Edition
Fairy Tales, Dreams And Reality... Where Are You On Your Path? Second Edition
Your Persona... The Mask You Wear
Archangel Michael's Soul Retrieval Guide
Tesla And The Future Of Energy Medicine
Beyond Tesla: Advancing The Science Of Energy Healing
Tesla's Code: Mastering Energy, Frequency, And Creative Power
Beyond The Mind: Harnessing The Power Of Astral Projection For Creative Awakening
Bend, Don't Break: Finding Your Way Back To Abundance
Ring Therapy: A Guide To Healing And Balance
Ring Therapy Pocket Guide
Floraopathy™: The Art And Science Of Vibrational Healing With Essential Oils
Dear Older Me: A Memoir... Of Sorts
It's Just Like Poker: A Spiritual Guide To Playing The Cards Life Deals You
Signs And Meanings: What The Feet Reveal About Health, Stress, And The Body's Story
Auricions: Unlocking Subconscious Healing Through Quantum Medicine
Quick Fix Acupressure Method
Manifestation – The DREAM Method in 5 Steps
Confidence- Mastering the Dream Method

REIKI WISDOM, SERIES:
Angelic Lifestyle, a Vibrant Lifestyle
Angelic Lifestyle 42-Day Energy Cleanse
Reiki and the Power of The Joint Points: Unlocking Energy Pathways for
Healing (Vol I)
Reiki and Karmic Healing: Releasing Patterns From Past Lives (Vol II)
Reiki and the Five Elements (Vol III)
Secrets of a Healer, Magic Of Reiki
The Reiki Master's Manual

CHAKRA SERIES:
Heart Chakra 101: The Bridge
Root Chakra 101: Building Safety, Survival, Foundation
Sacral Chakra 101: Creativity, Pleasure, Emotions
Solar Plexus Chakra 101: Power, Confidence, Will
Throat Chakra 101: Truth, Voice, Self-Expression
Third Eye Chakra 10: Intuition, Vision, Insight
Crown Chakra 10: Spiritual Connection, Transcendence.

SECRETS OF A HEALER, SERIES:
Magic Of Aromatherapy (Vol I)
Magic Of Reflexology (Vol II)
Magic Of The Gifts (Vol III)
Magic Of Muscle Testing (Vol IV)
Magic Of Iridology (Vol V)
Magic Of Massage (Vol VI)
Magic Of Hypnotherapy (Vol VII)
Magic Of Reiki (Vol VIII)
Magic Of Advanced Aromatherapy (Vol IX)
Magic Of Esthetics (Vol X)
The Reiki Master's Manual (Vol XI)

ADULT COLORING JOURNALS
SERIES-ZEN COLORING:
Quantum Energy and Mindful Living Journal (Vol 1)
Reiki Energy Journal (Vol 2)
Nine Spiritual Gifts Journal (Vol 3)
I Forgive Journal (Vol 4)

FOR CHILDREN
I am Big Tonight. I Don't Need the Light
The Magic Elf Book: 25 Days of Surprises

COOKBOOK
My Favorite Recipes, with a Hint of Giggle

BUISNESS
How To Use ChatGPT For Authors: From Idea To Published Book
Scaling Beyond 6 Figures: Strategies For Health & Wellness Professionals
The Academypreneur's Playbook: Turn Knowledge Into A
Revenue-Generating School

HUMOR/GIFT BOOK
How Do You Like Your Eggs? Crack Into Your Personality, Yolk and All

Contents

Throat Chakra 101: Truth, Voice, Self-Expression

"The power to express, the courage to be authentic, the peace to simply be."

(Vol V)

Dr. Constance Santego

Preface

Introduction: Speaking the Truth of the Soul

Our journey through the chakras is both ascent and integration — a spiral of energy weaving heaven and earth through the human experience. We began at the Heart Chakra, the bridge of compassion and love, then rooted ourselves in the foundation of the Root Chakra, where safety and belonging took form. From that stability, we flowed into the creative waters of the Sacral Chakra, awakening feeling, sensuality, and the dance of duality. Then we ignited the fire of the Solar Plexus, discovering the radiance of personal power and the courage to act with purpose and integrity.

Now, that energy rises once more — upward to the **Throat Chakra (Vishuddha)**, the sacred center of truth and self-expression. Here, vibration becomes voice, and energy becomes sound. The throat is where inner reality meets outer reality — where what we know within seeks to take shape through the breath, word, and resonance of being.

Vishuddha means *"especially pure."* This purity refers not only to speech but to the alignment of truth through all layers of self — thought, emotion, and action. To speak from this chakra is to speak from clarity and authenticity, where communication becomes a creative act, shaping the world around us with intention and integrity.

Its element is **ether**, or **space** — the vastness that allows sound to travel and expression to exist. Ether is both invisible and essential, like truth itself. When Vishuddha is balanced, our voice flows freely, we listen deeply, and we express ourselves with confidence and compassion. When blocked, we may feel unheard, anxious about speaking, or silenced by fear of judgment. And when overactive, words may pour forth without discernment, scattering rather than connecting.

The Throat Chakra governs not only the physical organs of speech and hearing but also the **energetic act of creation through sound**. Every word carries frequency; every tone carries intention. The vibrations we send out ripple into the collective field, affecting others — and returning to us. In this way, voice becomes both instrument and mirror.

Just as the heart teaches us to love and the solar plexus to act, the throat teaches us to express truth. True communication is not simply about talking — it is the resonance of alignment between heart, mind, and spirit. When we speak our truth with love, we become conduits for the divine voice moving through us.

In this book, we will explore the wisdom and healing practices of the Throat Chakra — the power of sound, silence, and authentic expression. Through mantra, chanting, journaling, breathwork, and mindful listening, you will learn to dissolve the blocks that silence your spirit and awaken the voice of your higher self.

As our journey continues upward, remember: **your voice is not separate from creation itself.** Every breath, every word, every song carries the power to shape the unseen into being.
Your truth is vibration — and vibration is the language of the soul.

About the Chakra 101 Series

The *Chakra 101 Series* is a journey through the seven primary energy centers of the human body — a guided exploration of how spirit expresses itself through matter, and how healing unfolds layer by layer. Each book in this series blends ancient wisdom with modern energy practices, bridging spirituality, psychology, and embodiment to help readers rediscover balance and wholeness.

The series began with *Heart Chakra 101: The Bridge*, where love and compassion opened the way for inner transformation. From there, *Root Chakra 101: Building Safety, Survival, Foundation* grounded that love into the physical world, teaching stability, trust, and the sacredness of belonging. *Sacral Chakra 101: Creativity, Pleasure, Emotions* then carried the journey forward — from stability to movement, from survival to creation, from love as an ideal to love as an experience felt through the body.

Next, *Solar Plexus Chakra 101: Power, Confidence, Will* ignited the inner fire — the energy of purpose, determination, and self-mastery. It taught how to transform fear into courage, uncertainty into action, and self-doubt into radiant confidence. Through this center, we learned what it means to stand in our power and direct our lives with intention and grace.

Now, *Throat Chakra 101: Expression, Authenticity, Truth* opens the gateway between the inner and outer worlds — where energy becomes vibration and truth finds its voice. It is the realm of communication, sound, and resonance, where we learn that to speak from the heart is to heal, to listen is to understand, and to express is to create. When balanced, the Throat Chakra becomes the conduit through which our higher wisdom takes form, shaping reality through the purity of sound and the honesty of expression.

Each book in this series builds upon the last, guiding you upward through the chakra system:

1. **Heart Chakra 101** – *The Bridge of Love and Compassion*
2. **Root Chakra 101** – *Building Safety, Survival, Foundation*
3. **Sacral Chakra 101** – *Creativity, Pleasure, Emotions*
4. **Solar Plexus Chakra 101** – *Power, Confidence, and Will*
5. **Throat Chakra 101** – *Expression, Authenticity, and Truth*
6. **Third Eye Chakra 101** – *Intuition, Vision, and Clarity*
7. **Crown Chakra 101** – *Spirit, Consciousness, and Unity*

While each volume stands on its own, together they form a complete map — a journey from earth to sky, from the physical to the divine. This path through the chakras mirrors the process of awakening itself: beginning with love, rooting into safety, awakening creative flow, discovering purpose, speaking truth, seeing clearly, and ultimately remembering our oneness with all that is.

Whether you are a student of energy medicine, a healer, or a seeker of self-understanding, the *Chakra 101 Series* is designed to guide you home — to your body, your energy, and your divine essence.

Chapter 1 – The Resonance of Truth

The Role of the Throat Chakra in the Chakra System

Every journey of energy moves in waves — expansion and release, silence and sound. After grounding in the Root, flowing through the Sacral, and igniting purpose in the Solar Plexus, energy now rises into the **Throat Chakra (Vishuddha)** — the sacred channel where thought becomes vibration, and vibration becomes creation.

Though our series began at the Heart, where love bridges heaven and earth, it is here, in the Throat, that love takes voice. The truths cultivated in the lower centers — safety, emotion, will — are now ready to be expressed into the world. The Throat Chakra is the meeting point between the inner and outer realms, where what you believe and feel becomes visible through word, sound, and presence.

If the Root Chakra whispers, *"You are safe; you belong,"* the Sacral responds, *"You may feel; you may create,"* and the Solar Plexus declares, *"You may act; you may become,"* then the Throat Chakra sings, *"Now you may speak; now you may express."*

Here, thought finds tone and emotion finds resonance. Vishuddha governs communication, truth, and authentic expression — the sacred right to speak, listen, and be heard. It invites us to align what we say with what we know, what we feel, and what we do. This is the energy of coherence — when inner truth and outer expression vibrate as one harmonious frequency.

Vishuddha's element is **ether**, or **space** — the expansive field through which all sound travels. Its color is **sky blue**, the hue of openness and infinite possibility. Its symbol, the **sixteen-petaled lotus**, encloses a downward-pointing triangle within a circle, signifying the descent of spiritual truth into the human voice. This is the portal of resonance — where vibration purifies, harmonizes, and reveals the truth of who we are.

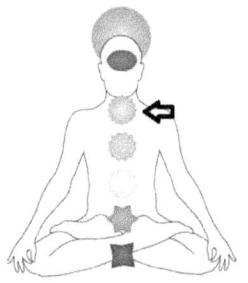

In the chakra system, Vishuddha builds directly upon Manipura. Without the confidence and willpower of the Solar Plexus, the voice cannot rise in strength or conviction. Likewise, without the grounding and emotional awareness of the lower chakras, our words lack authenticity or compassion. But when energy flows freely from root to heart, the Throat becomes a clear channel — pure, powerful, and creative.

Think of Vishuddha as the **bridge of vibration**. The Root provides the foundation, the Sacral adds movement, the Solar Plexus gives direction, and the Throat releases that energy as expression. It is the alchemy of sound — where silence turns to tone, and tone becomes truth. Every word, every song, every sigh is a pulse of creation rippling through the ether.

When Vishuddha is balanced, our voice flows naturally, carrying clarity and compassion. We listen as deeply as we speak, honoring both sound and silence. Our words become healing instruments, transmitting love and understanding. But when this chakra is blocked, we may fear judgment, struggle to express feelings, or silence ourselves to maintain peace. When overactive, speech can turn sharp or excessive, losing sensitivity and depth.

In the great ascent of the chakra system, the Throat represents **the will to express** — the transition from power to presence. It is where inner awareness begins to shape the outer world, and communication becomes creation. Vishuddha teaches that to speak truth is to free oneself; to listen deeply is to hear the divine within all things.

Balanced, the Throat Chakra brings authenticity, confidence, and clarity. Imbalanced, it may leave us voiceless, misunderstood, or disconnected. In its highest expression, it becomes the voice of the soul — resonant, healing, and true.

The Throat Chakra invites you to reclaim your right to speak, to sing, to express, and to be heard. For when your words align with your essence, your voice becomes more than sound — it becomes a vibration of truth that transforms both self and world.

TRADITIONAL SANSKRIT NAMES

Vishuddha (विशुद्ध) – The most common Sanskrit name for the Throat Chakra, meaning "especially pure" or "purest." The term derives from *vi* (especially) and *shuddha* (pure), signifying purification, clarity, and refinement. Vishuddha represents the energetic center where all vibrations are cleansed and transformed into truth. It is the sacred space of sound and resonance — where expression becomes the vehicle for spiritual awakening.

In ancient yogic texts, Vishuddha is described as a radiant lotus with sixteen petals, the color of a clear blue sky, shimmering with luminosity and depth. This chakra governs the purification of both inner and outer communication — transforming unspoken emotions, hidden thoughts, and unexpressed truths into higher vibration and understanding.

Vishuddha is associated with the **element of ether (ākāśa)**, the subtlest of all elements, representing space, sound, and infinite possibility. Ether is the container that allows all other elements to move, exist, and express. Through this expansive element, sound vibrations travel — making Vishuddha the energetic bridge between the physical and spiritual worlds.

This chakra is also regarded as the center of **nāda**, the cosmic sound current, symbolizing the divine frequency from which all creation arises. When Vishuddha is open and balanced, speech becomes sacred; silence becomes wisdom; and truth flows effortlessly from the soul through the voice. It purifies not by force, but by resonance — harmonizing all levels of being.

COMMON ENGLISH NAMES

- **Throat Chakra** – The most widely recognized English name, referring to its location at the throat and its connection to voice, sound, and self-expression. It is the energetic channel through which inner truth takes form as vibration and communication.
- **Center of Communication** – Highlights Vishuddha's role in governing not only verbal speech but all forms of expression — written, artistic, emotional, and energetic. It reminds us that every word, gesture, and tone carries frequency and influence.
- **Voice of Truth** – Symbolizes this chakra's power to align thought, emotion, and action with authenticity. It is where honesty transcends fear, and communication becomes an act of integrity and healing.
- **Gateway of Sound** – Reflects Vishuddha's function as the meeting point between vibration and consciousness. It is the threshold through which the spiritual realm

communicates with the physical, allowing divine inspiration to become audible, visible, and real.

- **Purification Center** – A poetic translation of *Vishuddha*, reminding us that expression is a form of cleansing. When we speak truthfully, sing, chant, or release unspoken emotion, we purify the subtle body and restore resonance between inner and outer worlds.

ELEMENTAL & SYMBOLIC ASSOCIATIONS

Ether Chakra – Associated with the element of **ether (ākāśa)**, representing space, sound, and the boundless field through which all vibrations move. Ether is the most subtle of the five elements, embodying openness, expansion, and connection. It is the bridge between the physical and spiritual realms — the silent medium that carries the resonance of truth. Through this element, the Throat Chakra governs expression, vibration, and the purification of energy through sound.

- **Center of Sound** – Linked to the principle of **nāda**, or the cosmic sound current, from which all creation arises. Just as every word or tone creates ripples in the air, the universe itself is said to have been born from primordial sound — the "Om." Vishuddha is the channel through which this creative vibration manifests, turning the invisible into the audible, the inner into the outer. It reminds us that speech is a sacred power — capable of healing, revealing, and transforming.
- **Blue Chakra** – Identified by its radiant **sky-blue hue**, symbolizing clarity, serenity, and spacious awareness. Blue reflects calm communication, inner peace, and the infinite expanse of truth. It is the color of openness — like a clear sky after a storm — inviting transparency and honest expression without fear or distortion.
- **Lotus of Sixteen Petals** – Represented by a **sixteen-petaled lotus** enclosing a **downward-pointing triangle within a circle**, symbolizing the descent of divine truth

into human expression. Each petal corresponds to one of the **sixteen Sanskrit vowels**, the purest sounds of speech, which vibrate freely without obstruction. Together, they signify the fluidity and resonance of clear communication — unbound, flowing, and luminous.

CULTURAL / ESOTERIC NAMES

- **The Purification Center** – Derived from the Sanskrit *Vishuddha*, meaning "especially pure," this title reflects the chakra's role as the energetic center of cleansing and refinement. It is where emotion, thought, and vibration are purified through expression, transforming lower frequencies into harmony and truth.
- **Voice of the Soul** – In mystical and esoteric traditions, the Throat Chakra is often viewed as the gateway through which the soul speaks into the world. It is the channel of authentic communication — where divine wisdom is translated into human language, and one's inner essence finds resonance in sound.
- **Gateway of Sound** – Recognized in yogic and Tantric systems as the center of *nāda*, or the cosmic sound current. This chakra represents the threshold between the subtle and material realms, where vibration gives birth to form. It is through this gateway that the creative Word (*Om*) continues to sustain all existence.
- **Blue Lotus of Expression** – A poetic name referencing Vishuddha's sixteen-petaled lotus and sky-blue radiance. The blue lotus symbolizes purity emerging through openness, reminding us that clarity of voice and thought arises from stillness, honesty, and inner alignment.
- **Temple of Truth** – In both Eastern mysticism and Western esoteric teachings, the throat is regarded as the sacred temple of *Satya*, the universal principle of truth. To speak truth is to honor the divine within, and to withhold or distort truth is to cloud the light of

consciousness. This center teaches that truth is not only spoken — it is lived through integrity.

- **Fifth Gate of Ascension** – Within Hermetic and alchemical systems, the Throat Chakra is known as the fifth gate — the portal through which the alchemist transforms knowledge into wisdom and energy into sound. It marks the passage from individual expression to divine communication, where words become carriers of light and vibration becomes revelation.

METAPHORICAL NAMES

- **The Bridge of Voice** – Symbolizing the connection between the heart and the mind, the Throat Chakra is the bridge through which emotion becomes understanding and thought becomes sound. It is the sacred passage where truth travels outward and inspiration flows inward, linking the visible and invisible worlds through vibration.
- **The River of Expression** – Representing the continuous current of communication that flows through every being. Like a river, expression must remain open and fluid; when dammed by fear or self-doubt, it stagnates, but when allowed to move freely, it nourishes creativity, clarity, and connection.
- **The Chamber of Echoes** – A metaphor for inner reflection and resonance. Within this chamber, we hear not only the words we speak but the vibrations they create. It teaches that every sound carries consequence, every thought leaves an echo, and every silence has meaning.
- **The Blue Horizon** – Evoking the infinite openness of the sky, this name reminds us that truth is vast, spacious, and liberating. Just as the horizon merges earth and heavens, the Throat Chakra unites the human voice with divine frequency — expanding awareness beyond limitation.

- **The Lyre of Truth** – Portraying the Throat Chakra as an instrument of harmony. When tuned to authenticity, it produces a clear, resonant sound that uplifts all who hear it. But when out of tune — distorted by fear or repression — it creates dissonance within the self. This chakra teaches us to keep our instrument pure, to let our voice be a melody of truth.
- **The Voice of Creation** – Reflecting the divine principle that through sound, worlds are formed. This chakra is the womb of vibration, where ideas are given breath and imagination becomes real. It is the reminder that your words are spells, your tone is energy, and your voice is sacred power made audible.

VISHUDDHA: THE VOICE OF TRUTH

The Sanskrit name for the Throat Chakra is **Vishuddha**, a word steeped in sacred symbolism. *Vi* means "especially," and *shuddha* means "pure." Together they form "the especially pure" or "the purifier" — the energy center through which truth is refined, vibration is cleansed, and consciousness becomes sound.

If the Solar Plexus Chakra teaches us to act, **Vishuddha** teaches us to express. It is the inner sanctuary where thought becomes vibration and emotion becomes resonance. Here, the energy that once burned as fire is carried upward into ether — expanded, liberated, and given voice.

From birth, our survival depends not only on strength and emotion but on our ability to communicate — to cry out, to connect, to be heard. As we mature, that instinct evolves into the deeper human need for authentic expression. The grounding of Muladhara roots us, the flow of Svadhisthana allows us to feel, the fire of Manipura gives us will, and Vishuddha transforms that will into word. It is where we speak our truth and vibrate with the harmony of who we are.

Vishuddha represents the **energetic intelligence of resonance**. It governs not only the voice and vocal cords but the subtler power of vibration itself — how we speak, listen, and emit frequency into the world. It teaches us that every sound carries energy, and that expression is a form of creation. Through this chakra, silence becomes wisdom, and speech becomes prayer.

When Vishuddha is balanced, our communication flows freely and authentically. We express ideas with confidence and compassion. Our voice is steady, our listening deep, and our presence peaceful. We no longer speak to convince or control but to connect and clarify. Our words carry the vibration of integrity — pure, grounded, and kind.

When imbalanced, this center may close or overextend. Too little energy, and we become silent, suppressed, or fearful of judgment. Our truth remains trapped in the throat, unable to emerge. Too much energy, and our words may spill without awareness — sharp, excessive, or dominating. In both extremes, we lose harmony between heart and voice, and truth becomes distorted.

Vishuddha is the **sky of the subtle body** — vast, open, and luminous. It draws strength from the fire below and channels clarity to the mind above. Without this open expanse, emotion has no outlet, and inspiration has no sound. But when Vishuddha vibrates in balance, it becomes the bridge between the inner and outer worlds — allowing the soul to speak and spirit to be heard.

Just as the open sky carries the songs of birds and the whisper of the wind, the Throat Chakra carries the vibrations of your being. It transforms confusion into clarity, repression into freedom, and silence into song. It reminds us that truth is not merely spoken — it is lived through the resonance of authenticity.

It is here, in the luminous ether of **Vishuddha**, that your journey into truth, voice, and self-expression begins.

What Is Sanskrit and Why Does It Matter for Chakras?

The language most closely intertwined with the chakras is **Sanskrit**, the ancient sacred language of India. Sanskrit is often called *the language of vibration* — each sound is more than a word; it is a precise energetic frequency. Its tones are designed to awaken resonance within the subtle body, harmonizing the physical, emotional, and spiritual layers of our being.

For the **Throat Chakra**, the Sanskrit name is **Vishuddha**. *Vi* means "especially," and *shuddha* means "pure." Together, they form *"the especially pure"* — a title that reflects this chakra's essence as the purifier of vibration and the gateway of truth. Vishuddha is the place where energy becomes sound, where the unseen transforms into expression, and where communication aligns with the soul's integrity.

Unlike ordinary language, Sanskrit words are not mere labels but living **vibrational codes**. Each syllable carries the energy of the concept it represents. To speak *Vishuddha* is to invoke purity, clarity, and resonance. The very sound vibrates through the throat and etheric field, clearing distortion and awakening authenticity.

Each chakra also has a **bīja mantra**, or *seed sound*, that activates its energy through vibration. For Vishuddha, that sound is **HAM** (pronounced "hum"). When softly chanted, HAM creates a gentle, humming resonance that can be felt throughout the throat, neck, and even the chest. This vibration clears energetic congestion, soothes tension, and balances communication. It encourages you to speak truthfully, listen deeply, and align your words with wisdom.

Sanskrit is more than sound — it is **consciousness made audible**. The letters of its alphabet correspond to subtle aspects of the human energy field, and in traditional chakra imagery, each lotus petal bears a Sanskrit syllable. The sixteen petals of Vishuddha are inscribed with sixteen *svaras* — the pure vowel sounds of the Sanskrit language. These vowels represent unbound resonance — open, flowing, and unobstructed — mirroring the Throat Chakra's purpose: to allow energy to move freely through vibration and space.

Why does this matter today? Because sound shapes energy, and energy shapes reality. When we speak, sing, or chant in Sanskrit, we are tuning into patterns of resonance that have harmonized body, mind, and spirit for thousands of years. To engage with the language of the chakras is to awaken within yourself a universal rhythm — a remembrance of harmony that transcends culture, time, and form.

When you chant **HAM**, you are not simply making a sound. You are affirming: **I express my truth. I listen with love. My voice is clear and aligned.**

Chanting this mantra awakens the **etheric vibration** that bridges heart and mind. It dissolves fear of judgment, heals patterns of silence or overexpression, and restores the natural flow of communication. HAM purifies the channel of voice, transforming distortion into resonance and confusion into clarity. It reminds you that your words carry power — that every sound you speak creates ripples in the field of existence.

In the traditional mandala of Vishuddha, sixteen Sanskrit syllables radiate from the center of the lotus like luminous waves of sound. They represent the full spectrum of vocal expression — from whisper to song, from silence to prayer.

Each syllable symbolizes an aspect of consciousness in motion, revealing that every vibration is part of one cosmic song.

Why does this matter today? Because when you give sound to your truth, you participate in creation itself. Sanskrit offers more than spiritual vocabulary — it provides a **vibrational pathway** back to wholeness.

When you chant **HAM**, you are not merely speaking an ancient word; you are **becoming** it.
You are declaring: **I speak. I resonate. I am the voice of truth.**

The Throat Chakra and Maslow's Hierarchy of Needs

In the mid-20th century, psychologist **Abraham Maslow** introduced his *Hierarchy of Needs*, a model outlining the progressive stages of human motivation and fulfillment. At its base lie physiological and safety needs — food, water, shelter, and security. Once these are met, human energy naturally ascends toward belonging, esteem, and ultimately self-actualization — the realization of one's fullest potential.

This psychological model mirrors the **chakra system** with remarkable precision. Long before modern psychology, yogic philosophy recognized that consciousness evolves through layered stages of development. Each chakra represents a dimension of human need — physical, emotional, mental, and spiritual — each one building upon the last. When a lower level is balanced, energy rises to awaken the next.

- **Root Chakra ↔ Physiological & Safety Needs**
  The Root Chakra, Muladhara, governs survival and stability. It mirrors Maslow's foundational needs — the

assurance of safety, security, and physical grounding that sustains all other growth.

- **Sacral Chakra ↔ Belonging, Intimacy & Emotional Flow**
  With stability established, energy rises to the Sacral Chakra, Svadhisthana, the realm of emotion, pleasure, and creativity. This reflects Maslow's need for connection — to love, to be loved, and to belong.
- **Solar Plexus Chakra ↔ Esteem, Confidence & Personal Power**
  Once belonging is secured, Manipura awakens — the center of self-esteem and personal autonomy. It represents Maslow's fourth level, the need for achievement, self-respect, and the confidence to act with purpose.
- **Heart Chakra ↔ Love & Compassion**
  When self-worth is integrated, the heart opens to unconditional love. Here, Maslow's hierarchy transitions from personal fulfillment to transpersonal awareness — from seeking love to *being* love.
- **Throat Chakra ↔ Authentic Expression & Truth**
  With the foundation of love and self-trust established, the natural next step is *expression*. The Throat Chakra, Vishuddha, corresponds to Maslow's movement toward **self-actualization** — the stage where authenticity and creativity emerge as living expressions of the true self. Vishuddha governs the human need to be heard, understood, and witnessed — not through performance, but through truth. It represents the integration of inner awareness with outer communication: the freedom to express what one genuinely thinks, feels, and believes.

Just as Maslow described self-actualized individuals as spontaneous, honest, and creatively expressive, the yogic system teaches that Vishuddha is the energetic portal where individuality and universality harmonize. To express truth is to embody alignment; to speak with authenticity is to live one's higher purpose through vibration.

- **Third Eye Chakra ↔ Vision & Intuition**
  When expression flows freely, perception deepens. The Third Eye, Ajna, refines awareness beyond the ego, opening intuitive insight and inner wisdom.
- **Crown Chakra ↔ Self-Realization & Transcendence**
  At the highest stage of both systems lies union — the realization of divine consciousness and the oneness of all existence.

In this way, Maslow's hierarchy and the chakra system reveal two perspectives of the same human journey: the evolution from survival to self-realization. Maslow mapped this ascent in psychological terms, while yoga expressed it through energy and vibration.

The **Throat Chakra** marks a pivotal threshold in this ascent — the passage from internal awareness to external creation, from knowing oneself to expressing that knowing. It is where authenticity becomes audible and individuality merges with the universal song of life.

When we cultivate Vishuddha, we strengthen the bridge between thought and sound, between the unseen world of feeling and the spoken world of form. Both psychology and spirituality affirm:

True freedom arises not just from thinking or feeling, but from expressing — clearly, honestly, and with love.

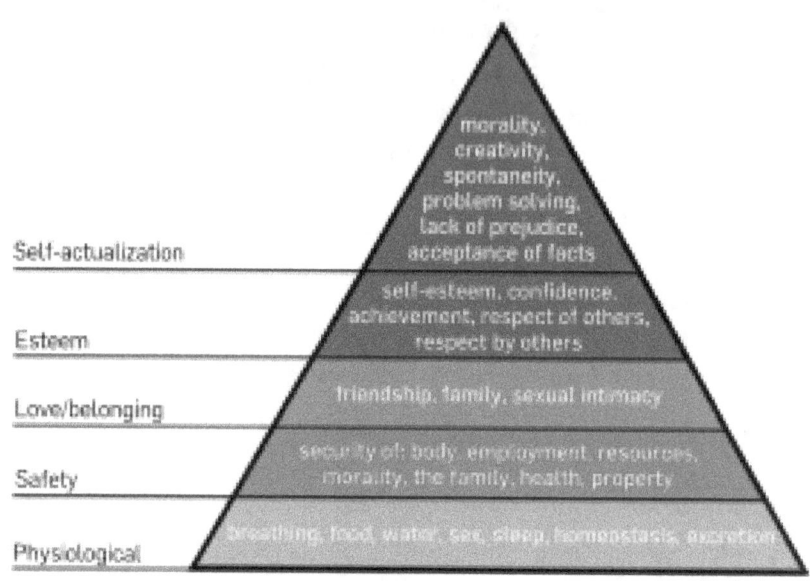

Mazlow's Hierarchy of Needs

Throat Chakra ↔ Authentic Expression & Truth

The **Throat Chakra (Vishuddha)** is the fifth energy center in the chakra system, corresponding to the next stage of human evolution after self-confidence and empowerment. Once personal identity and will are established through the Solar Plexus Chakra, the spirit naturally seeks **authentic expression** — the freedom to speak, create, and live in alignment with one's inner truth.

Just as esteem forms the bridge to self-actualization in Maslow's Hierarchy of Needs, Vishuddha forms the energetic bridge between the personal and the universal. Without open communication and self-expression, the higher centers of intuition and transcendence remain silent.

AUTHENTIC EXPRESSION: THE HUMAN DESIRE TO BE HEARD AND UNDERSTOOD

At its core, Vishuddha governs the **voice of the soul** — our ability to express thoughts, emotions, and insights in alignment with truth. It teaches that confidence alone is not enough; we must also share that confidence with integrity and clarity.

• **Honest Communication:** True expression begins with honesty. When Vishuddha is balanced, words flow with sincerity — not to impress, but to connect. We speak from awareness rather than reaction, and our communication uplifts rather than divides.

• **Active Listening:** Authentic expression also includes receptivity. This chakra teaches that listening is an act of love — a sacred space in which understanding is born. Listening deeply refines speech and transforms communication into communion.

• **Self-Expression:** Vishuddha is the creative bridge between thought and manifestation. Here we translate ideas into form — through speaking, writing, art, song, or silence. It is where the inner world meets the outer one through vibration.

• **Integrity of Speech:** Every word carries energy. This chakra reminds us that language can heal or harm, empower or diminish. Speaking truthfully and kindly aligns our vibration with higher consciousness.

TRUTH: THE RESONANCE OF INNER CLARITY

Beyond the need for recognition, the Throat Chakra represents the **freedom to live and speak one's truth**. It is where the energy of will (Manipura) ascends into vibration — transforming inner knowing into outer resonance.

> • **Authenticity:** Vishuddha encourages us to live without masks. When balanced, we no longer suppress our voice out of fear of judgment. We express ourselves clearly, confidently, and compassionately — allowing others to see who we truly are.

> • **Courage to Speak:** This chakra empowers the voice of truth, even when it trembles. To speak one's truth is an act of courage and faith — trusting that honesty brings liberation rather than rejection.

> • **Creative Resonance:** Vishuddha is the seat of sound and song. When energy flows freely here, inspiration becomes expression — art, writing, teaching, or communication that carries the vibration of soul.

> • **Alignment of Word and Action:** Just as integrity strengthens Manipura, it purifies Vishuddha. Speaking what we live and living what we speak harmonizes the inner and outer worlds, turning communication into sacred expression.

When Vishuddha is balanced, we no longer speak for approval but for **truth**. Our voice becomes a tool of creation, carrying the vibration of compassion, wisdom, and authenticity. When blocked, we may silence ourselves to keep the peace or speak excessively to be heard. Both are imbalances of resonance.

Ultimately, the Throat Chakra represents **the freedom to express the soul's harmony**.

When we speak from the heart and listen from stillness, our words become music — the vibration of truth flowing through the infinite ether of being.

AUTHENTIC POWER: THE ENERGY OF EXPRESSION

Vishuddha's element is **ether**, symbolizing expansion and vibration. It governs both the physical voice and the subtle resonance of truth that moves through every word, gesture, and intention. When balanced, it allows us to express life with clarity, harmony, and purpose.

- **Boundaries in Communication:** Authentic power includes the ability to speak truthfully without aggression and to remain silent without suppression. It is knowing when to express and when to listen — allowing words to flow from wisdom rather than reaction. Healthy communication honors both the self and the other.
- **Influence Through Resonance:** A balanced Throat Chakra radiates authenticity that naturally inspires trust. Just as clear sound travels farther, clear truth reaches deeper. True influence does not come from volume or persuasion but from the steady vibration of integrity.
- **Responsibility of Voice:** With expression comes accountability. Vishuddha teaches that words are energy in motion — each carrying the potential to heal or to harm. To speak consciously is to recognize that the voice is sacred power, shaping reality through vibration.
- **Transformation Through Sound:** This chakra refines inner experience into outer expression. When emotions, insights, and truths are voiced with awareness, they lose their heaviness and transform into wisdom. Speaking truth becomes a path of purification — where silence turns to song and resistance turns to resonance.

When Vishuddha is balanced, your words align with your essence. You no longer speak from ego or fear, but from a place of clear inner knowing. Authentic power is not about speaking louder — it is about speaking **truer**, resonating with the frequency of your soul.

WHY THIS MATTERS FOR ENERGY FLOW

Just as Maslow's hierarchy reveals that suppressed self-expression limits self-actualization, the chakra system teaches that blocked **Throat Chakra** energy disrupts the entire upward flow of consciousness. When **Vishuddha** is constricted or overactive, the communication channel between heart and mind becomes clouded, preventing truth from flowing freely through the system.

If Vishuddha is weak or unstable:
• **The Heart Chakra (Anahata)** may struggle to share love openly, for love unspoken can turn to longing or resentment. The voice of the heart must move through the throat to become compassion in action.
• **The Third Eye Chakra (Ajna)** may find its vision blurred, as intuition requires clear interpretation and expression. Inner wisdom, if never articulated, remains unrealized potential.
• **The Crown Chakra (Sahasrara)** may waver in its connection to the divine, for spiritual insight flows most purely through vessels of truth. Silence born from fear blocks revelation, while silence born from presence invites it.

When Vishuddha is balanced, the entire chakra system resonates in harmony. Energy flows upward with clarity and coherence, guided by the voice of truth. A pure Throat Chakra affirms: **"I speak with integrity. I listen with awareness. I express the truth of my being."**

With this alignment, communication becomes creation. Words carry light, silence holds peace, and expression becomes an act of spiritual service. The clear resonance of Vishuddha transforms vibration into revelation — turning sound into wisdom and the voice into the bridge between human and divine.

Chapter 2 – Foundations of Vishuddha

Throat Chakra Basics: A Gentle Recap

If you are new to chakra study, the **Throat Chakra**, or **Vishuddha**, is the fifth of the seven main chakras. It is located at the throat, extending through the neck, jaw, mouth, tongue, and shoulders, and energetically governs the thyroid and parathyroid glands. Vishuddha acts as a bridge between the heart's feeling and the mind's knowing — transforming inner truth into outer expression.

Where the Heart Chakra opens us to love and compassion, the Throat Chakra invites us to **communicate that love** — to give voice to what the heart feels and the soul knows. It is the center of communication, authenticity, and creative resonance, guiding how we speak, listen, and express ourselves in alignment with truth.

The energy here is expansive and subtle, like the open sky or the vibration of a song carried on the wind. Vishuddha governs our ability to express who we are — to let thought flow into word, emotion into tone, and inspiration into creation. When clear, it harmonizes the entire energy field, allowing life to move through us with ease and grace. When blocked, energy becomes trapped — truth remains unspoken, creativity is stifled, and the voice of the soul grows faint.

KEY QUALITIES OF VISHUDDHA

• **Element:** Ether (Ākāśa) — spacious, resonant, and expansive; the element through which sound travels.
• **Color:** Sky blue — symbolizing clarity, peace, and open expression.
• **Symbol:** A sixteen-petaled lotus enclosing a downward-pointing triangle within a circle, representing the descent of divine truth into human expression.
• **Sound (Bīja Mantra): HAM** — the seed syllable that vibrates through the throat, clearing the channel for truth, sound, and spiritual resonance.
• **Location in the Body:** Throat, neck, jaw, mouth, tongue, and shoulders.
• **Organs and Systems:** Thyroid, parathyroid, vocal cords, respiratory tract, and auditory system — all processes related to communication, metabolism, and vibrational balance.
• **Core Themes:** Expression, authenticity, communication, truth, creativity, listening, purification, and resonance.

THE VOICE OF AUTHENTICITY

When Vishuddha is balanced, your communication is clear, compassionate, and confident. You express your needs, ideas, and emotions with grace and integrity. Your words carry truth without force, and your silence holds peace. You feel comfortable being seen and heard, and you listen to others with genuine presence.

When it is **blocked or weak**, you may struggle to express yourself or feel unheard. Fear of judgment, shyness, or a tendency to "swallow your truth" can cause energetic congestion in the throat or even physical tension in the neck and shoulders. You may experience difficulty speaking up, creative blocks, or a sense that your voice has lost its resonance.

When it is **overactive**, the energy may manifest as excessive talking, criticism, gossip, or overpowering communication. The voice becomes reactive rather than responsive, and truth is spoken without compassion or awareness of impact.

BALANCING THE VOICE WITHIN

Vishuddha reminds us that **authentic communication is not just about speaking** — it is about listening, receiving, and aligning words with the heart's truth. True expression arises from stillness, where intention and vibration merge.

When we clear and balance the Throat Chakra, we restore the natural flow of energy between the heart and the mind. Love gains voice, wisdom gains resonance, and the soul gains freedom to express its essence.

From this center of communication, energy rises effortlessly into the **Third Eye Chakra**, where truth transforms into vision and sound becomes light.

The Throat Chakra is your invitation to express your truth with purity and grace — to speak with love, listen with awareness, and let your words become a vessel for healing and harmony.

Cross-Cultural Perspectives on the Throat Chakra

The concept of **voice, truth, and sacred sound** is not confined to yoga or Sanskrit philosophy. Across time and cultures, humanity has recognized the profound power of **vibration** — the creative force that shapes reality, bridges spirit and matter, and expresses the soul's essence through sound. Though symbols and languages differ, the essence of **Vishuddha** is universal: without sound, there can be no communication, no creation, and no connection between inner and outer worlds.

YOGIC TRADITION

In the yogic chakra system, **Vishuddha** is the fifth chakra — the center of communication, resonance, and purity. Its name means *"especially pure,"* representing the refinement of energy through sound and truth. Symbolized by the sixteen-petaled lotus and the downward-pointing triangle within a circle, it embodies the element of **ether (ākāśa)** — the vast space through which vibration travels.

Ancient yogic texts such as the *Shat-Chakra-Nirupana* describe Vishuddha as the **gateway of sound**, glowing like a pure sky. Here, the sacred vibration *HAM* governs expression, purification, and spiritual resonance. When awakened, Vishuddha allows one to speak from the higher mind and listen from the heart. It purifies not only speech but thought, serving as the bridge between emotion and wisdom, between the mortal and the divine.

SHAMANIC TRADITIONS

In many shamanic and animistic cultures, **sound** is regarded as the thread connecting the physical and spiritual realms. The voice of the shaman — through **chanting, drumming, toning, or whistling** — carries the vibration of intention into the unseen world. Sound is used to summon spirit allies, release stagnant energy, and restore harmony.

Just as Vishuddha represents the purification of vibration, shamanic healing employs **sacred song** as medicine. Every drumbeat, breath, or chant is a declaration of truth — a reminder that words themselves are living frequencies. When one's inner song fades, illness or disconnection may follow. Through ritual and resonance, the lost voice is retrieved, and the individual's vibration is restored to harmony with the greater web of life.

INDIGENOUS PERSPECTIVES

Across Indigenous traditions worldwide, **sound and voice** are revered as sacred instruments of creation. Words are considered powerful — prayers that carry intention and weave reality. The spoken word is treated with reverence, often accompanied by ritual silence or song to maintain balance and respect.

In many First Nations teachings, the **Voice of the Heart** is seen as the expression of truth and integrity. To "speak from the heart" means to communicate with respect, honesty, and purpose. The drum — often called *the heartbeat of Mother Earth* — echoes Vishuddha's teaching that sound unites the physical and spiritual worlds. Through song, storytelling, and ceremony, Indigenous wisdom keeps alive the understanding that sound is sacred and that every voice contributes to the harmony of creation.

SOUND AND SKY DEITIES

Across global mythologies, deities associated with **sound, song, and the heavens** embody the spirit of Vishuddha:

• **In Hinduism**, **Saraswati**, goddess of wisdom, speech, and music, flows through the river of sound known as *nāda*, the vibration from which all creation emerges.
• **In ancient Egypt**, **Thoth**, the god of words and wisdom, was said to have spoken the world into being, mirroring the divine act of sound shaping form.
• **In Greek mythology**, **Hermes**, the messenger of the gods, represents communication and eloquence — the bridge between divine knowledge and human understanding.
• **In many Indigenous and shamanic cosmologies**, the **Sky Spirit** or **Thunder Being** embodies the voice of nature itself —

the booming resonance that commands respect, awakens awareness, and restores balance.

Across these traditions, the **voice and vibration** represent the creative breath of the universe — the divine sound that animates all life. Just as Vishuddha governs the flow of energy between heart and mind, these myths remind us that communication is sacred — that words are not merely spoken but *sent forth as living currents of energy*.

Across cultures, Vishuddha's essence remains the same: **truth expressed through sound**. Whether through mantra, song, prayer, or silence, the Throat Chakra invites every soul to participate in the eternal act of creation — to speak, to sing, and to resonate with the harmony of the cosmos.

SOUND-BASED SPIRITUALITY

Sound-based spiritual traditions — from the Vedic chanting of mantras to Gregorian hymns, from the shaman's drumbeat to the Indigenous flute, from Buddhist prayer wheels to Sufi zikr — all express reverence for **the creative power of vibration**. To sit in sound is to commune with the rhythm of existence itself. Sound purifies, uplifts, and reminds us that life began not with form, but with frequency — *"In the beginning was the Word."*

The **Throat Chakra** resonates with this same principle: when we honor our inner voice, we align with truth and harmony. When we ignore it, communication falters and disconnection arises; when we misuse it, words wound rather than heal. Balance comes from *listening within* — expressing not to dominate, but to harmonize.

A Shared Understanding

Whether through yogic philosophy, shamanic chanting, Indigenous song, or sacred recitation, the message is the same: we are **beings of sound and resonance**. Our health and awareness depend on how we tune the instrument of our voice and our energy.

Vishuddha reminds us that the true measure of power is not how loudly we speak, but how purely we resonate. When the voice is aligned with heart and intention, it becomes a channel for truth — transforming fear into faith, confusion into clarity, and silence into understanding.

Origins & Hidden History Of Vishuddha

The concept of **Vishuddha** arises from the ancient yogic traditions of India, where the chakra system was first described in the Tantras. Classical texts such as the *Shat-Chakra-Nirupana* (circa 16th century) portray Vishuddha as a **sixteen-petaled lotus**, radiant like the color of a clear sky, located at the throat. Within this lotus lies a **downward-pointing triangle within a circle**, symbolizing the descent of spiritual truth into human expression.

The element associated with this chakra is **ether (ākāśa)** — the subtle space that allows sound to travel and life to vibrate. Vishuddha governs the **power of vibration**, encompassing voice, hearing, resonance, and creative communication. Yogic adepts viewed this center as the purifier of energy — the place where all that is dense becomes refined, and where silence births speech infused with spirit.

The Sanskrit name *Vishuddha*, meaning "especially pure," reflects the essence of this energy center: the **purification of thought, emotion, and sound** into truth. It is the temple of resonance, where communication becomes a sacred act of alignment between human and divine.

Vedic India

In the earliest Vedic hymns, **Vāc**, the goddess of speech, is honored as the voice of creation — the divine Word that gave rise to existence. The *Rig Veda* describes Vāc as both sound and consciousness, linking language to the unfolding of reality. The chanting of **mantras** (sacred syllables) was viewed as the act of harmonizing one's vibration with cosmic order (*ṛta*).

This understanding mirrors Vishuddha's purpose — the transformation of vibration into wisdom. Just as Manipura's fire refines matter, Vishuddha's sound refines consciousness. In both, purification leads to illumination.

Egyptian Mysteries

In ancient Egypt, **Thoth**, the god of words, wisdom, and magic, was believed to have spoken the world into being. Through the utterance of divine names, creation took form — a concept directly parallel to the yogic principle of *nāda brahma* ("the universe is sound"). Hieroglyphs themselves were considered living symbols, each carrying vibrational potency. Speech, writing, and truth (*Ma'at*) were intertwined as sacred acts of order and manifestation.

Greek Philosophy & Western Esotericism

Greek philosophers such as **Pythagoras** taught that sound and number underlie all creation — the *music of the spheres* — in which planets and stars vibrate in divine harmony. This cosmic symphony reflects the Throat Chakra's higher function: to attune the self to universal resonance.

In mystical Christianity, the *Logos* — "the Word" — represents the divine expression through which all things are made. The practice of **chanting psalms** and **intoning prayers** was intended not merely as devotion but as vibration — a way to align human voice with divine will.

In the Hermetic and Rosicrucian traditions, speech and sound are viewed as **alchemical forces**, capable of transmuting the inner and outer worlds. "As above, so below" becomes "As spoken, so made."

Chinese Medicine

In **Traditional Chinese Medicine (TCM)**, the **Throat** is closely associated with the **Metal element**, which governs communication, breath, and the ability to release through sound (crying, sighing, singing). The lungs and throat form the **gateway of expression**, where energy (qi) transitions between the inner and outer world. Sound therapy, breathwork, and toning practices in Qigong mirror Vishuddha's teaching of purification through vibration and air.

Kabbalistic Mysticism

In **Kabbalah**, the sefirah **Da'at**, meaning "knowledge," occupies the space of the throat on the Tree of Life. It serves as the link between wisdom (*Chokhmah*) and understanding (*Binah*), symbolizing revelation — the moment when divine knowing is expressed into form. The Hebrew creation story begins with sound: *"And God said, Let there be light."* The spoken word, therefore, becomes the medium of manifestation — an echo of Vishuddha's principle that speech is sacred creation in motion.

Across all traditions — from the **chants of the Vedas** to the **psalms of the West**, from the **medicine songs of shamans** to the **vibrations of Tibetan bowls** — humanity has always known that **sound is spirit moving through form**.

Vishuddha embodies this universal wisdom: the truth that what we speak, sing, and believe becomes the world we experience. To awaken the Throat Chakra is to remember that **our voice is divine** — the echo of creation itself, resonating in every word, every breath, and every silence.

THE HIDDEN HISTORY OF VISHUDDHA

Over time, **Vishuddha** came to represent more than communication or speech — it became the center of **truth, integrity, and divine resonance**. Yogic sages taught that the ether of Vishuddha, when purified, awakens wisdom, discernment, and expression — the very qualities needed to elevate consciousness from emotional reaction to spiritual awareness.

The "hidden history" of Vishuddha lies in how societies have treated **truth and voice**. Cultures that honored the spoken word as sacred fostered communities built on honesty, storytelling, and collective understanding. Those that silenced truth — through fear, censorship, or domination — often birthed generations marked by repression, secrecy, and disconnection. These imbalances persist today as the struggle between authentic expression and social conformity, between speaking truth and remaining silent to belong.

Understanding Vishuddha's origins is more than studying sound and symbol — it is an invitation to **reclaim the sacredness of voice**. True expression is not noise — it is resonance. It is the vibration that aligns heart and mind, harmonizes self and other, and communicates not just information, but spirit.

Vishuddha reminds us that **speech is sacred** when it flows from awareness. To awaken this chakra is to remember that communication and contemplation, expression and silence, are not opposites — they are the twin harmonies of the same eternal vibration. When aligned, they purify thought, heal division, and restore coherence between inner truth and outer world.

THE SYMBOLISM OF THE THROAT CHAKRA

Vishuddha is associated with the **element of ether (ākāśa)** — the most subtle and expansive of all elements. Ether represents space, sound, and the vibrational field that connects all life. It is the unseen thread through which energy, intention, and consciousness travel. Just as sound cannot exist without space, truth cannot exist without openness.

Its color is **sky blue**, the hue of serenity and infinite possibility. Blue cools the fires of ego and softens the weight of emotion, opening the mind to clarity and the heart to calm. It is the color of honesty, peace, and divine communication — the space where wisdom speaks in stillness.

The **sixteen-petaled lotus** of Vishuddha symbolizes the unfolding of pure sound. Each petal corresponds to one of the sixteen Sanskrit vowels — the open, unbound tones that carry resonance without restriction. Together, they represent the fluidity and freedom of expression when the voice flows from authenticity rather than fear.

Within the lotus rests a **downward-pointing triangle enclosed in a circle**, signifying the descent of divine truth into human form. The triangle mirrors the heart's upward aspiration meeting the divine's downward grace — a symbol of harmony between receiving and expressing, between the silence of knowing and the vibration of speaking.

Vishuddha's symbolism reminds us that the voice is not merely a human function — it is a divine instrument. Through sound, the invisible becomes known, and through truth, the soul becomes heard.

To awaken this chakra is to let your voice become light — clear, resonant, and aligned with the higher harmony of all things.

THE BLUE LOTUS

The lotus of **Vishuddha** is always depicted as **sky blue**, radiant like the expanse of a clear morning sky, shimmering with the peace of truth and the purity of sound. It is the **lotus of ether and vibration**, symbolizing the awakening of authentic expression through clarity, resonance, and divine communication.

Its **sixteen petals** represent the sixteen **Sanskrit vowels** — pure, open sounds that flow effortlessly from the breath. In yogic tradition, these vowels embody freedom of expression, the unbound resonance that moves without resistance. Each petal corresponds to a subtle quality of vibration — receptivity, honesty, creativity, clarity, patience, listening, and spiritual refinement. Together, they form the sacred architecture of communication: the harmonious balance between silence and sound.

At the heart of the blue lotus rests a **downward-pointing white triangle enclosed within a circle**, symbolizing the descent of higher truth into human awareness. The circle represents wholeness and the infinite expanse of ether (*ākāśa*), while the downward triangle signifies divine energy flowing into the realm of vibration and expression. This sacred geometry reveals Vishuddha's function as a **bridge** — where spirit becomes sound and consciousness takes form through the spoken word.

Unlike the red lotus of Muladhara, which roots us to the earth, or the yellow lotus of Manipura, which ignites our will, the **blue lotus of Vishuddha** teaches us to **resonate** — to give voice to our essence with integrity and grace. It is the flower of truth, harmony, and purification.

Where the heart reminds us to love, and the solar plexus empowers us to act, the throat declares that we **may express**. It is not the flower of control or silence, but of alignment — the sacred bloom of communication guided by higher awareness.

The Blue Lotus of Vishuddha invites us to speak with clarity, listen with compassion, and vibrate with the frequency of truth. It reminds us that **sound is not merely heard — it is felt, embodied, and lived.** When we align our voice with our soul, every word becomes a prayer, every breath a song, and every silence a return to divine resonance.

THE COLOR BLUE OF VISHUDDHA

When you close your eyes and visualize the **Throat Chakra**, the color that most often appears is **blue** — serene, vast, and luminous like the open sky or the calm depths of the ocean. This is more than imagery; it reflects a **vibrational reality** recognized in yogic, Tantric, and energy-healing traditions. Blue carries the resonance of **ether, purity, and expression** — the very essence of Vishuddha, the center of truth and communication.

Blue: Calm, Truth, And Expansion

• **The Color of the Sky and Spirit:**
Blue is the hue of infinity — the boundless space that holds all sound and all creation. It is the color of the sky stretching endlessly above and of the ocean reflecting the heavens below. Just as the sky allows light to travel and the sea carries vibration through its depths, blue represents the **ether element (ākāśa)** — the subtle medium through which consciousness moves and voice becomes vibration.

• **The Ether of Expression:**
Associated with sound and space, blue symbolizes **clarity and openness**. It invites expansion — the ability to speak, listen, and express without fear or tension. Like the air that carries song, blue energy allows communication to flow freely. When Vishuddha is balanced, words become clear, tone becomes calm, and silence becomes sacred.

• **The Vibration of Truth:**
Blue is the color of **truth and integrity**. It cools the fires of emotion, dissolving confusion and aligning thought with wisdom. When the Throat Chakra is in harmony, blue energy radiates as honesty — the ability to express what is real with compassion, without distortion or defense. Blue reminds us that truth is not harsh; it is healing.

• The Serenity of Presence:
Blue awakens the quality of **peaceful awareness**. It steadies the breath, slows the racing mind, and brings presence to the moment. In its gentlest form, it teaches that silence can speak as clearly as sound. When we embody the calm of Vishuddha's blue light, we communicate not only through words but through vibration — our presence itself becomes our message.

• The Frequency of Connection:
Blue carries the vibration of unity — it bridges the inner world and the outer, the heart and the mind, the human and the divine. It reminds us that communication is communion — a shared resonance that transcends words. When our energy glows with Vishuddha's blue, we become instruments of harmony in the orchestra of life.

Blue is the color of **purity and peace** — the vibration of the soul expressing itself clearly through sound and stillness. It bridges the warmth of the heart and the light of the mind, teaching that to **speak truth** is not rebellion but reverence.

To live in the radiance of Vishuddha's blue is to embody the calm clarity of consciousness itself — open, resonant, and free.

WHY BLUE BELONGS TO THE THROAT CHAKRA

Each chakra color vibrates at a unique frequency of light, forming part of the living spectrum that mirrors the evolution of human consciousness. **Blue** vibrates just above green — the color of the heart — representing energy rising from love into expression, from feeling into communication, from compassion into truth.

• The Fifth Color of the Rainbow

Just as blue follows green, **Vishuddha** follows **Anahata** in the chakra system — the natural next step after love is expression.

Once the heart opens and compassion flows freely, it seeks a voice. The calm blue of the Throat Chakra transforms emotion into understanding and turns the language of the heart into words that heal and connect.

• A Frequency of Clarity and Space

Blue holds a subtler, slower vibration than yellow or green, resonating with peace, spaciousness, and mental clarity. It bridges the emotional depth of the heart with the visionary insight of the Third Eye. This balanced frequency supports communication that is calm yet powerful — words that carry both wisdom and empathy. Blue energy reminds us that truth, like sound, travels best through open space.

• The Color of Resonance and Reflection

Blue is the color of reflection — the calm lake that mirrors the sky above. It embodies stillness that listens as much as it speaks. Within Vishuddha, blue represents the receptive aspect of communication: the ability to hear deeply, to absorb meaning beyond words, and to respond with presence.

• Expansive and Harmonizing

Blue is the hue of expansion and harmony — the vibration that brings order to sound and unity to diversity. Just as the vast sky holds all weather without judgment, the Throat Chakra holds all voices within the field of truth. When balanced, Vishuddha radiates serenity and coherence, allowing communication to become an act of alignment rather than reaction.

Blue belongs to Vishuddha because it is the color of truth made manifest — the vibration of sound moving through space.
It signifies the awakening of the inner voice, the calm resonance that turns silence into wisdom and speech into light. To live in

the blue of Vishuddha is to express with grace, to listen with the soul, and to let one's truth ripple outward in harmony with all that is.

BLUE IN DAILY LIFE

• **When you feel unheard or afraid to speak:**
Wear blue clothing, scarves, or jewelry to activate calm confidence and self-expression. Blue supports honest communication and helps you share your truth without fear. It encourages your voice to flow clearly and gracefully.

• **When your mind feels scattered or anxious:**
Visualize breathing in a soft, cool blue light. Let it fill your throat and chest, soothing your breath and steadying your thoughts. Blue clears mental noise and restores balance between thought and speech.

• **When communication feels strained:**
Hold or wear stones like **aquamarine**, **blue lace agate**, or **sodalite** to promote harmony and understanding. These crystals align with Vishuddha's energy, enhancing patience, listening, and compassionate dialogue.

• **In rituals of clarity and expression:**
Light blue candles or burn gentle incense such as sandalwood or lavender while setting an intention to speak truthfully and listen deeply. Surround yourself with blue fabrics, sky imagery, or soft sound frequencies to attune your energy to the vibration of truth.

MEDITATION WITH BLUE

1. Close your eyes and visualize a radiant **blue lotus** at your throat, glowing like a clear sky after rain.
2. See its blue light expanding outward, softening your jaw, neck, and shoulders — releasing tension, fear, and withheld words.
3. With each breath, feel this serene blue radiance purifying your voice and calming your mind as you silently repeat:

"I speak my truth with love.
I listen with peace.
I am the voice of calm clarity."

Blue invites stillness and flow — the perfect balance between expression and silence.
To live in its frequency is to speak only what uplifts, to listen with presence, and to let your words become instruments of healing and harmony.

WANT TO EXPERIENCE IT IN ACTION?...
Watch this video for the Throat Chakra Meditation.

Watch it here: https://youtu.be/LZ0ivyiUQjA

THE DEEPER LESSON OF BLUE

Blue teaches us that **truth, clarity, and expression** are not separate from the sacred. To speak with honesty, to listen with compassion, to live in harmony with one's word — these are all acts of devotion when guided by awareness. Just as silence gives meaning to sound, the soul finds peace through authentic expression.

The Throat Chakra's blue light is both a gift and a calling. It is the voice of spirit within matter, the resonance that whispers: **"You are truth. You are clarity. You are the voice of peace."**

It reminds us that our voice was never meant to dominate, but to harmonize — to become a bridge between heart and mind, between the human and the divine. When we honor the blue vibration within, we remember that to express truth is to live in alignment with the higher self, and that speaking light into the world is not vanity — it is **sacred service**.

THE SIXTEEN-PETALED LOTUS OF VISHUDDHA

At the heart of Vishuddha's symbolism lies a **sky-blue lotus with sixteen petals** — vast and ethereal, representing the subtle nature of sound and space. It is the lotus of **ether and purification**, where energy begins to move from expression through action (the solar plexus) into expression through vibration (the throat). Each petal unfolds as an aspect of consciousness seeking refinement — the evolution of speech from impulse to intention, from noise to truth.

This lotus signifies the **transformation of sound into awareness**, where communication becomes creation and words carry resonance beyond meaning.

THE SIXTEEN VOWELS OF SOUND

Each of Vishuddha's sixteen petals bears a **Sanskrit vowel**, the pure tones of the sacred alphabet —
aṁ, āṁ, iṁ, īṁ, uṁ, ūṁ, ṛṁ, ṝṁ, ḷṁ, ḹṁ, eṁ, aiṁ, oṁ, auṁ, aṁ, and aḥ.

These are not mere letters, but **vibrational frequencies** — the unbound sounds of the universe that flow freely through the breath. In yogic tradition, vowels are considered "open" energies: they carry life-force (*prāṇa*) without resistance, representing the soul's natural state of openness and expansion.

Chanting or meditating upon these vowels purifies the Throat Chakra, harmonizing the body's subtle currents and clearing the residue of unspoken truth. Each tone awakens a different nuance of expression — from softness to strength, from stillness to resonance — reminding us that sound, when conscious, becomes a pathway to liberation.

When these sacred syllables are intoned or visualized, they vibrate through the etheric body like waves across still water, awakening communication that is **authentic, healing, and clear**.

Vishuddha is the voice of the awakened soul.
It teaches that expression is not merely a human act — it is divine participation in creation itself.
To speak truth with love, to listen with openness, and to resonate with peace — these are the deepest lessons of blue.

THE SIXTEEN QUALITIES OF EXPRESSION

The sixteen petals of **Vishuddha** are associated with sixteen sacred qualities that must be refined for communication to become wisdom. These are the *echoes of ego* that arise as one learns to give voice to the soul. When purified, they become the harmonies of truth — the radiant tones of Vishuddha's **"lotus of pure sound."**

• **Silence Misused** – transformed into mindful stillness and inner listening.
• **Falsehood** – purified through honesty and self-awareness.
• **Gossip** – refined into speech that uplifts and unites.
• **Judgment** – balanced by compassion and understanding.
• **Self-Doubt** – healed through clarity and faith in one's authentic voice.

- **Harsh Speech** – softened into kindness and constructive truth.
- **Suppression** – released through courage and self-expression.
- **Confusion** – cleared through discernment and inner calm.
- **Over-Talking** – balanced by presence and receptivity.
- **Disharmony** – resolved through attunement and empathy.
- **Insecurity** – transcended by confidence grounded in peace.
- **Resistance to Feedback** – transformed into openness and growth.
- **Distortion** – purified by integrity and alignment with truth.
- **Fear of Being Heard** – healed through self-trust and divine support.
- **Manipulation Through Words** – transmuted into sincerity and service.
- **Spiritual Deafness** – awakened through devotion to inner guidance.

Together, these sixteen energies represent the **alchemy of pure expression**. When unrefined, they create misunderstanding, isolation, and imbalance. When transformed, they become **resonance, harmony, and spiritual communication** — the voice of wisdom expressed through love.

THE SIXTEEN DIRECTIONS OF RESONANCE

The sixteen petals can also be seen as **directions of sound and awareness**, radiating outward like ripples in water or the vibration of a struck bell. They symbolize the multidimensional flow of energy through voice and consciousness — forward and backward (speaking and reflecting), left and right (listening and expressing), above and below (heaven and earth), and the eight diagonals of balance (thought, feeling, word, and silence in harmony).

Vishuddha's vibration expands in all directions, reminding us that **authentic expression is not about volume, but alignment** — the ability to resonate with truth in every word, tone, and silence.

THE SIXTEEN CURRENTS OF ETHER

In Tantric tradition, the sixteen petals also correspond to the sixteen **vowels of Sanskrit**, known as the **open sounds of ether (ākāśa)**. These are the subtle tones that carry *prāṇa* through space, enabling communication between body, mind, and spirit. Chanting or meditating on these sounds purifies the energetic field, bringing speech and thought into coherence with the vibration of truth.

When sound is expressed from awareness — not too soft, not too forceful — it becomes the steady current of **divine communication**, the voice of one who speaks from essence rather than ego.

THE SACRED GEOMETRY OF SIXTEEN

The number **sixteen** holds profound symbolism in sacred geometry, representing **expansion, harmony, and resonance**. It is the multiple of four (stability) and four (expression) — the completion of the material and spiritual meeting in equilibrium. It signifies the perfected communicator: one who speaks with wisdom, listens with the soul, and vibrates in unity with the whole.

In the Throat Chakra, the sixteen-petaled lotus reflects this same harmony — the marriage of expression and silence, intellect and intuition, communication and contemplation. It teaches that **truth is not found in words alone, but in the vibration that carries them.**

When aligned with spirit, the voice becomes prayer, the breath becomes creation, and silence becomes communion.

The Triangle Of Sound: Vishuddha's Core Geometry

At the center of **Vishuddha's** sky-blue lotus lies a **downward-pointing white triangle**, encircled by a luminous ring. This sacred symbol represents the **descent of divine truth into vibration** — spirit entering sound, consciousness finding expression through voice. Unlike the Root Chakra's square of foundation or the Solar Plexus' triangle of fire, the Throat Chakra's triangle floats within a **circle of ether (ākāśa)**, signifying boundless resonance and infinite space.

THE TRIANGLE

• The three sides represent the trinity of **sound, silence, and resonance** — creation, rest, and reflection — the eternal cycle through which truth manifests.
• The downward point symbolizes the **flow of divine wisdom into human awareness**, the movement of higher consciousness into language and song.
• In meditation, this triangle becomes the **gateway of expression**, the point where thought transforms into vibration and the invisible becomes audible.

THE CIRCLE

• The surrounding circle embodies **ether — the element of space and vibration**. It signifies unity, openness, and the infinite field in which all sounds are born and eventually dissolve.
• The circle teaches receptivity: that communication begins not with speaking, but with listening — to the stillness within, where all true words originate.
• Together, the circle and triangle express the harmony between form and formlessness, the meeting of structure (intention) and flow (resonance).

THE UNION OF SOUND AND SPACE

Where the triangle of Manipura symbolized the fire of transformation, Vishuddha's triangle within the circle symbolizes **purification through vibration**. Fire refines matter; sound refines consciousness.
Through this sacred geometry, we learn that energy must first be refined (Solar Plexus) before it can be clearly expressed (Throat). Just as flame becomes light, intention becomes sound.

Vishuddha's geometry teaches that **truth is not forced — it is revealed through resonance**. When expression flows from alignment rather than ego, the voice becomes a vessel of spirit, not self.

RETURNING TO RESONANCE

While the Heart opens us to love and the Solar Plexus empowers us to act, the Throat Chakra **translates energy into expression**. It reminds us that sound, when purified by awareness, becomes wisdom — and that our task is not merely to act or feel, but to communicate from clarity, compassion, and peace.

This is the secret wisdom of Vishuddha: To be human is to speak as well as to listen, to resonate as well as to reflect, to express as well as to understand.

TRIANGLES IN TAROT SYMBOLISM

In esoteric traditions, triangles are among the most ancient symbols of creation and communication. Within the **Throat Chakra**, the downward-pointing triangle represents **the descent of divine truth into form**, while the circle surrounding it symbolizes the infinite field of **ether** through which sound and consciousness travel.

In the **Tarot**, this same principle — of spirit expressed through form, or vibration translated into awareness — appears repeatedly, particularly in cards that speak of revelation, communication, and spiritual alignment.

THE MAJOR ARCANA

• The High Priestess (II):
Seated between the pillars of duality, she forms the apex of an unseen triangle pointing downward, signifying divine wisdom descending into intuition. This is Vishuddha's principle of *inner listening* — truth revealed through silence, reflection, and the still voice within.

• The Hierophant (V):
His raised hand and the two acolytes below form the sacred triangle of teaching — divine knowledge transmitted through word and ritual. The Hierophant reflects the Throat Chakra's higher function: the channeling of universal wisdom into human understanding.

• The Lovers (VI):
Once again, the composition forms a triangle — the two figures below and the angel above. Here, the emphasis is communication and honesty within relationship. This card mirrors Vishuddha's truth principle: harmony through clear expression and spiritual transparency.

• Temperance (XIV):
The angel pours water from one cup to another, forming the triangle of flow and resonance. This symbolizes the purification of expression — the balance between speaking and listening, sound and silence, much like Vishuddha's harmonizing of vibration.

• The Star (XVII):

The star's rays create intersecting triangles — one descending, one ascending — uniting heaven and earth through light. This card perfectly embodies Vishuddha's purpose: divine inspiration flowing downward as guidance, and human hope rising upward as prayer. The Star is the *voice of faith* made visible.

• The Judgment (XX):

An angel blows a trumpet from above, awakening the sleeping below — the literal act of vibration awakening consciousness. This is Vishuddha's clarion call: the power of sound to resurrect truth, to awaken clarity, and to bridge heaven and earth through tone.

• The World (XXI):

Encircled by the four living symbols of the elements, the dancer at the center expresses the harmony of voice and movement, sound and form. It is Vishuddha realized — the complete communication between spirit and matter, microcosm and macrocosm.

THE MINOR ARCANA

• The Suit of Swords (Air):

Aligned with the element of **ether and intellect**, Swords resonate closely with Vishuddha's energy. Triangular compositions in this suit often depict moments of truth, choice, and clarity — representing the refinement of communication and the discernment born from honest reflection.

• The Suit of Cups (Water):

When the flow between vessels or figures forms a downward triangle, it reflects the harmonizing current of expression and empathy. Vishuddha's blue vibration refines emotion into understanding — turning feeling into compassionate speech.

• **The Suit of Wands (Fire):**
Though associated with Manipura's fire, triangular
arrangements of wands also symbolize the projection of energy
through space — the voice of intention. They remind us that
fire, when expressed through sound, becomes word: *the creative
declaration that shapes reality.*

• **The Suit of Pentacles (Earth):**
The pentacle's five-pointed star within a circle encloses subtle
triangular geometry, representing sound manifesting in matter
— ideas given form through articulation and skill. This echoes
Vishuddha's lesson: that true creation begins with
communication, and every manifestation starts as vibration.

THE VOICE OF SYMBOLS

Across the Tarot, triangles appear as **bridges of energy** —
linking higher and lower, thought and expression, silence and
sound. For **Vishuddha**, they represent the meeting point of
divine inspiration and human articulation.

Every triangle in the Tarot is a whisper of this truth:
What descends as revelation must rise again as expression.
In speaking, chanting, singing, or simply breathing with
awareness, we complete the triangle of creation — transforming
divine vibration into human truth, and human truth back into
divine harmony.

THROAT CHAKRA REFLECTIONS IN TRIANGULAR IMAGERY

• **Expression:**
Triangles in Tarot represent the movement of energy from
silence to sound, from inner knowing to outer expression. They
mark the moment when awareness finds its voice — when truth,
once hidden, becomes vibration. This is Vishuddha's gift:
expression through alignment.

• **Resonance:**
Unlike squares, which hold form, or circles, which encompass infinity, the triangle **directs vibration** — focusing energy toward a point of clarity. This directed resonance reflects the Throat Chakra's nature as the center of communication, bridging thought and feeling, heaven and earth, the divine and the human voice.

• **Revelation:**
The triangle's downward orientation within Vishuddha's lotus symbolizes the **descent of divine truth into human awareness** — illumination through vibration. It teaches that clarity is not forced; it is received through stillness and expressed through purity. True wisdom is not shouted; it **resonates**.

The triangle is the **sacred geometry of sound and purification**.
In Tarot, as in Vishuddha, it reveals that growth comes not from speaking more, but from **speaking truth** — from allowing vibration to refine consciousness until sound becomes serenity and expression becomes revelation.

To embody the Throat Chakra is to remember:
your voice is the echo of creation,
your silence is its source.

KEY CARDS TO MEDITATE ON FOR THE THROAT CHAKRA

• **The High Priestess (II):**
Inner knowing and sacred silence — the wisdom that arises when you listen deeply to the voice within.

• **The Hierophant (V):**
The act of teaching and transmitting truth — speaking from divine authority, not ego.

• **The Lovers (VI):**
Authentic communication and transparency in relationship —
truth spoken in harmony with love.

• **Temperance (XIV):**
Balanced expression — the alchemy of sound and silence,
where communication becomes healing.

• **The Star (XVII):**
Faith, inspiration, and divine communication — the voice of
Spirit made luminous through hope and clarity.

• **Judgment (XX):**
Awakening through sound — the trumpet call that reminds us
of our purpose and the power of truth.

• **Eight of Wands:**
Swift communication, momentum, and messages carried
through space — the flow of energy in motion.

• **Page of Swords:**
Curiosity, honesty, and the first spark of clear articulation —
the courage to speak truth as it forms.

Vishuddha is both the **echo and the ether** of the human
journey.
It is the fifth chakra to awaken — the point where
understanding seeks expression and awareness becomes
vibration. It marks the sacred transition from feeling (Heart) to
knowing (Third Eye), from emotion to articulation, from silence
to resonance.

From the moment we learn to speak our first truth, Vishuddha
carries the lifelong imprint of **communication, integrity, and
purpose**. It is the radiant center where sound becomes creation
— the bridge between mind and manifestation.

Without Vishuddha, the chakra system remains unexpressed — like a song never sung. With it, we gain the courage to **speak, listen, and live in truth**, allowing divine wisdom to flow freely through voice, action, and presence.

In this way, the Throat Chakra is not simply the realm of speech — it is the teacher of resonance.
Every word spoken with love, every silence held in awareness, every song that rises from authenticity is touched by its light.

As we ascend toward vision and unity, Vishuddha reminds us: **Enlightenment is not silence, but clear sound — the voice of the soul in harmony with the divine.**

VISHUDDHA IN YOGIC PRACTICE

In the earliest Tantric and yogic traditions, the chakras were understood not as physical organs but as subtle centers of consciousness — **vortices of vibration** that mediate between the seen and the unseen. Each chakra was viewed as a gateway to awakening, purifying, and harmonizing the various layers of being.

For **Vishuddha**, the Throat Chakra, practice centers upon **sound, truth, and resonance**. Its Sanskrit name means "especially pure," reflecting its role as the purifier of consciousness through vibration. The element of Vishuddha is **ether (ākāśa)** — the vast expanse through which sound travels and all creation resounds.

The **bīja mantra**, or "seed sound," of Vishuddha is **HAM (pronounced hum)** — the vibrational key that awakens the etheric field of communication, clarity, and divine connection. By meditating on the sixteen-petaled lotus and chanting "HAM," practitioners refine their inner frequency, aligning the voice with truth and the mind with serenity.

Yogis recognized Vishuddha as the **gateway between the lower centers of embodiment and the higher centers of consciousness**. Through its purification, the energies of the body, heart, and intellect become harmonized, enabling speech and silence to serve as tools of enlightenment.

Traditional practices for activating Vishuddha included **prāṇāyāma (breath control), ujjāyī breathing (the oceanic breath)**, and **nāda yoga (the yoga of sound)** — all methods that cultivate inner resonance and awareness of subtle vibration. Chanting sacred syllables, reciting mantras, or simply listening to the sound of one's breath were seen as acts of devotion, aligning the individual with the universal tone — the eternal *Om* that hums beneath all existence.

For the yogi, speech was never merely communication; it was **creation in motion**. Every word, sound, and breath carried the power to shape energy and consciousness. Therefore, mastery of Vishuddha required more than eloquence — it demanded integrity, awareness, and humility. The voice was to become a sacred instrument, tuned to truth.

When balanced, Vishuddha awakens the ability to express without distortion and to listen without judgment. The practitioner's voice becomes clear, compassionate, and courageous — not a projection of ego, but a transmission of spirit. In this purified state, **sound becomes silence in motion**, and silence becomes the wellspring of all sound.

THE INNER SYMBOL OF VISHUDDHA

At the center of Vishuddha's lotus lies a **downward-pointing triangle** set within a **circle of radiant white or sky-blue light**. The triangle represents the descent of spiritual energy — divine wisdom entering the field of communication — while the circle signifies the infinite expanse of ether through which vibration travels.

Surrounding this central geometry are **sixteen petals**, each inscribed with one of the Sanskrit vowels. These sounds represent the pure tones of creation — the fundamental frequencies that shape all speech and all form. The vowels, being breath-born and open, symbolize the unconditioned flow of expression, truth spoken without obstruction.

At the heart of the triangle rests the **bīja mantra HAM (हं)** — the seed syllable of purification. HAM is the resonance of the higher mind descending through the channel of expression. When chanted, it vibrates gently in the throat and chest, clearing energetic blockages, soothing emotional constriction, and awakening the flow of prāṇa through the voice.

To intone "HAM" is to align with clarity — to speak, sing, or remain silent with awareness of divine presence. It dissolves the fog of confusion and opens the inner ear to subtle truth.

Vishuddha's symbol teaches that **sound is sacred** — that every vibration carries the potential to heal or to harm, to conceal or to reveal. When guided by compassion and integrity, the voice becomes a tool of liberation — a living mantra that connects the finite self with the infinite.

To purify Vishuddha is to reclaim the holiness of one's own expression — to remember that truth, when spoken in love, is the highest form of prayer.

WHAT HAM REPRESENTS

• **Vibrational Key:**
HAM (हं) is the sacred sound that unlocks the Throat Chakra, activating the element of **ether (ākāśa)** — the space through which all vibration travels. It attunes the voice to truth, purifies the channel of communication, and harmonizes inner and outer expression. Through HAM, one awakens the resonance of

authenticity — the power to speak clearly, listen deeply, and live in alignment with divine vibration.

• **Sound of Ether and Purification:**
When chanted, HAM vibrates gently within the throat and upper chest, creating a cooling, expansive sensation. It clears congestion — both physical and energetic — dissolving tension, suppressed emotion, and miscommunication. This sound purifies the subtle pathways of expression, allowing energy to flow freely from the heart to the mind and beyond.

• **Dissolver of Falsehood and Fear:**
Ancient yogic texts describe HAM as the mantra that burns away distortion — the unspoken fears, withheld truths, and inner noise that obscure clear expression. It transforms repression into resonance, anxiety into openness, and silence born of fear into silence born of peace. Through HAM, the practitioner learns that to speak truth is not rebellion but liberation.

• **Link to the Ether Element:**
Each chakra corresponds to one of the five **tattvas** (elements). Vishuddha aligns with **ether**, the subtlest of all — the boundless expanse that carries sound and consciousness. Ether represents both space and presence: the stillness from which sound emerges and to which it returns. By meditating on HAM, we harmonize with this element — cultivating spacious awareness, clarity of mind, and serenity of spirit.

By meditating on **Vishuddha's sixteen-petaled lotus** and chanting **HAM**, yogis attuned themselves to the sacred vibration of truth. They discovered that the spoken word is an act of creation — that to speak consciously is to shape the world through frequency and intention.

The Throat Chakra was never seen as merely the seat of voice, but as the **temple of vibration** — the bridge between inner wisdom and outer reality. It is the sacred resonance that transforms silence into song, thought into expression, and communication into communion with the divine.

THE SEED SOUND OF VISHUDDHA: HAM

At the very center of the Throat Chakra's symbol lies not only sacred geometry, but **sacred sound**.
In Tantric and yogic philosophy, each chakra resonates with a *bīja mantra* — a "seed sound" that carries the pure vibrational essence of its energy center.

For **Vishuddha**, the Throat Chakra, that sound is **HAM** (pronounced "hum," with a gentle vibration in the back of the throat).

Why Sound Matters

In Sanskrit tradition, sound (*nāda*) is considered the fabric of creation — the vibration from which all form arises. The ancient seers taught that the universe itself was born from the primordial resonance of **OM**, and that every living being continues to echo this eternal sound within.

Each chakra represents a distinct tone within this cosmic symphony — a harmonic field that governs both energetic and emotional expression. Chanting the *bīja* mantra of a chakra is therefore not mere repetition, but a tuning process — aligning the human instrument with the frequency of divine order.

For Vishuddha, that resonance is **HAM**, the sound of **purification and truth** — the vibration that clears distortion, refines awareness, and allows pure expression to flow through voice and breath.

THE POWER OF HAM

• Resonance in the Throat and Chest:
When chanted, HAM vibrates in the hollow of the throat, resonating through the vocal cords, larynx, and upper chest. It opens the channel between heart and mind, uniting feeling with thought and emotion with clarity.

• Purifying the Channel of Expression:
Vishuddha can become clouded by unspoken truths, fear of judgment, or withheld emotion. HAM clears this energetic congestion, releasing what has been silenced and restoring the natural rhythm of communication and trust.

• Awakening Authentic Voice:
HAM awakens the voice of the soul — not the voice that seeks attention, but the one that seeks truth. It empowers you to speak with integrity, listen with compassion, and express from a place of inner peace rather than reaction.

• Honoring the Element of Ether:
Each chakra corresponds to one of the five elements (*tattvas*). Vishuddha aligns with **ether (ākāśa tattva)** — the boundless space through which all sound travels. Ether is both the silence before creation and the resonance that sustains it. Through HAM, we attune to this infinite expanse — finding stillness within sound and presence within silence.

CHANTING HAM

Chanting HAM is a practice of **alignment and release**.
It teaches that purification does not come from denial, but from expression — from allowing truth to move through you as vibration, clear and unforced.

With each repetition, HAM dissolves constriction in the throat, softens the heart, and quiets the mind, leaving behind a sense of spaciousness and serenity. It connects you to the etheric dimension — the awareness that everything spoken, whispered, or sung carries energy into the world.

HAM is the **vibrational key to clarity**, opening the gateway between inner wisdom and outer expression.
It is the mantra of freedom through authenticity — the sound of the soul remembering its true voice.

How To Chant Ham

Step 1 – Prepare the Body

• Sit comfortably with your spine tall and your shoulders relaxed.
• Rest your hands lightly on your throat or place one hand on your heart and one on your throat.
• Take 3–5 slow, deep breaths, feeling the gentle rise and fall of your chest. Allow your breath to soften the muscles of your neck and jaw, opening the gateway of your voice.

Step 2 – Focus on the Throat Center

• Visualize a soft **blue lotus** at your throat, glowing like the sky at dawn.
• See its sixteen petals gently unfolding, shimmering with light and sound.
• Imagine a stream of clear, blue energy flowing through your throat, cooling, calming, and cleansing — freeing your voice and your breath.

Step 3 – Chant the Sound

• Inhale deeply. As you exhale, chant slowly and clearly:
HAAAAAHHHHMMMmmmm…
• Let the "Ha" emerge softly from the back of your throat, airy and open, like a breath moving through space.

• Allow the "mmm" to vibrate gently through your throat, chest, and head — a soothing hum that harmonizes your inner and outer voice.

Step 4 – Repeat Rhythmically

• Chant **HAM** 7, 12, or 108 times.
• With each repetition, visualize your blue lotus expanding with luminous vibration — each petal radiating purity, honesty, and serenity.
• Feel your throat clearing, your breath deepening, and your words aligning with truth.

Step 5 – Silent Resonance

• After chanting, sit quietly and feel the subtle vibration lingering in your throat and heart.
• Sense the spaciousness of ether — calm, clear, infinite.
• Rest in this silence as you affirm:
"I speak truth. I listen deeply. I express with clarity and peace."

WAYS TO USE HAM IN PRACTICE

• **Morning Clarity:**
Begin your day by chanting **HAM** three times to open your voice and clear your mind. Let its soft vibration awaken calm confidence and invite clarity into your words and thoughts.

• **Before Communication:**
When preparing for an important conversation, meeting, or presentation, chant **HAM** to align your energy with truth and ease. Feel the resonance clear hesitation, allowing your voice to flow naturally and sincerely.

• **Emotional Release:**
If emotion feels trapped in your throat or chest, hum or chant

HAM until the energy softens and releases. Let sound become your medicine — transforming silence into freedom and heaviness into harmony.

• Healing Sessions:
Practitioners can chant **HAM** softly or inwardly while working near the neck, shoulders, or upper chest to promote energetic flow, relaxation, and authentic expression. The vibration supports clearing blockages tied to unspoken truth or withheld emotion.

• Breath & Movement Integration:
Pair chanting with gentle, open-throat poses such as Fish Pose (*Matsyasana*), Supported Bridge, or Cobra (*Bhujangasana*). Let each inhale expand your throat and chest, and each exhale carry the sound of **HAM** into spacious resonance.

• Group Practice:
Chanting **HAM** together creates a harmonic field of unity and serenity. Collective voice amplifies the vibration of truth — dissolving boundaries and cultivating peace within and between all who participate.

Ether-Centered Affirmation With Ham

"As I chant HAM, my voice aligns with truth.
I express clearly. I listen deeply.
I am the calm space where sound becomes peace."

THE ANIMAL SYMBOL OF VISHUDDHA: THE WHITE ELEPHANT

At the base of each chakra lotus rests a sacred animal, representing the instinctual or elemental force that animates its energy.
For the **Throat Chakra**, this guardian is the **White Elephant**, or *Airavata* — the celestial elephant of purity, wisdom, and

gentle power.

It embodies the element of **ether (ākāśa)** — the vast space through which sound travels, where thought becomes voice and vibration becomes creation.

Why the White Elephant?

• Ether Element:

The elephant's presence is grounding yet spacious, mirroring the quality of ether — stillness that carries all sound, form, and movement.

Just as the White Elephant moves with silent strength, Vishuddha teaches that true communication flows from calm awareness and inner space.

• Wisdom and Sacred Sound:

In Indian and Buddhist traditions, the White Elephant symbolizes divine insight and the power of sacred speech.

It represents the transmission of truth — words that uplift rather than wound, sounds that heal rather than divide.

• Strength in Serenity:

Unlike the Ram of Manipura, whose fire burns bright with action, the Elephant's strength lies in stillness.

Its vast presence radiates stability and grace, reminding us that true power does not need to shout — it simply *is*.

• Purity and Higher Consciousness:

White is the color of spiritual clarity and purification. The White Elephant, born from the clouds, reflects Vishuddha's purpose — to cleanse distortion, release falsehood, and return expression to its pure essence.

It carries the rains of truth that nourish both heart and mind.

• Divine Messenger:

In yogic symbolism, the White Elephant serves as the carrier of *Indra*, the god of the heavens and the wielder of thunder and

voice.
It bridges the realm of silence and sound, carrying divine communication into human consciousness.

The White Elephant teaches that speech, like thunder, holds power — it can destroy or awaken, depending on its purity. It reminds us to listen deeply before we speak, to move deliberately before we act, and to honor the sacredness of our words.

Gentle yet unyielding, humble yet majestic, the Elephant embodies the awakened throat — **where strength becomes serenity, and truth becomes sound.**

THE SHADOW OF THE ELEPHANT

The White Elephant symbolizes purity, calm strength, and the sacred power of voice. Yet even the gentlest energy can cast a shadow when imbalanced.
When Vishuddha's etheric flow is blocked or misdirected, expression becomes distortion — sound loses its clarity, and truth becomes veiled.

• Silence and Suppression:

When fear or self-doubt constricts the throat, words remain unspoken.
This shadow manifests as withholding truth, people-pleasing, or suppressing emotion to maintain peace.
The voice fades, and with it, authenticity and vitality.

• Dishonesty and Manipulation:

The gift of communication becomes a weapon when used without integrity.
Half-truths, gossip, or persuasive falsehoods cloud the clarity of

Vishuddha, turning the sacred act of speech into illusion.
What was meant to liberate begins to bind.

• **Overexpression and Noise:**

Just as silence can wound, so can overuse.
When the need to be heard outweighs the willingness to listen,
expression becomes chaos.
The overactive Throat Chakra speaks without awareness —
flooding space with sound rather than resonance.

• **Disconnection from Inner Voice:**

In the shadow of the Elephant, we may lose touch with intuition
— speaking from intellect rather than truth.
This dissonance between mind and spirit breeds confusion,
anxiety, and the haunting sense of being unheard, even when
words are many.

When Vishuddha's light dims, communication becomes either
too loud or too absent — noise without meaning, or silence
without peace.
The White Elephant teaches us to restore balance through
awareness: to speak with purity, to listen with presence, and to
honor silence as deeply as sound.

**The true voice is not found in volume, but in vibration —
the resonance of truth unspoken as much as spoken.**

THE WISDOM OF THE ELEPHANT

When balanced, the White Elephant embodies the majesty of
calm presence — strength guided by truth, and power expressed
through peace.
Its wisdom lies not in volume, but in resonance: a reminder that
the purest sound emerges from stillness.

• **Grace in Expression:**

Like the Elephant that moves slowly yet surely, we are called to speak with intention.
Measured words carry more weight than hurried noise.
Through conscious speech, we learn that truth, when spoken gently, can move mountains.

• **Listening as Strength:**

The Elephant's great ears remind us that communication begins with listening.
To truly hear — the self, others, and the silence in between — is an act of humility and power.
Vishuddha's wisdom teaches that silence is not absence, but presence made profound.

• **Purity of Voice:**

When speech aligns with the heart, words become prayer.
The Elephant's trumpet resounds not for dominance, but for truth — a declaration of life's harmony.
To speak with purity is to give sound to the divine within.

• **Peaceful Power:**

True authority does not roar; it resonates.
The White Elephant teaches us to express strength through serenity — to let truth flow like water through air, steady and unshakable.
Its voice heals because it carries no harm.

The Elephant's wisdom is a song of balance — strength wrapped in gentleness, truth carried in stillness.
Its trunk reaches both earth and sky, just as the awakened throat bridges silence and sound.
When we honor Vishuddha's energy with awareness, we

discover that **the voice is not merely to speak, but to harmonize — to bring heaven and earth into resonance through truth.**

THE ELEPHANT IN TANTRIC SYMBOLISM

In Tantric depictions of the sixteen-petaled lotus of Vishuddha, the **White Elephant (Airavata)** rests beneath the lotus as its **vāhana**, or sacred vehicle. The Elephant carries **Indra**, the Vedic god of thunder and the heavens — the divine voice that speaks creation into being.

Just as Agni's Ram represents fire, Airavata embodies **ether (ākāśa)** — the vastness in which sound is born. It is through this element that vibration becomes voice and silence becomes song.

Airavata's whiteness symbolizes purity of expression — speech freed from distortion, truth untangled from fear. Its mighty form moves with the grace of space itself: vast, unhurried, and resonant.

Where Manipura's Ram teaches transformation through action, Vishuddha's Elephant teaches transformation through expression — the alchemy of vibration. It reminds us that **sound is not mere communication; it is creation.** Every word, every tone, shapes reality.

In Tantric wisdom, Airavata carries the rains that cool the fires of Manipura, bringing clarity and peace to the inner world. The breath, the voice, and the silence between — all are sacred vehicles through which consciousness reveals itself.

The Elephant thus becomes the **embodiment of spiritual communication** — the voice as offering, the breath as prayer, and truth as the bridge between heaven and earth.

MEDITATING ON THE ELEPHANT

• **Visualization:**
Imagine a luminous White Elephant standing upon a field of
blue ether, its trunk lifted toward the sky. A soft light glows
from its heart, expanding with each breath, filling the space
around you with calm strength and radiant truth.
This is your inner voice — vast, clear, and unbound.

• **Affirmation:**
"I honor my voice as sacred. I speak truth with grace, and I
listen with wisdom."

• **Integration:**
Work with the element of sound — chant, sing, hum, or simply
breathe with awareness.
Visualize sound waves flowing like ripples through space,
carrying harmony into every cell of your being.
Feel your voice as vibration — the meeting place of spirit and
form, silence and sound, truth and love.

**The Elephant teaches that true expression is not loud, but
luminous.** It is the sound of soul — the resonance of
authenticity moving freely through the open sky of awareness.

THE DEITIES OF THE THROAT CHAKRA

In the Tantric tradition, every chakra is enlivened by divine
energies — archetypal forces that express the spiritual qualities
of that center.
These deities are not separate beings to be worshipped, but
luminous aspects of consciousness within us, waiting to be
awakened.
For **Vishuddha**, the Throat Chakra, these energies represent
**truth, purity, communication, and expansion through
sound.**

They teach us that the voice is sacred — a bridge between thought and manifestation, silence and creation.

Sadashiva – The Lord Of Pure Consciousness

• Sadashiva, the eternal aspect of Shiva, presides as the masculine deity of Vishuddha. He is the silent witness — the infinite awareness that underlies all vibration.
• In Tantric imagery, Sadashiva is depicted as tranquil and radiant blue, seated upon a white lotus, with five faces representing the five elements and directions.
• His presence embodies stillness and truth — the soundless source from which all sound arises. In the Throat Chakra, he governs communication infused with consciousness, teaching that every word should echo the silence from which it is born.
• Meditating on Sadashiva within Vishuddha awakens the higher mind, dissolves illusion, and clears the way for authentic expression. His blessing is **clarity** — the power to speak with integrity and to listen with wisdom.

Shakini – The Goddess Of Purity And Expression

• The feminine guardian of the Throat Chakra is **Shakini**, radiant goddess of sacred speech (*vak*), creativity, and intuition. She is often depicted with five faces and six arms, adorned in blue or white garments, holding musical instruments, prayer beads, and a skull symbolizing transcendence of illusion.
• Shakini represents the divine voice — the power of vibration to shape reality. She governs *mantra shakti*, the creative energy of sound that gives form to consciousness.
• Her nature is serene yet dynamic: she listens deeply, speaks truthfully, and harmonizes the currents of thought and emotion into clear communication.
• Meditating on Shakini awakens purity, eloquence, and insight. She reminds us that the highest form of expression is not performance, but presence — the alignment of heart, mind, and soul through sound.

Together: Sadashiva And Shakini

Together, Sadashiva and Shakini represent the sacred polarity of Vishuddha — **the stillness that listens and the sound that speaks.**
• Sadashiva is the space — the infinite ether (ākāśa) in which vibration moves.
• Shakini is the voice — the divine resonance that awakens creation within that space.
Their union embodies the eternal balance between silence and expression, consciousness and creation, spirit and sound.

When these deities awaken within us, the voice becomes a channel for the soul.
Words gain power not through volume but through vibration, not through intellect but through truth.
In this union, we remember that **speech is prayer, sound is creation, and silence is the womb from which all wisdom is born.**

Vishuddha, the "Pure Place," becomes the temple of sacred sound — where every breath, word, and silence can reveal the divine.

DEITIES OF SOUND AND EXPRESSION IN OTHER TRADITIONS

While Tantra names **Sadashiva** and **Shakini** as the presiding energies of **Vishuddha**, many cultures throughout history have honored divine figures who embody **truth, voice, wisdom, and the sacred power of sound.**
Though their names and symbols vary, each expresses the essence of the Throat Chakra — the bridge between thought and creation, silence and expression.

• **Saraswati (Hindu Tradition):**

The goddess of speech (*vak*), music, and learning, Saraswati
flows with the pure vibration of truth.
Her veena represents the harmony of sound, her white swan
discernment, and her waters the fluidity of divine expression.
Saraswati reminds us that all creation begins with a word — and
that to speak truth is to participate in divine order.

• **Hermes / Mercury (Greek & Roman Mythology):**

Messenger of the gods, guide of travelers and souls, Hermes
embodies the quicksilver current of communication.
He bridges worlds — mortal and divine, seen and unseen —
reflecting Vishuddha's role as the channel between mind and
spirit.
His caduceus, crowned with wings and serpents, mirrors the
rising energies of kundalini uniting through the central channel
of the throat.

• **Thoth (Egyptian Mysticism):**

Scribe of the gods and master of sacred words, Thoth represents
wisdom, truth, and the creative power of speech.
He records every thought and action, teaching that the spoken
word carries weight and consequence.
Through Thoth, we learn that language is a form of magic —
each word shaping the world through intention.

• **Brigid (Celtic Tradition):**

Goddess of poetry, inspiration, and the sacred flame of
creativity, Brigid represents the awakening of voice through
heart and spirit.
She blesses poets, healers, and artisans alike — all who give
form to inspiration through sound or craft.

Her fire burns not for destruction, but for illumination — the warmth of truth spoken in love.

• **Odin (Norse Mythology):**

Seeker of wisdom and master of runes, Odin's sacrifice upon the World Tree granted him the power of words imbued with spirit.
His runes are vibrations made visible — symbols of divine utterance and the courage to speak destiny into being.
Odin's story reminds us that truth requires surrender: to gain the voice of spirit, one must first listen deeply to silence.

• **Archangel Gabriel (Christian & Islamic Mysticism):**

Herald of divine revelation, Gabriel is the messenger of sacred words — the angel who brings light through language.
His voice carries inspiration, prophecy, and peace, echoing Vishuddha's gift: to communicate truth as an act of love.
Gabriel's trumpet represents not alarm, but awakening — the soul remembering its divine sound.

• **Benzaiten (Japanese Shinto-Buddhist Tradition):**

Also known as Benten, she is the goddess of music, eloquence, and flowing wisdom.
Often depicted playing the biwa (lute), she governs both the beauty of expression and the emotional depth of communication.
Her waters symbolize the purity and fluidity of sound, uniting intellect with intuition.

Across all traditions, the **Throat Chakra** is mirrored by deities who honor sound as sacred — whether through music, speech, prayer, or prophecy.
Each reminds us that **truth is vibration**, and every act of expression carries the potential to heal, awaken, or create.

Where the Solar Plexus burns with fire, **Vishuddha breathes with air and echoes through ether — the space in which all sound lives.**
The universal message endures:
When we speak from the heart and listen with the soul, we become the voice of the divine — clear, resonant, and infinite.

THE ELEMENT OF VISHUDDHA: ETHER (ĀKĀŚA)

Each chakra corresponds to one of the five great elements (*Pancha Mahabhutas*). For the **Throat Chakra**, that element is **Ether** — *Ākāśa* in Sanskrit.

More than emptiness, Ākāśa is the field of potential — the subtle dimension in which all vibration, sound, and thought arise. It is the essence of Vishuddha: **expansive, resonant, and pure** — the element of communication between the finite and the infinite.

ETHER AS THE SPACE OF RESONANCE

Ether is not nothingness — it is the space that holds everything. It is the vast silence before sound, the unseen medium through which all energy moves.
Where fire transforms and water flows, Ether simply allows — it **receives, carries, and connects**.
Through Ākāśa, voice becomes vibration, and vibration becomes creation.

QUALITIES OF ETHER

• **Purity and Clarity:**
Ākāśa is called *Vishuddha*, meaning "pure."
It filters out distortion and returns us to clarity — of thought, word, and being.
When this element is balanced, communication flows with ease, truth resonates, and silence itself feels alive with awareness.

• **Space and Expansion:**
Ether is the infinite sky of consciousness — boundless, open,
and receptive.
When Vishuddha expands, we feel spacious within;
constriction, tension, and fear dissolve into calm presence.
Through this spaciousness, creativity and wisdom naturally
arise.

• **Vibration and Sound:**
Ether carries *nāda*, the cosmic sound that sustains the universe.
Every word, chant, or song moves through Ākāśa — giving
shape to thought and emotion.
The Throat Chakra, as the seat of sound, translates vibration
into meaning, and silence into expression.

• **Connection and Communication:**
Just as space connects all things, Ether unites inner and outer
worlds.
It is the bridge through which we express our truth and receive
the truths of others.
Through balanced Vishuddha, we learn that communication is
not only speaking — it is listening, harmonizing, and being
fully present.

BALANCE AND IMBALANCE

When the element of Ether is **blocked**, communication feels
constrained — words may be stifled, misunderstood, or
withheld. Silence becomes heavy rather than peaceful.

When Ether is **overactive**, expression becomes excessive —
speech may lose grounding, truth becomes diluted, and energy
disperses in all directions.

When **balanced**, Ākāśa is spacious, radiant, and resonant.
The voice flows freely from the heart; the mind is calm yet
awake.

We become a clear vessel for truth — speaking, listening, and creating from stillness.

THE SACRED TEACHING OF ETHER

Ether reminds us that **space is not emptiness — it is potential**. It is the silent womb of creation, the breath between thoughts, the pause between sounds.
When we honor this stillness, we remember that communication begins not with speech, but with presence.

Through Ākāśa, the Throat Chakra teaches us the most subtle of all powers — **the power to create through sound and to heal through silence.**

WHY ETHER BELONGS TO THE THROAT CHAKRA

The chakras rise through the five great elements — earth (Root), water (Sacral), fire (Solar Plexus), air (Heart), and finally **ether (Throat)** — each one expanding into subtler, more refined states of consciousness.

After the movement of air through the heart, **ether is the next evolution** — the open expanse in which all vibration, sound, and thought arise. It is the element of communication, connection, and expression.

Ether belongs to Vishuddha because this chakra governs sound, resonance, and truth — the voice of the soul moving through the space of being.
Just as fire transforms matter into light, **ether transforms sound into meaning** — giving consciousness a voice and silence a purpose.

Through ether, the infinite becomes intimate: what is unseen finds expression, and what is internal becomes shared.

Vishuddha asks us to:

• Speak truth rather than seek approval.
• Listen deeply rather than simply hear.
• Create space for silence as much as sound.

Ether is the element of **spiritual communication** — the power
to connect, clarify, and harmonize.
It reminds us that the voice is not merely to speak, but to
resonate — to bridge heaven and earth through vibration.
When we honor ether, we discover that **every word is energy,
every breath is prayer, and every silence is sacred.**

MEDITATING ON ETHER

Bringing the element of ether into Throat Chakra practice
awakens calm, spacious awareness and clear self-expression.

1. Ether Visualization:
Sit comfortably and visualize a vast blue sky within your throat
and upper chest — open, luminous, and infinite.
With each breath, feel that sky expanding, clearing away
constriction, allowing your voice to move freely like wind
through space.

2. Humming Meditation (Bhramari Pranayama):
Inhale deeply, and as you exhale, hum softly, feeling the
vibration in your throat and chest.
The sound unites breath and vibration, clearing stagnation and
harmonizing your inner resonance.

3. Sound & Silence Practice:
Chant the seed sound **HAM** (pronounced "hum") three to
twelve times.
Then sit in silence, listening to the echo fade into stillness.
This teaches you that expression and silence are not opposites

— they are partners in balance.
Whisper: *"I speak truth. I listen deeply. I express with grace."*

When we meditate with the ether element, we align with the sacred truth of Vishuddha:
You are the voice of the divine made human.
Your words have the power to heal, to harmonize, and to awaken.

ETHER IN DAILY LIFE

• **When your voice feels blocked:**
Sing, hum, or chant freely — not for perfection, but for release. Let sound move through you until space returns to your breath.

• **When you feel unheard:**
Pause and listen to the silence beneath all noise. In that stillness, your inner voice will remind you: *"Truth does not need to shout."*

• **When overwhelmed by noise or emotion:**
Imagine a vast sky above and within you — endless, peaceful, and clear. Let distractions dissolve into that boundless space.

• **When you need clarity in conversation:**
Before speaking, take one full breath into your throat. Feel your words forming from your heart, guided by peace, not reaction.

• **When seeking divine connection:**
Spend a few minutes in silent meditation, listening for the subtle hum of life around you — the resonance of the universe itself.

Ether teaches that **space is not emptiness, but possibility**.
In Vishuddha, this sacred space becomes the channel of truth — where every sound, word, and breath can return to its source as light.

THE LESSON OF ETHER

Ether teaches that true expression is not about speaking more —
it is about **resonating with truth**.
It clears confusion and fear, opening the vastness of
understanding, peace, and authentic communication.
Just as open space holds all sound without judgment, **balanced
ether** allows the voice to express without distortion.

Vishuddha reminds us that clarity, expression, and silence are
sacred harmonies of the soul's vibration.
When aligned with awareness, your inner voice becomes a song
of truth — calm, luminous, and expansive.
A Throat Chakra attuned to ether becomes the **sky itself**: vast,
infinite, and filled with the music of creation.

BRINGING THE SYMBOLS TOGETHER

Taken together, these symbols form the complete picture of the
Throat Chakra's essence — the **pure center of
communication, truth, and resonance**:

• **The sixteen lotus petals** represent the many frequencies of
sound and expression — the layers of language, emotion, and
insight refined through awareness and purity.

• **The downward-pointing triangle within a circle** symbolizes
the descent of divine truth into human form — sound made
flesh, spirit made voice.

• **The White Elephant (Airavata)** represents strength through
serenity, carrying Indra, the god of divine communication —
the peaceful power of truth that flows through silence.

• **The color blue** radiates peace, clarity, and vastness — the
open expanse of ether that connects all beings through sound
and understanding.

• **The seed sound HAM (हं)** vibrates through the throat, harmonizing voice and consciousness, clearing distortion, and awakening the resonance of divine expression.

To meditate on these symbols is to awaken your inner sky — the clear, boundless field where all words are born and all silence returns.
Each image reminds you that voice, truth, and listening are sacred acts of alignment — the harmonious expression of your divine resonance.

When the symbols of Vishuddha unite, they whisper one eternal truth:
You are the space. You are the sound. You are the voice through which the divine speaks.

THE THROAT CHAKRA AS THE SACRED SOUND

Long before chakras were depicted as spinning wheels of light, ancient sages described **Vishuddha** as the **sacred sound** — the pure vibration of consciousness that bridges heaven and earth.

This sound was not imagined as mere speech, but as the **primordial resonance of truth** — the divine voice that gives creation form and meaning.
It is the etheric field through which spirit becomes sound and silence becomes revelation.

The Voice Within

Where the Solar Plexus was envisioned as a flame, the Throat was seen as a **sky** — vast, open, and luminous.
It is the inner expanse through which sound travels — the **space of communication, creativity, and expression.**

Yogis taught that when awareness rests in the throat, one can hear the subtle vibration of the soul — the **nada**, the inner

sound current that hums behind all existence.
This vibration is infinite yet intimate — it carries truth beyond words, expressing what the heart feels and what the spirit knows.

Here resides Ākāśa, the element of ether — the **sacred field of resonance** that connects all beings through vibration.
It is the source of expression, intuition, and divine communion — the space where thought becomes voice, and voice becomes creation.

Why the Throat Chakra?

The Throat Chakra is the seat of communication and creative expression — the **celestial ether** through which awareness speaks and listens.
To enter this space is to remember that sound is sacred — every word, whisper, and silence shapes reality.

• **In Tantra:** Vishuddha is the realm of purification through vibration — the inner temple where truth resonates and illusion dissolves.

• **In Yoga:** It is the "center of divine sound," the channel of sacred communication where silence and expression unite.

• **In Alchemy:** Ether is the fifth element — the quintessence that contains all others, transforming density into subtlety, form into frequency.

• **In Mystical Traditions Worldwide:** Sound is seen as creation itself — the first word, the original tone, the vibration that called the universe into being. Chant, song, and prayer become bridges between the human and the divine.

To meditate on **Vishuddha** is to listen — not only to your voice, but to the silence behind it.

It is to recognize that **you are both the sound and the space through which it moves** — the clear channel of divine expression, where truth vibrates as light, and silence speaks as love.

THE WORD AND THE THROAT CHAKRA

"In the beginning was the Word, and the Word was with God, and the Word was God."
— *John 1:1*

Long before language shaped human thought, there was vibration — the pure sound of creation itself.

Every tradition holds a version of this truth: that the universe began not with form, but with **frequency**, not with matter, but with **the Word** — the divine resonance that spoke existence into being.

In yogic and Tantric philosophy, this primordial sound is known as **Nada Brahma** — *"Sound is God."*

It is the same sacred principle that the Gospel of John reveals: the Word, or *Logos*, as the creative essence of the Divine.

Both teachings point to the same truth — that all creation begins with **vibration**, and that **sound is the bridge between the unseen and the manifest.**

Vishuddha: The Gateway of Divine Expression

The Throat Chakra, **Vishuddha**, is the energetic embodiment of that Word — the place where the **divine vibration becomes audible,** where spirit finds voice through human breath.

Just as God spoke the universe into existence, we shape our reality with every word we utter. Speech, song, prayer, and silence all carry creative force; they are modern echoes of that first cosmic utterance — the sound that set galaxies spinning.

To speak truthfully is therefore an act of creation.
Each word born from the Throat Chakra is a **spark of divine will**, sent into the ether to form new possibilities. When we align speech with wisdom and love, we reclaim the sacred power of the Word — not to control, but to harmonize; not to dominate, but to bring light into being.

The Sacred Parallel

- In **Genesis**, "God said, 'Let there be light,' and there was light."
  The Word *preceded* light — vibration became illumination.
- In **Vishuddha**, the same law unfolds within us: when we speak from the soul, vibration awakens light within and around us.

The Throat Chakra is therefore not only the center of communication — it is the **altar of creation** within the human body, the place where divine energy passes through the voice to shape the world.

The Inner Revelation

To awaken Vishuddha is to rediscover that the **Word still speaks** — not only in scripture, but through every breath, tone, and truth we share.
When our voice is aligned with Spirit, we become co-creators in the divine story — living expressions of the eternal truth:

In the beginning was the Word — and the Word still lives in you.

A SHARED WISDOM

Across traditions, the Throat Chakra has always been linked to **ether, sound, and the Word that creates worlds.**
Where the Heart feels and the Third Eye perceives, **Vishuddha expresses** — it is the moment of revelation, when truth becomes vibration and awareness becomes communication.

The lesson of the Throat Chakra is clear: **Tend your voice. Speak with truth, listen with openness, and let your words carry light.** When the sound of Vishuddha flows clear and free, you stand as your own resonance — calm, luminous, and in harmony with all that is.

THE THROAT AS A SACRED RESONANCE

The Throat Chakra's sixteen-petaled lotus — encircling a silver-blue sphere and the seed sound **HAM** — can be seen as a **map of divine vibration.** The petals are the many tones of expression, the circle is the infinite sky of consciousness, and the sound is the pulse of creation itself. Together, they guide awareness into the sacred space of Vishuddha, where honesty, creativity, and communication dwell — carrying the memory of truth and the seed of divine voice.

A Practice: Entering the Sound

1. Close your eyes. Place your hand gently over your throat or heart.
2. Visualize a **soft blue light** swirling in your throat — vast and calm, like an open sky after rain.
3. As you breathe, hear the faint hum of creation within — the subtle vibration behind all sound.
4. Begin to chant softly, **Haaaaaammmm...**, feeling the vibration expand through your neck, jaw, and chest.
5. Let the sound dissolve into silence. Rest in that stillness — the space where truth speaks without words.

In this stillness, feel your energy harmonize — your thoughts becoming clear, your voice steady and compassionate, your truth effortless and kind.

THE DEEPER LESSON

The voice of Vishuddha reminds us that **spirituality is not about silence alone, but about the sacred harmony between silence and sound.** The world may misunderstand you, your truth may tremble at first — but within you resounds a note that cannot be silenced.

To return to this sound is to return to truth.
To live from this sound is to speak with clarity, integrity, and peace. When you trust your inner voice, you do not seek truth — **you become its resonance.**

THE WESTERN ADAPTATION

When the chakra system reached the West in the late 19th and early 20th centuries, its profound Tantric roots were translated into a language that reflected Western views of consciousness, psychology, and personal growth. Early Theosophists such as **C.W. Leadbeater** and **Alice Bailey** reinterpreted the chakras not only as esoteric centers of energy, but as symbolic gateways to psychological and spiritual evolution.

In this adaptation, the **Throat Chakra (Vishuddha)** came to represent **communication, authenticity, and self-expression** — the bridge between thought and manifestation. Rather than being seen purely as the etheric center of vibration or divine sound, it became understood as the seat of the **voice, creativity, and personal truth** — the place where one learns to speak, listen, and live in alignment with inner integrity.

Western psychology found an immediate resonance with this interpretation. Freud's exploration of repression and expression, and Jung's work with the *Self* and *individuation*, both reflect Vishuddha's evolution — the transformation of unconscious emotion into articulated understanding. The voice became a metaphor for the psyche: to speak was to reveal, to silence was to suppress, and to express truth was to heal.

By the mid-20th century, as the **New Age movement** emerged, Vishuddha was widely recognized as the **center of communication and creative authenticity**. Therapists, writers, and spiritual teachers began linking the Throat Chakra with themes of **truth-telling, expression, boundaries, and artistic flow**. Speaking one's truth, journaling, affirmations, and vocal meditation became modern adaptations of ancient sound practices once reserved for sacred mantra and mantra yoga.

In this Western view, Vishuddha came to represent not only divine communication but also **psychological integration** — the healing that occurs when inner experience finds outward voice. It was described as the chakra of expression without fear, of the courage to speak, sing, write, and live one's truth.

Workshops, therapies, and healing practices began to center around **communication awareness** — from improving listening and self-expression to releasing the "blocked throat" caused by suppressed emotion or unspoken truth. Through this lens, the Throat Chakra became both a **spiritual and psychological gateway**: where clarity of mind meets authenticity of heart.

While the Western approach often simplifies Vishuddha's deeper mystical roots — reducing the vast ether of divine sound (Ākāśa) to the human act of communication — it still honors an essential truth: **without voice, there is no connection; without truth, there is no freedom.**

The journey of the Throat Chakra in the West reminds us that expression is not merely sound — it is a sacred act of

alignment. To speak with awareness is to create resonance between the inner and outer worlds.
And to live authentically is to let one's voice become an instrument of harmony, guided not by ego, but by Spirit.

As we continue in this book, we will weave together both the **ancient yogic wisdom of Vishuddha** and the **modern psychological understanding of communication**, bridging the sacred art of sound with the contemporary quest for authenticity — so that this chakra may once again be seen as what it truly is: **the voice of the soul and the breath of creation itself.**

SCIENTIFIC CORRELATIONS OF THE THROAT CHAKRA

While ancient yogic texts described the chakras as subtle energy centers, modern science recognizes clear anatomical and physiological parallels.
The **Throat Chakra (Vishuddha),** located at the base of the throat, corresponds to the **laryngeal plexus** and is closely associated with the **thyroid gland, vocal cords, respiratory system, and vagus nerve** — all structures responsible for vibration, regulation, and communication within the body.

The Thyroid Gland: Regulator of Vital Energy

The thyroid, a butterfly-shaped gland positioned in the neck, governs metabolism and the body's energy regulation.
Just as Vishuddha refines expression and flow, the thyroid refines the body's internal rhythm — maintaining balance between activity and rest, creation and conservation.
When thyroid function is balanced, we feel vibrant, clear, and expressive; when it is imbalanced, fatigue, anxiety, or stagnation may result, mirroring energetic blocks within the Throat Chakra.

In this sense, the thyroid acts as the **biological counterpart to Vishuddha's spiritual role**: both sustain equilibrium, translating inner intention into outward vitality.

The Vocal Apparatus: The Instrument of Expression

The **larynx (voice box)** and **vocal cords** give physical form to the energetic principle of sound.
Every word, hum, or tone originates as vibration — air passing through the cords, shaped by resonance and articulation.
This process mirrors Vishuddha's function as the **transformer of energy into vibration** — where unspoken thought becomes audible frequency.

Modern acoustics confirms that sound literally alters energy fields; resonance creates measurable waves that influence emotion and environment alike.
This scientific understanding echoes the yogic truth that **sound (nāda)** is not metaphorical, but elemental — vibration shaping reality.

The Vagus Nerve: The Bridge Between Speech and Calm

The **vagus nerve**, one of the body's primary communication pathways, passes directly through the throat, connecting brain, heart, and lungs. It governs the parasympathetic nervous system — the body's capacity for calm, relaxation, and repair.

When we chant, hum, or speak rhythmically, the vagus nerve is gently stimulated, lowering heart rate and blood pressure while releasing soothing neurochemicals like oxytocin.
Scientific research confirms that **chanting and vocal toning** increase vagal tone — supporting immunity, emotional regulation, and overall well-being.
This physiological response mirrors the spiritual teaching that **sound heals** — that the sacred vibration of voice restores harmony within the nervous system and the soul.

Breath: The Conduit of Sound and Spirit

Every sound begins with a breath.
In both yogic and medical understanding, breath is life's
messenger — the bridge between body and consciousness.
When breath flows freely, the voice carries resonance and
confidence; when restricted, speech falters, and expression
contracts.

Pranayama (yogic breathwork) directly supports Vishuddha by
synchronizing respiration, tone, and awareness.
Modern studies show that mindful breathing calms the limbic
system, enhances oxygenation, and promotes coherent heart-
brain rhythms — physiological harmony reflected in a balanced
Throat Chakra.

Breath, vibration, and consciousness are thus inseparable —
each one amplifying the other, forming the triad through which
the voice becomes sacred.

Modern Resonance: The Science of Sound Healing

Recent studies in **vibrational medicine** reveal that sound
frequencies can alter brainwave patterns, reduce inflammation,
and promote emotional release.
The human voice, with its rich harmonic range, acts as both
transmitter and receiver of these healing vibrations.
When one hums, chants, or sings intentionally, the oscillations
of the vocal cords generate frequencies that entrain the body's
cells and biofield into coherence — a modern reflection of the
ancient concept of **mantra as medicine**.

In this light, Vishuddha is not only symbolic — it is
anatomically active and scientifically verifiable.
The same energy that moves through the larynx to form sound
also regulates the body's internal harmony.

Each vibration we create ripples through the nervous system and beyond, shaping both physiology and consciousness.

The Unified Understanding

From the yogic view, the Throat Chakra refines the energy of the lower centers — transforming emotion (Heart), will (Solar Plexus), and instinct (Root) into sound and expression.
From a scientific view, it integrates the systems of **breathing, metabolism, and communication** — refining the life force into articulate vibration.

Together, they reveal a single truth:
Expression is biology and spirituality intertwined.
To speak your truth is to align breath, brain, and being — to let energy become sound, and sound become creation.

ARCHETYPES OF THE THROAT CHAKRA

Every chakra expresses itself through distinct psychological patterns — universal roles that shape how energy manifests in our lives.
These patterns, or **archetypes**, reveal both the light and the shadow of the chakra's essence.

For the **Throat Chakra (Vishuddha)**, the energy of **expression, truth, and resonance** unfolds through two primary archetypes: **The Communicator** and **The Messenger.**

The Communicator

The Communicator embodies Vishuddha's central purpose — the power of expression, honesty, and authentic dialogue.
This archetype represents the part of us that translates inner truth into outer voice, that bridges thought and emotion through language, and that creates harmony through understanding.

The Communicator teaches that **words are sacred instruments of creation** — capable of healing, connecting, and transforming when spoken with awareness.

In Balance:

The balanced Communicator speaks with clarity and compassion.
They listen deeply and express truth without fear or aggression.
Their words carry presence — steady, thoughtful, and aligned with heart and wisdom.
They understand that silence, too, can be communication when held with intention.
A balanced Communicator does not seek to convince; they seek to connect.

In Shadow:

When unbalanced, the Communicator may distort or suppress expression.
In one shadow, they become **The Silenced** — fearful of judgment or rejection, withholding truth until their voice fades into invisibility.
In the other, they become **The Talker** — speaking without listening, filling silence with noise rather than meaning.
In both, energy is trapped — the truth unspoken or the word unrooted.

The lesson: **speech without awareness is as harmful as silence without truth.**
The Communicator reminds us that to express is sacred — but to express consciously is divine.

The Messenger

If the Communicator gives voice to the self, the Messenger gives voice to Spirit.

This archetype represents Vishuddha's higher expression — the channel of divine inspiration, artistic creation, and sacred communication.

The Messenger speaks not only for themselves but as a vessel for universal truth, allowing higher wisdom to flow through sound, art, or presence.

In Balance:

The balanced Messenger lives in alignment with divine timing and inspiration.

They express truth with humility and grace, knowing their words are guided by something greater than ego.

Their art, teaching, or presence carries resonance — awakening understanding in others.

They are the poets, healers, and visionaries who translate vibration into meaning.

In Shadow:

When unbalanced, the Messenger may fall into distortion.

They become **The Preacher** — speaking truth without listening to its source, seeking validation instead of alignment.

Or they may become **The Doubter** — mistrusting their own voice, silencing divine guidance out of fear of being misunderstood.

Both shadows reflect disconnection from inner resonance — the loss of faith in one's truth.

The Messenger teaches that authentic expression is not performance but **presence.**

When the voice is attuned to the higher self, every word becomes a prayer — a vibration that heals and harmonizes both speaker and listener.

The Deeper Lesson

The archetypes of Vishuddha reveal that **the voice is both mirror and bridge** — it reflects our inner truth and connects us to the world around us. When expression flows freely, the soul resonates with life itself; when blocked, energy stagnates, and spirit dims.

The Communicator and the Messenger together remind us that the voice is a sacred channel — one that must be purified by awareness, balanced by heart, and guided by wisdom.

To speak truth is to align heaven and earth through sound.
To listen deeply is to hear the divine in all things.
And when both are honored, the Throat Chakra becomes what it was always meant to be — **the clear sky of consciousness through which truth travels freely, carried on the wind of Spirit.**

TOGETHER: THE COMMUNICATOR AND THE MESSENGER

Together, these archetypes reveal the dual expression of Vishuddha's truth:
• **The Communicator** brings the courage to speak.
• **The Messenger** brings the wisdom to channel.

One gives voice to personal truth; the other, to divine inspiration.
When balanced, they form the sacred harmony of the Throat Chakra — the resonance of authenticity joined with higher guidance.

The Communicator grounds expression in honesty and clarity.
The Messenger lifts it into grace and vision.
Together, they awaken the sacred art of conscious

communication — speaking not to impress, but to express the truth that liberates both self and others.

LIVING ARCHETYPALLY

Both the Communicator and the Messenger dwell within us. At times, one voice rises louder — the human voice that longs to be heard, or the spiritual voice that whispers with divine clarity.
Recognizing which speaks allows us to balance expression and listening, language and silence, individuality and intuition.

Living archetypally with Vishuddha means **aligning speech with spirit** — blending the Communicator's honesty with the Messenger's devotion.
It is learning to speak from awareness rather than reaction, to listen with presence rather than impatience, and to let words become carriers of light rather than noise.

When these archetypes unite, communication becomes sacred. The throat no longer struggles to be heard — it resonates as a clear instrument of truth. Expression becomes an act of creation, and every word, a vibration of awakening.

THROAT CHAKRA ARCHETYPE REFLECTION EXERCISE

Find a quiet space where you can sit comfortably.
Lengthen your spine and take slow, conscious breaths.
Place one hand gently on your throat, feeling the subtle rise and fall with each inhale and exhale.
With every breath, imagine a soft blue light glowing in your throat — cool, calm, and expansive — spreading clarity through your voice and peace through your mind.

Allow this light to expand until you feel your entire being resonating with openness and truth.

Then, reflect on the questions below and record your insights in your journal.

Exploring the Communicator

1. When do I feel most authentic and confident in expressing myself?
2. How often do I truly listen — to others, and to my own inner voice?
3. What truths am I holding back out of fear of judgment or rejection?
4. How does my tone — the energy behind my words — reflect my inner state?
5. What would it feel like to speak from calm honesty rather than defensiveness or silence?

Exploring the Messenger

1. When have I felt that something greater than myself was speaking through me — inspiration, intuition, or creative flow?
2. How do I honor the guidance I receive from within or from Spirit?
3. In what ways do I share messages of healing, wisdom, or encouragement with others?
4. Where might I doubt or distort my message — trying to please, impress, or convince rather than simply express?
5. What practice helps me attune my voice to higher truth — prayer, writing, song, or meditation?

Integration

• Which archetype feels stronger in me right now — the Communicator or the Messenger?
• Where do I notice tension or hesitation in expressing my truth?

• What small, loving step can I take this week to honor my authentic voice?

Reflection Mantra

"I honor the **Communicator** within me for speaking my truth with clarity and compassion.
I honor the **Messenger** within me for allowing divine wisdom to flow through my voice.
Together, they awaken my true resonance — clear, calm, and free."

Chapter 3 – The Energetic Blueprint of the Throat Chakra

The Throat Chakra and the Aura

The Throat Chakra (Vishuddha) is more than the organ of speech — it is the energetic bridge where vibration becomes expression and truth becomes resonance.
If the Heart radiates love and the Solar Plexus ignites purpose, then the Throat refines that energy into communication — transforming intention into frequency and awareness into sound.

When Vishuddha is open and balanced, the aura shimmers with a luminous **blue light** — soft yet radiant, like the sky at dawn. This energy radiates outward from the throat, neck, and shoulders, blending serenity with strength.
It carries the frequency of authenticity — a vibration that feels calm, trustworthy, and clear.
Others sense it as integrity, harmony, and presence — the unmistakable resonance of someone whose words, actions, and energy are aligned.

Energetically, a balanced Throat Chakra expresses as ease in communication and freedom in self-expression.
You speak truthfully without fear, listen deeply without defense, and allow inspiration to flow naturally through you.
Your aura expands, smooth, and coherent, like ripples moving evenly across still water — every word, thought, and gesture harmonized with intention.

When Vishuddha is **blocked or underactive**, the aura around the neck and upper chest may appear clouded or compressed. The individual may struggle to articulate feelings, doubt their voice, or fear judgment.

Energy stagnates at the throat, creating a sense of being "choked back" or unheard.

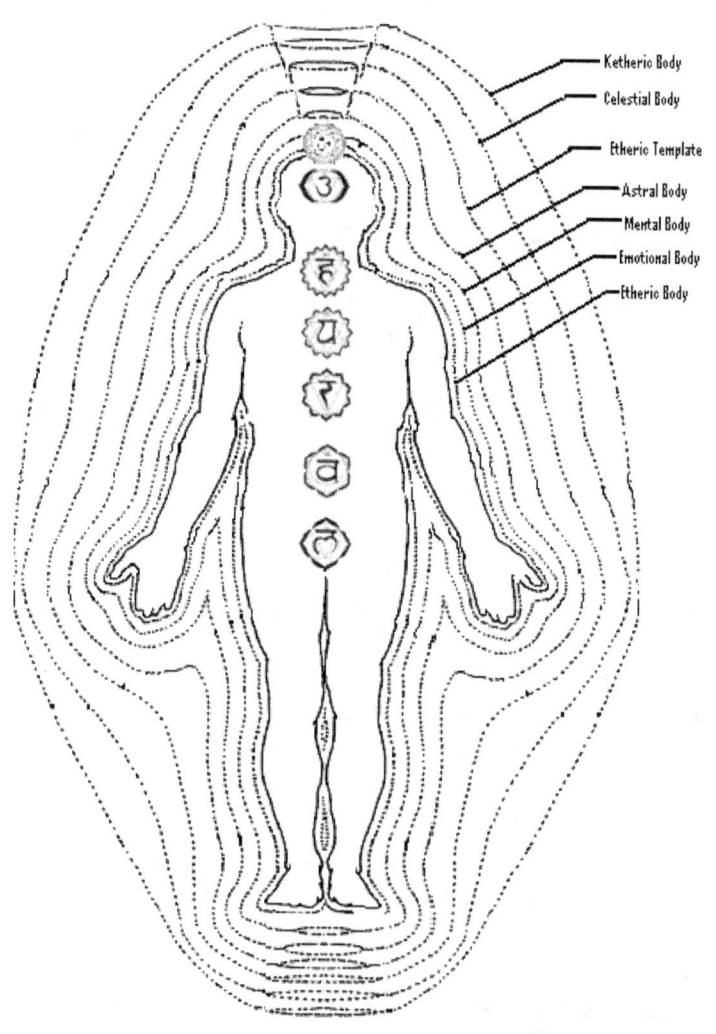

Conversely, when Vishuddha is **overactive**, the aura can flare with sharp or restless blue energy — expression that overwhelms rather than connects.
Words may become reactive or scattered, carrying more force than truth.
In both extremes, sound loses harmony — the voice either silenced or strained.

THE THROAT AS THE RESONANT FIELD OF THE AURA

The Throat Chakra acts as the **harmonic tuner** of the energy field.
Just as the Solar Plexus organizes vitality through fire, Vishuddha organizes vibration through sound.
It refines emotional and mental energy into frequency — shaping how your presence is "heard" by the world.

When balanced, the entire aura vibrates in coherence, resonating like a perfectly tuned instrument.
This is why sound healing, mantra chanting, humming, singing, or gentle breathwork can immediately bring the aura back into alignment.
Practices such as chanting the **bīja mantra HAM**, toning gentle "Ah" or "Om" sounds, or visualizing a radiant blue lotus at the throat send a clear energetic message through the field:
"I am heard. I am clear. I speak truth in harmony with my soul."

In response, the aura expands and brightens, its edges soft yet defined — like a calm sky after a storm, radiant with peace.

From an energetic practitioner's perspective, Vishuddha represents the **blueprint of resonance** within the aura — the pattern of coherence that reveals whether one's energy flows freely through truth or becomes distorted through suppression.
Even when the lower chakras are strong and the higher ones

awakened, if the Throat is constricted, energy cannot express its purpose.
It becomes trapped — felt but not shared, known but not spoken.

To clear the Throat Chakra is to restore alignment between inner and outer worlds.
It allows the soul's frequency to sing freely through the body and into the field.

When Vishuddha is awakened, the aura becomes music —
a field of luminous blue radiance that speaks without words.
It is the energetic signature of truth in motion,
the clear sky through which spirit communicates.

The Throat Chakra is the **energetic blueprint of resonance** —
the space where vibration becomes creation,
and where your voice becomes the song of your soul.

THE AURA OF SOUND: HOW VISHUDDHA RADIATES THROUGH THE ENERGY FIELD

When the Throat Chakra (Vishuddha) is balanced, its soft blue resonance expands beyond the physical body — not as brightness, but as tone.
It is the subtle hum of authenticity, the peaceful vibration of presence that fills the space around you even before a word is spoken.
This is the energy people feel when someone "speaks truth" — not through volume or force, but through clarity, calm, and coherence.

It is expression without performance, wisdom without superiority, communication without noise.
In the aura, this appears as a **gentle, luminous blue field** surrounding the neck and shoulders, rippling outward like waves across a clear lake.

It feels spacious, clean, and cool — the energetic signature of truth in harmony.

THE QUALITY OF SOUND

Vishuddha's energy expresses through the element of **ether (ākāśa)** — the subtlest of all elements, where sound becomes the vehicle of vibration.
When balanced, this etheric field shimmers in tones of **blue, turquoise, and silvery-white**, often with pearlescent edges of violet where communication meets intuition.
Its presence feels soothing, open, and expansive.

Others may describe sensing peace, calm, or clarity in your presence, as though your energy carries the sound of stillness itself.
When the Throat Chakra is **underactive**, the aura appears muted or compressed around the neck — communication feels blocked, and one may struggle to express truth.
When **overactive**, the field may vibrate erratically — speech becomes overanxious, excessive, or forced.
True balance lies in resonance: sound that vibrates freely, neither withheld nor overwhelming.

THE FIELD OF COMMUNICATION

The Throat Chakra governs expression and resonance — how your truth flows into the world.
Its light in the aura reflects coherence between thought, feeling, and word.
When balanced, Vishuddha refines the raw energy of the lower chakras into frequency — meaning you not only speak clearly but *emit* clarity.

This coherence creates an energetic integrity in communication. You no longer absorb others' confusion nor project your own — you respond with equanimity.

Your energy field becomes a resonant chamber of truth, holding space for honesty and understanding.

This is the **aura of presence**: it doesn't demand attention; it invites trust.

It says to the world:
"I am in harmony with my voice and my truth."

INFLUENCE AND RESONANCE

A balanced Throat Chakra magnetizes through vibration rather than force.

It attracts opportunities and people by the purity of tone, not by persuasion.

Your words carry frequency — they uplift, soothe, or awaken simply because they come from alignment.

When Vishuddha is radiant, communication flows like music — others feel safe, inspired, and more attuned in your presence.

This resonance is why teachers, healers, and artists with awakened Throat Chakras often influence deeply: they transmit not information, but vibration.

Their voices become instruments of transformation, tuning others to harmony and higher truth.

ENERGY EXCHANGE AND LISTENING

Vishuddha is also the center of **energetic dialogue** — the exchange not only of words, but of subtle frequencies through tone, silence, and intention.

When balanced, communication is reciprocal — giving and receiving truth in equal measure.

When weak, one may withhold expression or internalize others' voices; when excessive, one may dominate conversations or speak without listening.

Awareness restores harmony.
Pausing before speech, breathing deeply into the throat, and
visualizing a serene blue light can instantly recalibrate the
energy field — allowing your words to emerge from peace, not
pressure.

THE RADIANCE OF SACRED COMMUNICATION

At its highest vibration, the Throat Chakra becomes the **light of
divine expression** — communication as prayer, truth as
offering, sound as creation.
In this state, the aura expands in subtle blue-white radiance,
encompassing both presence and peace.
Your voice becomes an extension of consciousness — clear,
kind, and resonant with love.

To live from this center is to communicate as the soul does:
honestly, humbly, and harmoniously.

This is the essence of a balanced Vishuddha —
a sky that neither storms nor hides its light,
but opens vast and clear, a living field of sound where truth
becomes music and communication becomes grace.

FLOW OF ENERGY FROM THE THROAT UPWARD

The Throat Chakra (Vishuddha) is far more than the center of
speech — it is the **gateway of resonance**, where energy
becomes vibration and truth becomes sound.
It is the bridge between the heart's compassion and the mind's
clarity, transforming emotion into expression and insight into
understanding.

In yogic and Tantric tradition, Vishuddha marks a pivotal stage
in the ascent of Kundalini through the **sushumna nadi**, the
central channel of awakening.
Here, prana — the vital life force — is purified by sound and

refined into frequency.
It is said that when energy reaches Vishuddha, the soul begins
to hear its own voice — the divine sound within all creation.

At this level, the warmth of the Solar Plexus (Manipura)
evolves into tone and resonance — the **fire of will** becomes the
ether of expression.
The courage once used to act now matures into the courage to
speak, to reveal, and to share one's truth with grace.

The Upward Flow of Expression

• **From Vishuddha (Throat) → to Ajna (Third Eye):**
Sound refines into silence. Expression matures into insight.
What is spoken with awareness deepens into understanding and
vision.

• **From Ajna → to Sahasrara (Crown):**
Insight transcends form and merges into stillness.
The voice of intuition becomes the Word of the Divine — truth
beyond language, vibration beyond sound.

• **From Anahata (Heart) → to Vishuddha (Throat):**
Love rises to find its voice. Compassion becomes
communication.
The emotions of the heart take shape through expression,
revealing wisdom through words, art, and song.

The Path of Resonance

This upward flow mirrors the evolution of consciousness itself:
Feeling becomes expression, expression becomes perception,
and perception dissolves into realization.
Each chakra refines the energy it receives, lifting vibration
higher — from emotion to empathy, from empathy to truth,
from truth to pure awareness.

When Vishuddha is balanced, this ascent is **clear and harmonious**.
The will of Manipura flows effortlessly into the truth of the Throat, and expression becomes both creative and sacred.
The aura vibrates with serenity and coherence — a calm blue resonance that communicates peace even in silence.

But when Vishuddha is **blocked or unbalanced**, the current falters.
Truth becomes fear, voice becomes suppression, or words spill uncontrolled, scattering energy instead of transmitting clarity.
When the Throat is closed, energy from the Heart cannot express, and wisdom from the Mind cannot integrate.
The bridge between feeling and knowing collapses into disconnection.

The Voice as the Bridge of Light

Practitioners often describe Vishuddha as the **sky of the subtle body** — the open expanse where all elements dissolve into ether.
Here, the life force no longer burns or flows — it vibrates.
It sings, hums, and resounds through every layer of being.

When the Throat Chakra opens, sound becomes light.
Your words carry frequency, your silence carries presence.
Energy rises with purity, no longer distorted by fear or pride.
This is the stage where communication becomes communion — where your personal voice unites with divine resonance.

The Essence of the Flow

The Throat does not hold energy — it transmits it.
It transforms the emotional waters of the Heart into vibration and the insight of the Mind into understanding.
Like a flute through which the wind of Spirit plays, Vishuddha resonates with whatever frequency you allow to pass through it.

When balanced, it radiates the pure sound of truth —
calm, compassionate, and free. It reminds us that expression is
not noise but alignment; that the purpose of the voice is not
persuasion but revelation. Through Vishuddha, the life force
becomes language, and the soul learns to sing its eternal song.

The Throat Chakra As The Seat Of Truth And Expression

If the heart is the seat of love, and the solar plexus is the seat of
power, then the throat chakra is the **seat of truth and
expression**.
Vishuddha governs the element of ether — the pure field
through which vibration becomes voice, and consciousness
takes form through sound.
It is the sacred space where energy transforms into
communication, where inner truth meets outer reality.

This chakra represents **the evolution of awareness from action
to articulation** — from the will to do, to the wisdom to express.
At Vishuddha, power refines into resonance. It is no longer
about control or direction, but about alignment and authenticity
— allowing your inner truth to flow freely through word, tone,
and presence.

From an evolutionary perspective, the Throat Chakra mirrors
the stage when human beings began to articulate thought — not
just survival, emotion, or power, but **meaning**.
When early humans discovered language, song, and story, they
awakened the ability to connect consciousness across space and
time.
Likewise, when Vishuddha awakens within us, we rediscover
the creative force of the Word — the voice that bridges heart
and mind, heaven and earth.

THE BRIDGE OF COMMUNICATION

The Throat Chakra serves as the energetic bridge between the heart's compassion and the mind's clarity.
It is through this center that love becomes expression and wisdom becomes communication.
Where the Solar Plexus gives us confidence to act, the Throat gives us courage to **speak** — to declare our truth, to share our gifts, and to create harmony through voice and vibration.

When Vishuddha is **balanced**, energy flows like a calm, resonant current.
You express yourself clearly and truthfully, with kindness and conviction.
Your words uplift, your silence comforts, and your presence carries calm authority.
You communicate not to be heard, but to connect.

When Vishuddha is **underactive**, energy becomes constricted.
You may struggle to express yourself, fear judgment, or hold back your opinions to maintain peace.
Suppressed truth collects like pressure behind the voice, creating tension, self-doubt, or even physical tightness in the throat.

When **overactive**, energy disperses.
Speech becomes excessive or reactive — words overflow without clarity, or truth is spoken without compassion.
In both imbalances, communication loses resonance: the voice either fades into silence or overpowers without harmony.

THE BODY OF SOUND AND SPIRIT

Just as Manipura governs digestion of food and experience, Vishuddha governs the digestion of **vibration and meaning**. It filters the energy we take in through sound, words, and thought — transforming information into wisdom, and expression into understanding.

Physiologically, this center influences the throat, neck, thyroid, and respiratory system — all structures that regulate air, tone, and vibration.
Energetically, it determines how we balance listening and speaking, silence and sound.
When aligned, communication becomes effortless — an exchange of truth flowing through you rather than from you.

MODERN CHALLENGES TO VISHUDDHA

In the modern world, Vishuddha often suffers from overstimulation and suppression at once.
Constant noise, digital communication, and fear of vulnerability distort authentic expression.
People speak without presence, or remain silent to avoid conflict.
The result is disconnection — words without meaning, and silence without peace.

Healing the Throat Chakra restores the harmony between **voice and truth**.
It reminds us that speech is sacred — a creative act that can heal, inspire, or awaken when aligned with the heart.
To speak consciously is to weave vibration into the fabric of creation.

THE LIGHT OF AUTHENTICITY

When balanced, Vishuddha glows with a tranquil blue light —
vast as the open sky.
Your voice becomes calm, clear, and true.
You no longer force or withhold expression; you simply allow
truth to move through you with grace.

In this state, the Throat Chakra becomes the temple of divine
communication — the meeting place of heaven and earth within
you.
Here, you remember that your words are not just sound — they
are **frequency**, shaping the energy around you.

To honor Vishuddha is to speak with integrity, to listen with
presence, and to live as a vessel of truth.
It is to know that your voice is sacred, your silence powerful,
and your expression divine.

When you live from this center, you do not seek to convince —
you seek to connect.
You do not speak to be heard — you speak to harmonize.

Vishuddha teaches that truth is not something we possess, but
something we express —
the living resonance of spirit through sound,
the eternal echo of the soul saying, "I am."

A UNIVERSAL UNDERSTANDING OF SOUND

Though the chakra system arises from the yogic and Tantric
traditions of India, the experience of **sound** — both audible and
symbolic — is universal. Across cultures and epochs, humanity
has understood that vibration gives birth to creation. Before
light, there was resonance; before form, there was frequency.
Sound is the bridge between the seen and unseen — the breath
of the divine shaping silence into existence.

To live with sound is to live in harmony. It is the awareness that every word, tone, and rhythm carries energy — capable of building or breaking, healing or harming. Whether through chant, music, prayer, or poetry, cultures throughout history have honored sound as the voice of creation itself — the vibration that turns spirit into form.

CROSS-CULTURAL EXPRESSIONS OF SOUND

Indigenous Traditions:
For many Indigenous and First Nations peoples, sound is medicine — the voice of the earth and spirit intertwined. Drums echo the heartbeat of Mother Earth, songs call upon ancestors, and chants realign the soul with natural harmony. Sound ceremonies are not performances, but pathways — tools for healing, remembering, and reconnecting with the sacred rhythm of life.

Eastern Systems:
In yogic philosophy, Vishuddha's element is **Ākāśa (ether)** — the field of space through which all vibration moves. The universe itself is said to be woven of **Nada Brahma** — "sound is God." Every mantra, every word, is a wave in this ocean of creation. Chanting, toning, or silent prayer awakens the Throat Chakra, tuning the individual consciousness to the universal hum — the *Om* that underlies all existence.

Ancient Egypt:
To the Egyptians, the spoken word held the power of **heka** — divine magic. Creation began when the god Ptah spoke the world into being, and names were thought to hold the essence of what they described. Words were not merely sounds; they were living forces, shaping destiny through vibration.

Greek Philosophy:
Pythagoras taught that the universe was structured through **harmony and proportion** — that celestial bodies moved in

musical intervals known as the *Music of the Spheres*. This cosmic sound, though inaudible, was believed to sustain the order of creation. The Greeks understood that to live virtuously was to be "in tune" with this divine harmony.

Biblical and Mystical Traditions:
In Genesis, creation begins not with touch, but with a word:
"And God said, Let there be light."
The Word precedes light — sound gives rise to illumination. In Christian mysticism, the "Word made flesh" reflects the descent of divine vibration into matter, echoing Vishuddha's function as the bridge between heaven and earth. In Sufi practice, chanting the *Names of God* refines consciousness through rhythm and repetition, turning the heart into an instrument of divine remembrance.

Eastern and Western Alchemy:
Just as fire transforms matter, sound refines energy. Alchemists and mystics recognized the voice as a sacred tool of transmutation — the power to invoke, to heal, and to manifest. The spoken incantation, the chant, or the sacred tone all mirror Vishuddha's essence: vibration directed by consciousness.

Western Mysticism and Tarot:
The element of ether corresponds to the **Suit of Swords** — representing thought, language, and truth. Just as Manipura's fire becomes the flame of purpose, Vishuddha's ether becomes the breath of clarity. The Sword cuts through illusion, much like the voice of truth that frees the soul from silence.

THE SACRED VIBRATION

Across time and tradition, sound has been revered as the divine communicator — the subtle current through which all life converses.
It connects breath to being, thought to form, soul to Source.

To speak is to create; to sing is to awaken; to listen is to commune.
Sound reveals that the universe is not a collection of things, but a symphony of vibrations — each being, each word, each heartbeat a note in the eternal song of existence.

The Throat Chakra reminds us that truth is not just something we think — it is something we **resonate**.
When the voice aligns with the heart and the mind, speech becomes sacred, silence becomes peace, and life itself becomes music.

THE UNIVERSAL LESSON OF SOUND

In every culture, **sound** is a teacher of truth and resonance.
It reminds us that creation begins not in noise, but in vibration — the subtle hum that connects all life.
When we silence our voice, we block the current of expression; when we misuse it, we distort harmony.
Balance lies in sacred communication — speaking with integrity, listening with presence, and allowing silence its rightful place between words.

Across traditions, this same wisdom endures:
• Sound awakens.
• Sound harmonizes.
• Sound creates.

Whether we call it *Om*, the *Word*, *Nada Brahma*, or the voice of Spirit, the essence is the same:
When our inner sound resonates clear and true, we awaken the light of Vishuddha — the power to express, to align, and to create harmony between heaven and earth.

To honor sound is to honor connection.
To speak with awareness is to shape reality through vibration.

To listen deeply is to hear the voice of the divine — whispering through wind, water, and the beating heart.

When our words flow from truth and our silence rests in peace, we become instruments of the sacred —
resonating not with fear or ego,
but with the eternal tone of creation itself.

How Practitioners Work with the Throat Chakra

For healers and energy practitioners, the **Throat Chakra — Vishuddha —** is known as the center of **truth, expression, and resonance.**
Located at the base of the throat, it governs communication, authenticity, and the ability to align speech, thought, and feeling.
It is where inner truth becomes outer expression — where energy transforms into vibration, and vibration into voice.

When Vishuddha is balanced, a person speaks clearly and listens deeply. Their words carry calm authority and kindness, and their energy feels open, honest, and connected.
When blocked, communication falters — truth is withheld, misunderstood, or distorted. The person may feel unheard, anxious to speak, or unable to articulate what is true for them.

ASSESSMENT

Practitioners begin by tuning into a client's relationship with **truth, communication, and self-expression.**
They may explore questions such as:
• Do you feel safe expressing your thoughts and emotions?
• Do you often remain silent to keep peace or avoid judgment?
• Are your words aligned with your true feelings, or do you say

what others want to hear?
• Do you feel tension or tightness in your throat, neck, or jaw when speaking?
• Are you able to listen openly, or do you find yourself reacting before truly hearing others?

Energetically, healers sense Vishuddha as a luminous **blue field** radiating from the throat and extending into the upper chest and jaw.
• A **balanced center** feels open, cool, and flowing — like clear air or a resonant tone.
• An **underactive Vishuddha** may appear dim, compressed, or constricted, reflecting fear of speaking or difficulty expressing emotions.
• An **overactive Vishuddha** may feel sharp, scattered, or forceful — words spill out without awareness, or energy projects outward without harmony.

Practitioners may also notice how the **Throat Chakra interacts with the Heart and Solar Plexus** — the two centers most closely linked to its function.
When Manipura's willpower rises through a balanced heart, Vishuddha becomes the voice of love guided by purpose.
When the lower chakras are imbalanced, speech may either lack conviction or overflow with untempered emotion.

ENERGY HEALING TECHNIQUES

• Reiki & Hands-On Healing:
Energy is channeled into the throat and upper chest to clear blockages and restore the natural flow of expression.
Practitioners often visualize a radiant blue light expanding through the neck, jaw, and shoulders — dissolving tension, fear of speaking, or withheld emotion. The energy moves gently upward, harmonizing communication between heart and mind.

• **Sound Healing:**
The bija mantra **HAM** resonates with the Throat Chakra, aligning its vibration with truth and clarity. Practitioners may tone HAM aloud or use singing bowls, chimes, or crystal instruments tuned to the frequency of Vishuddha. Sound becomes a cleansing current, sweeping away energetic residue and awakening authentic resonance.

• **Crystal Healing:**
Blue-hued stones — such as **aquamarine, blue lace agate, turquoise, sodalite, and lapis lazuli** — are placed over the throat or worn as pendants to enhance communication, intuition, and calm self-expression. These crystals carry cooling, clarifying energies that support both confidence and serenity in speech.

• **Aromatherapy:**
Balancing and clarifying oils such as **eucalyptus, peppermint, chamomile, frankincense, and lavender** are diffused or applied gently to the throat area. Their light, airy essence opens the respiratory system and clears stagnant energy, inviting the breath — and the voice — to flow freely.

BODYWORK PRACTICES

Because **Vishuddha** governs breath, vibration, and communication, bodywork for this chakra focuses on opening the throat, freeing expression, and aligning posture so energy can flow between the heart and mind.

• **Neck and Shoulder Release:**
Gentle stretches, circular neck rolls, and shoulder openers release physical tension that constricts the voice. Tension here often reflects withheld words or emotional suppression.

• **Breathwork — Ujjayi or Ocean Breath:**
This controlled, wave-like breathing technique creates a soft

internal sound that soothes the nervous system and strengthens the vocal and respiratory pathways. Breath becomes vibration — a bridge between silence and sound.

• **Vocal Toning or Humming:**
Simple humming, chanting **HAM**, or softly toning vowel sounds stimulates the vocal cords and clears stagnant energy in the throat. The goal is not performance but resonance — feeling the vibration ripple through the body.

• **Yoga Poses for Vishuddha:**
Heart and throat openers such as *Fish Pose (Matsyasana)*, *Shoulderstand (Sarvangasana)*, *Plow Pose (Halasana)*, and *Cat-Cow (Marjaryasana-Bitilasana)* enhance circulation through the neck and chest, supporting open, honest communication.

• **Movement Expression:**
Practices such as singing, chanting, dancing, or even speaking affirmations aloud move energy through the throat channel. When the body moves with breath and rhythm, the voice naturally becomes freer and more authentic.

SPIRITUAL AND ANCESTRAL HEALING

Practitioners working at the **Throat Chakra (Vishuddha)** often focus on clearing generational or karmic imprints related to **silence, suppression, or fear of speaking one's truth.** Across many lineages, individuals have inherited energetic patterns of restraint — vows of silence, persecution trauma, or collective conditioning that discourages authentic expression. Healing the throat often means freeing the ancestral voice.

Common practices include:
• **Guided visualizations** to release past-life or ancestral vows of silence and reclaim the right to speak truthfully and lovingly.
• **Sound and breath release**, allowing suppressed emotion to

move out through toning, sighing, or spontaneous vocalization.
• **Cord and vow clearing** to dissolve energetic ties to judgment, guilt, or fear of being misunderstood.
• **Voice activation ceremonies** — chanting, singing, or reading sacred words aloud — to reawaken the power of expression.
• **Blue flame or smoke rituals** (using candlelight or incense) to symbolize purification of the throat and transmutation of unspoken truths into light.

INTEGRATION

Healing Vishuddha is the art of turning **truth into vibration** — bringing what lives within into alignment with what is spoken and shared.
Practitioners encourage clients to honor their voice as sacred, using daily practices that merge awareness, authenticity, and grace.

• Begin each day by **speaking one truth aloud** — something simple but real: "I feel…," "I believe…," or "I need…."
• Practice **mindful listening** — allow silence to speak, and hear beyond words.
• Chant **HAM** or hum softly for five minutes to harmonize the throat and heart energies.
• Wear or visualize the **color blue** to invite clarity, calm, and openness.
• Journal daily — not just to record events, but to give the inner voice space to speak freely.
• Spend quiet time near **sky, wind, or open water** — the natural elements of ether and air that resonate with Vishuddha's vastness.

For healers, the Throat Chakra represents the **alchemy of truth** — the point where wisdom becomes word, and inner clarity becomes outer expression.
It reminds us that communication is sacred; every word carries vibration.

When Vishuddha resonates clear and bright, we do not speak to
be heard —
we speak because truth is the song of the soul,
and silence, too, is its sacred rhythm.

Chapter 4 – Signs of Imbalance

Shadow Aspects of the Throat Chakra

Every chakra carries both light and shadow.
The **Throat Chakra — Vishuddha** — governs communication, truth, and expression. It is the sacred bridge between inner knowing and outer voice, translating feeling into sound and intention into word.

When balanced, Vishuddha is the vibration of authenticity — clear, compassionate, and free.
When misaligned, its energy contracts or distorts, silencing truth or scattering words without meaning. The voice becomes withheld or overused; expression becomes either suppressed or dominating.

These shadows are not failures — they are invitations. Each imbalance reveals where fear, shame, or distortion has interrupted the flow of truth. They call us to listen deeply, to realign speech with integrity, and to remember that voice is sacred vibration — a creative force meant to liberate, not to wound.

SILENCE AND SUPPRESSION

When Vishuddha is **underactive**, the voice dims. You may struggle to speak up, express needs, or share emotions. Words feel caught in the throat, or conversations replay endlessly in the mind, but never leave the lips.

This suppression often begins early — being told to stay quiet, to please others, or that your truth is "too much."
Physically, tension gathers in the neck, jaw, or shoulders; energetically, breath becomes shallow, cutting off flow between heart and mind.

Healing begins with gentle release — humming, sighing, journaling, or simply naming what has long been unspoken. The act of giving voice to truth rekindles confidence and restores flow.

OVEREXPRESSION AND VERBAL DOMINANCE

When Vishuddha burns too brightly, words overflow without awareness. The desire to be heard becomes control; speech loses empathy.
Overactive throat energy manifests as talking over others, defensiveness, gossip, or the compulsion to explain or justify every feeling.
This imbalance stems from fear of silence — the belief that stillness equals invisibility or loss of influence.
Healing requires returning to the sacred balance between speaking and listening — remembering that wisdom arises as much from silence as from sound.

FEAR OF JUDGMENT AND SELF-CENSORSHIP

At the root of many throat imbalances lies the fear of rejection. You may withhold truth, soften your opinions, or alter your words to maintain approval. This self-censorship dims the authentic frequency of Vishuddha, creating dissonance between inner knowing and outer expression.
The result is energetic tension — a feeling of "swallowing" your truth or of being unseen even when you speak.

Healing comes through honesty without aggression — speaking gently but clearly, trusting that authenticity creates alignment rather than conflict.

LYING OR MISALIGNMENT WITH TRUTH

When Vishuddha's energy becomes distorted by fear or ego, communication loses integrity. Half-truths, exaggerations, or people-pleasing distort the frequency of the voice.
Energetically, this creates heaviness in the throat and confusion in the aura — a static that blocks intuition and trust.
To realign, practice radical honesty: speak only what feels true in your body, and listen when silence feels wiser than speech.

MENTAL NOISE AND DISCONNECTION FROM SPIRIT

The Throat Chakra also governs inner dialogue — the voice that narrates life.
When imbalanced, this voice becomes harsh, critical, or chaotic.
Mental chatter drowns out intuition, and inspiration feels distant.
This overactivity reflects blocked energy between the throat and crown, where truth becomes tangled in overthinking.
Healing lies in stillness: meditative breathing, mantra repetition, and deep listening allow inner noise to dissolve into spacious awareness.

THE HIDDEN WOUND

At the heart of every Throat Chakra imbalance lies a simple truth: a wound to **authentic expression**.
Somewhere along the journey, you may have learned that it wasn't safe to speak — or that your truth didn't matter. The result is hesitation, self-censorship, or overcompensation through excessive talking.

Healing Vishuddha is not about volume; it is about resonance.
It is the courage to speak when truth calls — and the wisdom to
be silent when the soul listens.

Each conscious word spoken in integrity reopens the channel
between heart and voice.
Each pause honored in awareness clears space for truth to
vibrate freely.

When the Throat Chakra is healed, communication becomes
communion.
Your words no longer strive to impress — they exist to express.
And in that resonance, you rediscover the power of the divine
voice within you: the voice that creates, liberates, and heals.

Excess or Overactive Throat Chakra Energy

When the Throat Chakra (Vishuddha) becomes overstimulated,
its clear vibration of truth can distort into noise.
Instead of expressing with authenticity, the voice begins to
dominate — words spill faster than awareness, sound overtakes
silence, and communication becomes a weapon rather than a
bridge.

An overactive Vishuddha can manifest as overtalking, verbal
defensiveness, self-righteousness, or excessive intellectualizing.
The person may appear articulate and confident, yet beneath the
surface lies anxiety — the need to prove, explain, or control
through words.
This excess often develops when speaking becomes a survival
strategy: when one has learned that being heard equals safety, or
that silence once led to invisibility.

The result is sound without stillness — expression without
listening.

VERBAL DOMINANCE AND FORCEFUL COMMUNICATION

When Vishuddha overfires, the natural flow of dialogue becomes one-sided.
You may find yourself talking over others, needing to have the last word, or struggling to listen fully. The voice seeks control rather than connection, mistaking volume or intellect for truth.

This imbalance often hides fear — fear of not being heard, understood, or respected.
Healing begins with the sacred pause: letting silence complete the conversation that words cannot.

SELF-RIGHTEOUSNESS AND DOGMATISM

When the Throat Chakra becomes excessive, conviction hardens into rigidity.
Opinions become absolute, dialogue becomes debate, and the desire to express turns into the need to be right.
The tone sharpens, and words lose their compassion.

Vishuddha's true power is discernment — not persuasion.
When speech serves truth rather than ego, language becomes medicine instead of fire.

NERVOSITY AND OVEREXPLANATION

Overactive Vishuddha energy often feels like restlessness in the jaw, throat, or mind — an anxious need to fill silence.
You may overexplain, justify feelings, or talk to relieve discomfort.
This pattern reflects an inner disconnection between the heart (Anahata) and voice — the fear that stillness might expose vulnerability.

The remedy is presence. Slow the breath, soften the jaw, and let words arise naturally instead of chasing them.

GOSSIP, CRITICISM, AND INFORMATION OVERLOAD

Excess throat energy can scatter into idle talk, gossip, or criticism.
The voice, untethered from awareness, disperses energy outward instead of channeling it into meaningful creation.
In the digital age, this may manifest as compulsive communication — texting, posting, or explaining — a modern echo of the ancient imbalance of uncontrolled sound.

To heal, practice sacred speech: speak only what uplifts, clarifies, or honors truth. Silence, when conscious, is the most powerful mantra.

OVERSTIMULATION OF THE MIND

Because Vishuddha bridges the heart and higher centers, overactivity here can overstimulate the intellect. The result is racing thoughts, scattered focus, and mental fatigue. The voice of intuition becomes buried beneath analysis and chatter.
Balance returns through meditation, chanting, and conscious breathing — practices that calm the nervous system and restore the resonance of stillness.

THE HIDDEN LESSON

Overactive Throat Chakra energy teaches that expression without awareness becomes distortion.
Just as wind can carry a melody or scatter it into chaos, Vishuddha's energy must be tuned with intention.

Healing begins not by silencing the voice, but by refining it — learning when to speak, when to listen, and when to let silence reveal what words cannot.

Meditation on sound — chanting *HAM*, humming, or listening to the breath — helps the vibration of the throat become pure again.

When expression aligns with inner truth and sound flows from awareness rather than reaction, the Throat Chakra returns to its highest function: **the clear voice of the soul — resonant, compassionate, and free.**

The Experience of an Imbalanced Throat Chakra

When the Throat Chakra (Vishuddha) is out of balance, life feels like a song that cannot find its rhythm — sometimes too quiet to be heard, other times too loud to be understood. Because this chakra governs **communication, truth, self-expression, and the bridge between thought and feeling**, its imbalance echoes through every aspect of being: how we speak, how we listen, how we express our needs, and how we honor our own truth.

An imbalanced Throat Chakra often reveals itself in the struggle between silence and overexpression — between saying too little and saying too much.
You may feel unheard yet afraid to speak, full of thoughts yet unable to articulate them. The voice wavers — sometimes constricted, sometimes forced — never quite finding its true tone.

EMOTIONAL SIGNS

Emotionally, an unbalanced Vishuddha can feel like being trapped between truth and fear.
You may experience anxiety around confrontation, fear of

rejection, or guilt for speaking your mind.
Suppressed feelings often accumulate in the chest and throat, creating tension, frustration, or even tears without words.

Alternatively, an overactive Throat Chakra can manifest as defensiveness, argumentativeness, or compulsive talking — using words to fill silence rather than express meaning.
In both cases, the emotional current of truth is blocked, leaving expression either muted or distorted.

MENTAL AND BEHAVIORAL SIGNS

On the mental level, imbalance may appear as **self-doubt about expression**, difficulty finding the right words, or an overactive inner critic that censors thoughts before they're spoken.
When underactive, you may withdraw, holding back ideas or emotions for fear of misunderstanding.
When overactive, you might dominate conversations, overanalyze every word, or speak impulsively without reflection.

The mind becomes either guarded or scattered — one extreme protecting silence, the other drowning in sound.
In both, communication loses coherence, and the voice disconnects from the heart.

VOCAL AND CREATIVE SYMPTOMS

Vishuddha governs not only speech but all forms of creative expression — writing, singing, teaching, storytelling, and art.
When imbalanced, creative flow feels blocked; inspiration fades, or self-judgment prevents sharing ideas.
You may feel that what you create isn't "good enough" or that your words will be misunderstood.
Conversely, an overstimulated Throat Chakra may lead to overproduction — speaking, creating, or performing without rest, driven by the fear of silence or invisibility.

RELATIONAL DYNAMICS

Because the Throat Chakra bridges self and others through communication, imbalance often appears in relationships as misunderstanding or misalignment.
When excessive, you may talk over others, interrupt, or dominate dialogue, mistaking expression for connection.
When deficient, you may avoid confrontation, agree outwardly while disagreeing inwardly, or carry resentment from unspoken truths.

Both patterns create emotional distance.
Healthy relationships require balanced exchange — speaking truth with compassion and listening with presence.

PHYSICAL MANIFESTATIONS

Physically, Vishuddha corresponds to the throat, neck, jaw, thyroid, and respiratory system.
Imbalance may show as tightness in the throat or shoulders, chronic sore throats, jaw tension, thyroid imbalance, or shallow breathing.
Energetically, these symptoms mirror unspoken truths, repressed creativity, or stress from overuse of voice.

Breath and sound are the medicine here — humming, chanting, or simply breathing consciously through the throat begins to release held tension and restore flow.

THE INNER EXPERIENCE

At its core, an imbalanced Throat Chakra feels like being disconnected from your authentic voice — uncertain whether it's safe to speak or whether anyone will truly listen.
You may silence yourself to maintain peace or speak too loudly to feel seen.
The result is the same: the truth remains unmet.

The lesson of Vishuddha is that expression is sacred only when it is aligned.
Authentic voice is not loud — it is clear.
Healing begins when words match feeling, when listening equals speaking, and when silence becomes part of the dialogue.

When the Throat Chakra returns to balance, expression feels effortless.
Words carry wisdom, not reaction.
Listening becomes communion, not obligation.
You no longer speak to prove your worth — you speak to share your truth.

Balance at Vishuddha is not about having power over the conversation; it is about harmony within communication.
It is the gentle strength to express with honesty, to listen with openness, and to let truth move through you like breath — steady, spacious, and free.

Chapter 5 – Causes of Disturbance

Childhood Silence and Suppressed Expression

If the Root Chakra is where we learn that life is safe, and the Sacral is where we learn that life can be felt, and the Solar Plexus is where we learn that life can be directed, then the **Throat Chakra** is where we learn that life can be *spoken*. Vishuddha begins to awaken in late childhood — the years when language, honesty, and creativity intertwine. This is the stage when we first learn to voice our needs, to ask questions, and to express what we know and feel.

When this natural growth of communication is supported — when we are heard, encouraged, and allowed to speak freely — a healthy Throat Chakra develops.
We learn that truth is safe, that words carry power, and that our voice matters.
But when our early environment suppresses, distorts, or punishes expression, the voice contracts. The clear blue current of Vishuddha becomes tangled in silence, shame, or overcompensation.

The result is a fractured relationship with communication — an adult who either fears to speak or speaks without being truly heard.

AUTHORITARIAN ENVIRONMENTS AND FEAR OF SPEAKING

Children raised in households where authority outweighs empathy often learn that silence equals safety.
When expression is punished, ridiculed, or dismissed, the message becomes internalized: *"My words are dangerous."*

Over time, the child's natural voice retreats. They begin to measure every word, anticipating rejection before it occurs. As adults, this may appear as fear of public speaking, avoidance of confrontation, or difficulty expressing needs.
Alternatively, some may overcompensate — becoming loud, argumentative, or overly talkative to assert the voice once silenced.
Both responses stem from the same wound: a loss of trust that truth can coexist with safety.

CRITICISM, RIDICULE, AND SHAMING OF EXPRESSION

Few wounds cut deeper than being mocked for one's voice — being told to "be quiet," "stop talking," or "don't be dramatic."
For a child, ridicule for self-expression translates as humiliation of identity.
Each criticism compresses the throat energy until the natural flow of communication becomes strained.

As adults, this can manifest as chronic self-censorship, fear of "saying the wrong thing," or a compulsive need to explain and justify every word.
The individual struggles to trust their intuition or opinions, constantly editing themselves for acceptance.

CONDITIONAL LISTENING AND EMOTIONAL INVALIDATION

When parents or caregivers listen only selectively —
responding with approval when the child says what they want to
hear — the Throat Chakra develops under tension.
The child learns to shape their truth to fit others' expectations,
sacrificing authenticity for belonging.

In adulthood, this becomes the pattern of the people-pleaser:
speaking what is expected rather than what is real. Over time,
the voice loses its natural tone, replaced by careful diplomacy or
quiet resentment.

SECRETS, TABOOS, AND FAMILY SILENCE

In families where truth is avoided — where conflict is hidden,
pain is denied, or appearances must be maintained — children
internalize the unspoken rule: *"We don't talk about that."*
This suppression lodges deeply in Vishuddha, creating energetic
blocks that later manifest as tightness in the throat or difficulty
speaking openly about emotions.

As adults, such individuals often carry unexpressed grief, guilt,
or confusion. They may feel compelled to "keep the peace,"
even at the cost of honesty, fearing that truth will unravel the
fragile harmony they were taught to protect.

OVERSTIMULATION AND PERFORMANCE PRESSURE

Conversely, some children are encouraged to *perform* rather
than *express* — praised for eloquence, talent, or intellect, but
not for authenticity.
They learn to use words to impress rather than connect. The
voice becomes an instrument of validation rather than truth.

In adulthood, this manifests as perfectionism in communication — the need to sound right, appear confident, or maintain authority. Behind the polished expression lies a deep fear of vulnerability: the terror of saying something raw, imperfect, or real.

EMOTIONAL NEGLECT AND UNHEARD VOICES

When a child's feelings are ignored or minimized — "Don't cry," "You're fine," "It's not a big deal" — the emotional current that feeds Vishuddha dries up.
The child learns that their inner world has no audience. The result is a disconnection between emotion and expression: they may feel deeply but struggle to articulate it.

As adults, they often appear calm or composed, but beneath the surface lies loneliness — the ache of never having been heard.

THE LASTING IMPACT

Childhood experiences that distort communication teach the body that speech is dangerous, truth is conditional, and silence is survival.
As adults, this creates patterns of repression or overcompensation: either the chronic self-silencing of the timid voice, or the relentless overexpression of the anxious one.

Healing Vishuddha begins with reclaiming the right to speak — and the right to be silent with choice.
Through mindful communication, journaling, chanting, and heart-centered listening, we remind the inner child that expression is safe, that their words have value, and that truth can be spoken gently without fear.

Each time we voice a feeling honestly, sing without judgment, or share a truth long buried, we clear the channel of Vishuddha a little more.

The voice grows stronger, softer, and truer — not as performance, but as presence.

When we remember that authenticity is sacred, the Throat Chakra opens again — clear, resonant, and free to express the soul's wisdom through the language of truth.

Ancestral Patterns of Silence, Suppression, or Distorted Truth

The Throat Chakra (Vishuddha) does not carry only your personal voice — it holds the collective echo of your lineage's relationship with truth, expression, and silence.
Just as we inherit physical DNA, we also inherit energetic memory — the unspoken histories of how our ancestors used their voices, where they stayed silent, and how they were heard or silenced by the world.

When generations before us endured persecution, colonization, censorship, or patriarchal control, their ability to speak freely was often stripped away.
That trauma lingers. It becomes an energetic imprint within Vishuddha — the place where sound becomes expression and truth seeks resonance.

Even in peaceful times, descendants may carry subtle echoes of ancestral silence — the hesitation to speak honestly, the fear of saying "too much," or the deep fatigue of holding words unspoken for generations.
What our ancestors could not express becomes the weight our throats unconsciously bear.

INHERITED SILENCE AND FEAR OF SPEAKING

Vishuddha governs the right to express truth.
When ancestors lived in environments where honesty brought
danger — where speaking against authority, culture, or religion
meant punishment or exile — they learned to survive by silence.

Generations later, that silence manifests as constriction in the
throat, timid communication, or self-censorship.
You may feel the urge to speak up, yet find your words freeze
in your throat — not because of present danger, but because of
inherited memory.
It is the ancestral whisper: *"Stay quiet. It's safer not to be
heard."*

Healing begins with remembering that your voice is not
rebellion — it is restoration.
Each time you speak your truth, you release the unspoken
prayers of those who could not.

INHERITED DISTORTION OF TRUTH

In some lineages, survival required secrecy, diplomacy, or
silence.
Over time, this necessity can morph into habitual inauthenticity
— the subtle patterns of half-truths, emotional masking, or
saying what keeps peace rather than what brings clarity.

Descendants may carry this distortion as a chronic struggle
between honesty and harmony — wanting to speak freely but
fearing the consequences of truth.
The result is energetic confusion: words that sound calm but
feel heavy, voices that speak yet remain unheard.

Healing arises through courageous honesty — learning that
truth can coexist with kindness, and clarity does not destroy
connection.

FAMILY SHAME AND TABOOS OF EXPRESSION

When families carry generational shame — whether around social status, religion, race, or trauma — the Throat Chakra bears the brunt of the silence.
Entire subjects may become "off-limits," creating energetic blockages that span generations.

As descendants, we may feel guilt for asking questions or discomfort discussing family history.
The energetic body remembers: *"We don't talk about that."*
Yet healing Vishuddha requires precisely this — the gentle unveiling of what was buried, not to expose or blame, but to bring light to truth.
When we give voice to the unspoken, the ancestral line breathes again.

INHERITED CONTROL AND SPEECH DOMINANCE

Not all ancestral wounds are silent — some overexpress to compensate for centuries of repression.
In families marked by strict hierarchies or patriarchal control, certain voices dominated while others were muted.
Descendants may inherit the pattern of speaking *over* others, mistaking control for communication, or using words as protection.

This is the other side of silence — speech without listening, expression without awareness.
Healing this lineage means learning the sacred rhythm of dialogue: the dance between sound and stillness, between voice and ear.
As we practice listening as deeply as we speak, we restore the balance of expression across generations.

ANCESTRAL RELIGIOUS OR CULTURAL CONSTRAINTS

In many lineages, devotion and tradition were tied to obedience — to "right speech" dictated by authority or faith.
Over time, this can condition descendants to associate authenticity with sin or disrespect.
The soul learns to filter truth through dogma, until the voice no longer feels like one's own.

Healing begins with reclaiming the sacred nature of direct communication with the Divine — through prayer, chant, or meditation not as submission, but as communion.
When the Throat Chakra opens in alignment with Spirit, words become sacred offerings rather than obligations.

THE LEGACY OF VOICE AND SILENCE

Just as the Solar Plexus carries ancestral stories of power, the Throat carries ancestral stories of truth.
Every generation either strengthens or suppresses the collective voice.
If your ancestors were silenced, your authentic expression becomes an act of liberation.
If they misused their words, your mindful speech becomes an act of redemption.

You are the bridge between what was unspoken and what must now be said.
Every word spoken from integrity — every song, prayer, or honest conversation — heals the ancestral line of distortion and restores harmony between truth and love.

HEALING THROUGH THE VOICE

To heal ancestral patterns within the Throat Chakra:
• Honor the silence that once kept your ancestors safe — then release it with compassion.
• Speak aloud family truths that were hidden, allowing acknowledgment to replace shame.
• Write letters to ancestors, expressing gratitude and forgiveness for what was unsaid.
• Chant or sing to awaken Vishuddha's vibration — transforming silence into sound, and sound into light.
• Affirm:
"I honor the truths my ancestors could not speak. Through my voice, their wisdom rises in clarity and peace."

THE DEEPER LESSON

Where the Root carries the memory of survival and the Solar Plexus the story of power, the Throat carries the legacy of truth — how our lineage spoke, listened, and was heard.

When ancestors were silenced, Vishuddha learned fear.
When they used their voices with courage or prayer, it learned resonance.

By transforming inherited silence into authentic expression, you become the voice of renewal — the harmonic note that brings your lineage back into balance.
The Throat Chakra no longer carries the story of repression, but the song of remembrance: **the voice that heals generations through the courage to speak truth in love.**

Inherited Beliefs About Expression And Truth

Across many lineages, beliefs about communication are polarized — either truth is exalted as sacred or feared as dangerous.
Families who lived under censorship or persecution may equate silence with safety, while those who held influence may have used speech as control rather than connection.
Both distort the Throat Chakra's natural harmony between honesty and compassion.

If your lineage carries fear of speaking, you may hesitate to share ideas or opinions, choosing peace over authenticity.
If it carries patterns of domination through words, you may unconsciously use speech to defend, persuade, or overpower rather than to understand.

Healing this polarity begins by remembering that true expression serves — it connects rather than conquers.
Vishuddha, in its essence, is not a weapon or a whisper, but a channel — a conduit through which truth flows with clarity, kindness, and purpose.

INHERITED SILENCE AND THE FEAR OF BEING HEARD

Many families carry ancestral vows of silence: *"It's better not to speak," "Don't make trouble,"* or *"Keep your thoughts to yourself."*
For generations, this silence preserved safety in oppressive times, but over centuries it becomes suffocating.

Descendants may feel nervous when sharing opinions, apologetic when speaking, or uncomfortable when their voice draws attention.

This inherited hesitation constricts the Throat Chakra — the energy of sound withheld before it can form.
You may even find yourself speaking softly, hesitating mid-sentence, or censoring emotions without knowing why.

Healing this belief involves reclaiming the right to voice your truth with gentleness.
Speech does not endanger you now — it liberates you.
Each time you speak from authenticity rather than fear, you dissolve generations of silence and restore your lineage's freedom to express.

INHERITED DEFERENCE TO AUTHORITY AND SELF-CENSORSHIP

In lineages where social status, religion, or culture demanded obedience, truth became selective.
Children learned to speak in ways that pleased or protected — to filter truth through hierarchy.
This conditioning teaches the body that honesty threatens belonging.

As adults, this may appear as difficulty challenging injustice, holding back insights, or deferring to authority even when you know you are right.
The voice stays small out of respect, yet the soul aches to speak.

Healing begins with honoring the wisdom of both humility and integrity — recognizing that reverence does not require repression.
You can respect tradition while still giving voice to what is real.

INHERITED VERBAL DOMINANCE AND THE FEAR OF LISTENING

Some families pass down not silence but noise — the belief that speaking louder ensures survival.

In such lineages, the Throat Chakra learns expression without listening.
Words become tools of persuasion, performance, or defense rather than understanding.

Descendants may inherit impatience in dialogue, interrupt frequently, or feel uncomfortable in silence.
This imbalance burns through Vishuddha like static — constant sound without resonance.

Healing this pattern means remembering that silence, too, can be sacred.
Listening does not weaken expression; it deepens it.
When we allow space between words, truth can breathe again.

INHERITED BELIEF THAT VULNERABILITY IS WEAKNESS

Where ancestors survived by restraint, emotion and truth were separated.
The heart felt deeply, but the throat learned restraint.
Tears, needs, and truth were hidden beneath composure.

Generations later, descendants may struggle to share personal feelings — especially love, pain, or fear — believing that openness invites rejection or loss of dignity.
But Vishuddha's higher purpose is the union of strength and sincerity: to speak truth with an open heart.

Healing begins when you allow softness in your words — when honesty is guided by compassion rather than armor.
Vulnerability does not weaken your voice; it sanctifies it.

INHERITED LIMITATION AND SELF-SILENCING

When families carry beliefs like *"No one listens to us"* or *"Our words don't matter,"* the vibration of defeat settles over

Vishuddha.
You may find yourself withdrawing in groups, struggling to express creative ideas, or giving up mid-conversation — not because of a lack of wisdom, but because of ancestral fatigue.

These moments are not failures; they are echoes seeking resolution.
Each time you affirm, *"My voice matters,"* you rewrite the family story.
You speak not only for yourself but for every ancestor who swallowed their words.

Healing the Throat Chakra at this level means embodying a new truth: that expression is not rebellion, it is remembrance — a way of bringing ancestral wisdom back into resonance with love.

THE DEEPER LESSON

Where the Root carries ancestral memory of survival, and the Solar Plexus holds inherited stories of power, the Throat carries the legacy of communication — how truth was expressed, feared, or withheld.

When past generations equated silence with safety, Vishuddha learned suppression; when they equated dominance with speech, it learned distortion.
Now it is your turn to harmonize both — to speak and listen, to express and receive.

Your healing voice becomes the bridge across generations — turning silence into song, and fear into freedom.
The Throat Chakra no longer carries the story of control or repression, but the **living vibration of truth — clear, compassionate, and eternal.**

Environmental and Energetic Toxins: Noise, Dishonesty, and Collective Disconnection

The Throat Chakra (Vishuddha) is the energetic bridge between inner truth and outer expression — the etheric channel through which thought becomes vibration and vibration becomes creation.

While the Heart connects us to compassion and the Third Eye to vision, the Throat determines how truth moves between them — whether it is spoken with clarity or distorted by noise.

In a world saturated with misinformation, constant chatter, and emotional volatility, Vishuddha often becomes both the messenger and the casualty — struggling to speak clearly amid the static of collective confusion.

Where the Heart feels empathy like water, the Throat absorbs the world's dissonance like sound.

It constricts in response to lies, manipulation, or hostility — tightening to protect itself, yet in doing so, muting authentic expression.

Over time, this imbalance leads to exhaustion, cynicism, and a growing disconnect between what we know and what we say. Vishuddha's sacred current — truth — becomes clouded in a culture of contradiction.

THE REACTIVE NATURE OF VISHUDDHA

The element of Vishuddha is ether — vast, expansive, and sensitive to vibration.

It thrives in honesty, integrity, and open dialogue, but falters in noise, deceit, and emotional chaos.

When surrounded by dishonesty, arguments, or constant verbal assault — whether in personal life, media, or society — the Throat Chakra reacts instantly.

It may constrict, manifesting as tightness, hoarseness, or a lump in the throat.
Or it may overcompensate, producing overtalking, defensiveness, or compulsive speech.
Each lie heard, each truth withheld, creates tension in the energetic channel that longs for resonance.

The body reflects it — shallow breathing, jaw tension, neck stiffness, or chronic sore throats.
Vishuddha begins to whisper through discomfort: "Speak what is true. Release what is false."

EXPOSURE TO VIOLENCE, NOISE, AND VERBAL AGGRESSION

Violence does not always strike through action — sometimes it comes through words.
Constant exposure to shouting, blame, or harsh communication erodes Vishuddha's clarity.
Even the background noise of aggression — in homes, workplaces, or media — can teach the nervous system that speech equals conflict.

In such conditions, the voice becomes cautious or strained.
We may fear saying the wrong thing, defaulting to silence to maintain peace.
Or we may lash out defensively, our words carrying the same heat that wounded us.

Vishuddha burns unevenly — sometimes too sharp, sometimes barely audible.
Healing begins by recognizing that the world's noise is not your truth — that you can hold peace within even as discord surrounds you.

CHRONIC STRESS AND COMMUNICATION FATIGUE

Modern life rarely pauses for silence.
We speak, type, scroll, and consume language endlessly —
rarely listening deeply.
This constant output taxes Vishuddha, whose natural rhythm
depends on both sound and stillness.

Under continual stress, words lose meaning.
We repeat patterns of communication — reacting instead of
responding, speaking to fill space instead of sharing truth.
The voice becomes mechanical, the ears grow numb, and
genuine dialogue fades.

Just as the Solar Plexus burns out from overuse, the Throat
burns out from overexpression without resonance.
Healing begins with spaciousness: silence as medicine.
True communication arises not from pressure, but from
presence.

SOCIETAL DISHONESTY AND COLLECTIVE DISSONANCE

Vishuddha is humanity's collective voice — the resonance of
truth across consciousness.
In times of misinformation, corruption, or moral confusion, this
chakra absorbs the discord of false narratives.
We feel it as confusion, mistrust, or apathy toward
communication itself.

When the collective forgets how to speak truth, individuals
begin to doubt their own intuition.
The result is a society of echo chambers — everyone speaking,
few listening, and truth lost in the noise.

Healing Vishuddha in such times requires discernment: the
ability to hear the subtle vibration beneath the volume — to

recognize sincerity amid distortion.
Truth always vibrates differently; it feels light, clear, and
freeing, even when uncomfortable.

ENERGETIC CONTAMINATION THROUGH SPEECH AND THOUGHT

Because Vishuddha governs sound and frequency, it is
especially sensitive to environments heavy with gossip, lies,
criticism, or manipulation.
Words are energy, and every vibration leaves a trace in the
subtle field.
Harsh or dishonest communication can linger like smoke,
dulling the brilliance of the throat's natural resonance.

You may feel physically drained after arguments or notice
fatigue after engaging with negativity.
This is energetic residue — an overload of distorted vibration.

Energetic hygiene for Vishuddha includes conscious speech,
intentional listening, and vocal cleansing.
Speak words that align with truth.
Decline to engage in gossip or complaint.
Use sound to restore harmony — humming, chanting, or toning
clears residual dissonance from your field.

HEALING THROUGH SOUND AND SILENCE

The antidote to Vishuddha's energetic pollution is purification
through sound, breath, and stillness.
• Limit exposure to noise, conflict, and misinformation.
• Begin each day with silence before engaging with media or
conversation.
• Practice conscious speech — pause before speaking, ask, "Is it
true? Is it kind? Is it necessary?"
• Use mantra or vocal toning to restore resonance. The bija
mantra *HAM* vibrates the Throat into alignment.

• Incorporate listening meditations — hearing the wind, music, or another's words without judgment — to attune awareness to subtle sound.
• Visualize a soft blue light expanding in your throat, clearing distortion and restoring peace.

THE DEEPER LESSON

Vishuddha teaches that communication without consciousness becomes noise, and silence without truth becomes suppression. The goal is not to withdraw from the world's sound, but to refine your inner resonance — clear, calm, and truthful.

To speak without harm, to listen without fear, to express without distortion — this is the mastery of the Throat Chakra. When the voice aligns with the heart and mind, it becomes medicine.
When silence holds presence, it becomes prayer.

In a world of chaos, Vishuddha asks not that we speak louder, but that we speak truer — becoming tuning forks of truth in a collective field, still learning how to listen.

Silencing, Manipulation, and the Violation of Voice

The Throat Chakra (Vishuddha) is the seat of truth — the sacred bridge between inner knowing and outer expression.
It governs the right to speak, to be heard, and to express one's authentic self without fear or distortion.

When that right is violated — through shaming, gaslighting, ridicule, or suppression — the core of Vishuddha contracts.
Its natural vibration of clarity becomes muffled by fear, confusion, or disbelief in one's own truth.

Just as the Solar Plexus governs the sacred flame of will, the Throat governs the sacred resonance of voice.

When this resonance is silenced through manipulation or domination, the individual may lose trust in their perception, their words, and even their right to speak.
It is a wound not only of communication but of identity — the distortion of one's inner frequency.

ENERGETIC IMPACT OF VOICE VIOLATION

When words are used as weapons — through mockery, lies, or coercion — Vishuddha absorbs the shock directly.
The throat tightens, breath shortens, and the body instinctively suppresses sound as a form of protection.

People who have been silenced or verbally abused often describe a lump in the throat, chronic tension in the neck and jaw, or recurring sore throats that seem to have no physical cause.
Energetically, the aura around Vishuddha may appear dim, fragmented, or constricted — as though the flow between thought and expression has been interrupted.

This trauma leaves the individual questioning:
"Is it safe to speak?"
"Will my truth be believed?"
"Does my voice even matter?"

Some withdraw into silence, internalizing the belief that peace is safer than honesty.
Others overcompensate — speaking loudly, interrupting often, or dominating conversation — not from confidence, but from fear of being unheard.
Both reactions arise from the same wound: a loss of trust in the sanctity of one's own voice.

THE LEGACY OF RIDICULE AND GASLIGHTING

Few injuries cut deeper than the distortion of truth.
When words are twisted, or reality is denied, the Throat Chakra
learns confusion — the painful fracture between what is felt and
what is allowed to be spoken.

Gaslighting, sarcasm, and humiliation create dissonance
between inner knowing and outer validation.
The mind begins to doubt itself, and the voice follows —
hesitant, uncertain, self-censoring.
You may replay conversations long after they end, wondering if
you said too much, too little, or the wrong thing altogether.

Culturally, many systems of hierarchy and control perpetuate
this injury by rewarding conformity and punishing authenticity.
People learn to speak in ways that maintain approval, even if it
means betraying truth. But Vishuddha's power is not
compliance — it is coherence: the alignment of speech, thought,
and soul.

When your words match your truth, the throat becomes a
channel of liberation, not limitation.

THE WOUND OF PUBLIC SHAMING AND DISBELIEF

Public humiliation, gossip, or betrayal of confidence can deeply
scar the Throat Chakra.
To be exposed, mocked, or not believed after speaking truth is
to have one's resonance shattered.
The body remembers — tightening each time the possibility of
exposure arises again.

In such wounds, Vishuddha closes its gates, guarding the heart
from further pain.
But this self-protection can imprison authenticity.

The person may develop patterns of speaking vaguely, avoiding opinion, or deflecting emotion through humor or deflection.

Healing begins by reclaiming the right to clarity — to speak plainly and truthfully without apology.
Every time you express what is real, you reweave trust between voice and spirit.

THE COST OF MANIPULATIVE COMMUNICATION

When communication is used to control rather than connect — through guilt, deceit, or intimidation — Vishuddha's natural rhythm collapses. This form of energetic violation replaces resonance with distortion, teaching the body that language is unsafe.

Children raised in such environments often grow into adults who fear confrontation or overanalyze every word.
They may speak in ways that please rather than express, using language to manage emotion instead of revealing truth.
Over time, authenticity erodes, leaving only performance.

Yet Vishuddha's purpose is expression, not perfection.
To reclaim your voice is to accept imperfection as part of communication's beauty.
Truth does not require polish — only presence.

THE SACRED RESTORATION OF VOICE

Healing the Throat Chakra after manipulation or suppression involves re-teaching the body that your voice is safe and sacred.
• Begin with breath — inhaling deeply through the nose, exhaling through open sound (a hum, sigh, or tone).
• Speak to yourself in the mirror daily — small truths at first, until your reflection feels like an ally again.
• Write unsent letters to those who silenced you, releasing words that were never allowed to live.

• Surround yourself with people and spaces where your truth is received with respect.
• Affirm: *"My voice is a divine expression. My words carry truth and light."*

Each act of honest communication repairs the energetic bridge between your inner knowing and outer world.
As Vishuddha clears, your voice gains resonance — no longer a reaction to pain, but a reflection of peace.

THE DEEPER LESSON

Where Manipura teaches sovereignty through will, Vishuddha teaches sovereignty through truth.
The violation of voice is the attempt to erase presence itself — yet even silence holds vibration.
Every unspoken truth waits patiently for its return to sound.

Healing does not mean shouting over others; it means reclaiming harmony — the courage to let your truth vibrate freely through the ethers once more.
When your words align with love and integrity, the world remembers how to listen.

Vishuddha's ultimate alchemy is this: **to turn silence into song, pain into resonance, and the broken voice into the sacred echo of truth.**

EMOTIONAL AND PSYCHOLOGICAL VIOLATION

Not all Throat Chakra wounds are spoken.
Emotional manipulation, gaslighting, or coercive communication can gradually erode trust in one's own voice.
When someone's truth is constantly dismissed, twisted, or used against them, the psyche learns to equate honesty with danger.

This subtle violation teaches the body to constrict the throat, to withhold expression, to replace authenticity with silence.
It manifests as self-censorship, chronic fear of being misunderstood, or a deep hesitation to speak one's feelings.
In time, Vishuddha learns suppression as safety — confusing quiet with peace.

Gaslighting and emotional invalidation create a fracture between inner knowing and outer expression.
The person begins to doubt what they feel, question what they know, and mistrust what they say.
Each swallowed truth tightens the throat a little more, until the body forgets the sensation of honest expression.

Healing begins with permission — the right to speak again, even imperfectly.
To name experiences without justification.
To believe your perception, your words, and your reality.
When Vishuddha reclaims this right, the voice trembles at first — but it trembles with truth, not fear.

PHYSICAL MANIFESTATIONS

Because the Throat Chakra governs the vocal cords, thyroid, mouth, and breath, emotional suppression often reveals itself physically.
Symptoms may include chronic sore throats, thyroid imbalances, jaw tension, tightness in the neck and shoulders, or a sensation of "something stuck" in the throat.

The body literally "chokes" on unspoken truth — holding words that were never allowed release.
Long-term suppression can even affect breathing patterns, leading to shallow respiration or anxiety around speaking.
In energy terms, the current between heart and mind becomes congested; emotion rises but cannot pass into articulation.

Vishuddha's healing comes through release — through sound, through breath, through truth made audible.

Humming, singing, toning, or speaking your experiences aloud (even privately) begins to reopen the channel.

As the voice returns to flow, the entire energy system begins to harmonize — the heart's emotion and the mind's wisdom meeting once more in sound.

When the Throat Chakra clears, expression feels effortless again — not loud, not forced, simply real. The breath deepens, the voice steadies, and the truth moves freely through you — the vibration of healing itself.

PATHWAYS TO HEALING THE THROAT CHAKRA

Healing Vishuddha after experiences of suppression, silencing, or emotional manipulation is the sacred act of reclaiming your voice — the ability to express truth with clarity, compassion, and courage.

It is not about speaking louder or proving yourself right; it is about remembering that your voice is divine — an instrument of truth, creation, and alignment.

The process unfolds gently, as honesty replaces fear, and resonance restores the bridge between heart and mind.

Each word spoken in authenticity becomes a note of healing.

Key Approaches Include:

• Ground in Inner Silence:
Begin not with words, but with listening.
Silence is Vishuddha's medicine — it clears static and prepares the channel for truth.

• Open the Channel of Breath:
Breathe deeply into the throat and chest. Feel the flow of air as a reminder that your voice begins with life itself.

Conscious breathing restores rhythm and calms the nervous system, allowing words to flow with ease.

• Sound as Liberation:
Use gentle toning, humming, or chanting "HAM," the bija mantra of Vishuddha.
Let the vibration move through your neck and jaw, dissolving old constrictions and activating clarity.

• Speak Truth Without Defense:
Practice sharing feelings and needs without apology.
Honesty does not require explanation — it requires presence.
Each time you speak your truth calmly, you rebuild trust in your own voice.

• Boundaries of Communication:
Choose conversations that honor mutual respect.
Step away from gossip, verbal aggression, or environments that distort truth.
Protecting your energy field preserves the purity of your voice.

• Reframe Fear of Judgment:
Remind yourself that expression is not about perfection; it is about connection.
Speak even when your voice shakes — it strengthens with use.

• Supportive Guidance:
Work with vocal coaches, energy healers, or therapists who value authentic communication.
Healing Vishuddha thrives in environments that encourage listening as much as speaking.

• Affirmations of Truth:
"My voice is sacred."
"I speak with clarity, love, and integrity."
"My truth vibrates in harmony with divine wisdom."

THE DEEPER LESSON

Violations of Vishuddha — whether through ridicule, suppression, or manipulation — reveal how deeply humanity fears truth.
Yet within this fear lies our greatest lesson: the voice, once reclaimed, becomes not a weapon, but a bridge.

Vishuddha's gift is transmutation — the power to turn silence into song, confusion into clarity, and pain into expression.
Every word spoken in authenticity heals the throat, the heart, and the world it touches.

To reclaim your voice after silence is not defiance — it is devotion.
It is to remember that:

I am not voiceless.
I am not bound by fear.
My truth is light,
and I speak it with peace.

Chapter 6 – Signs of Balance

Authentic Expression: Truth, Clarity, and Resonance

When the Throat Chakra (Vishuddha) is balanced, your words flow from a deep well of truth.
There is ease between thought and expression, feeling and articulation.
You speak not to impress, but to connect — not to control, but to convey.

Your voice becomes a bridge between your inner and outer worlds, carrying a vibration that aligns with integrity.
You listen with openness and respond with presence.
Like a clear sky after a storm, your energy feels spacious and light — transparent, yet full of meaning.

A balanced Vishuddha is not loud; it is luminous.
It resonates through calm confidence, through words that uplift and silence that nourishes.
In this state, expression becomes effortless authenticity — the soul speaking through sound.

CLARITY AND HONEST COMMUNICATION

A harmonious Throat Chakra reflects mental and emotional coherence.
You know what you feel and can express it clearly without fear

or aggression.
Your communication carries honesty and empathy in equal
measure — truth delivered through kindness.

There is no need to overexplain or defend your perspective;
authenticity speaks for itself.
You honor your truth while allowing others theirs, recognizing
that multiple voices can exist in harmony.

A balanced Vishuddha makes communication sacred — not
performance, but communion.
Words become prayers of alignment, each one a declaration of
who you truly are.

SELF-EXPRESSION AND CREATIVE FLOW

When Vishuddha is open, expression feels effortless and
inspired.
Ideas, art, and insight flow freely — as though the universe is
speaking through you.
Whether through writing, teaching, singing, or simple
conversation, your voice carries clarity and grace.

You no longer fear being seen or heard; visibility feels natural
because it arises from authenticity, not ego.
Your creativity is guided by purpose rather than perfectionism.
Expression becomes an act of devotion — the spirit of truth
moving through form.

INTEGRITY AND TRUTH IN ACTION

The balanced Throat Chakra unites speech with action — your
words reflect your values, and your choices follow suit.
Integrity becomes second nature.
You say what you mean and follow through with compassion
and consistency.

There is no longer a gap between your inner and outer worlds; what you express aligns with what you believe.
Dishonesty, gossip, and manipulation lose their appeal because they disrupt the harmony of your energy field.
Truth becomes your natural vibration, and in truth, there is peace.

LISTENING AND RECEPTIVITY

Vishuddha's balance is not measured only by how you speak, but by how you listen.
In deep listening, you hear not just words, but essence — the heart behind the voice.
You hold space for others without losing yourself in their stories.

Balanced communication flows in both directions:
You receive as clearly as you express.
This receptivity nourishes connection and cultivates wisdom — the understanding that silence, too, has a voice.

VIBRATIONAL HARMONY AND PHYSICAL BALANCE

Because Vishuddha governs sound and vibration, balance manifests as a sense of inner resonance.
Your breath is steady, your tone natural, your voice clear.
The physical throat feels open and unstrained — energy flows smoothly from heart to head, linking love with wisdom.

This harmony often reflects in physical vitality: healthy thyroid function, relaxed shoulders and jaw, and rhythmic breathing.
Your energy feels light but grounded — as though every word spoken is both anchored and free.

THE FEELING OF TRUTHFUL FLOW

When the Throat Chakra is balanced, there is no inner conflict between thought and speech.
Truth moves freely through you — gentle yet powerful, like a river of sound.
You no longer rehearse your words or silence your instincts.

Communication becomes communion — the meeting of souls through the language of authenticity.
You express yourself with humility and confidence, knowing your words are guided by the heart and refined by awareness.

To live with a balanced Vishuddha Chakra is to embody clarity, honesty, and grace.
You become a vessel of truth — a voice of peace that speaks with purpose, listens with love, and resonates with the harmony of the soul.

Physical Vitality: Breath, Voice, and the Element of Ether

The Throat Chakra (Vishuddha) governs the realm of communication and vibration — the bridge between the heart's emotion and the mind's thought.
Where the Solar Plexus burns with fire, Vishuddha expands with ether — the spacious, invisible element that carries sound and connects all life through frequency.
It is the center of resonance, breath, and expression — the subtle field where vibration becomes voice and truth takes form.

When this center is balanced, the voice feels clear, breathing effortless, and the body aligned in both sound and spirit.
You speak with authenticity, listen with openness, and move

through the world with a sense of spacious ease — as though your very breath were prayer.

RESPIRATORY SYSTEM: THE BRIDGE OF BREATH AND SPIRIT

The lungs, trachea, and diaphragm form the physical landscape of Vishuddha — the gateway through which life-force (prana) flows.
Breath is the language of spirit, and each inhale and exhale mirrors the exchange between self and universe.

When the Throat Chakra is balanced, breathing is full and rhythmic; the voice carries calm authority and clarity.
When constricted, breath becomes shallow, the throat tightens, and expression feels forced or fearful.
Energy cannot rise smoothly through the body if the breath — the carrier of sound and emotion — is blocked.

Conscious breathing practices, such as Ujjayi ("ocean breath") or alternate nostril breathing (Nadi Shodhana), open this channel, restoring both vitality and inner peace.
As breath deepens, so does truth — and the voice once again becomes a sacred instrument of alignment.

VOCAL CORDS AND THROAT MUSCLES: THE INSTRUMENT OF EXPRESSION

The physical voice — the larynx, vocal cords, and throat muscles — reflects the energetic state of Vishuddha. When the chakra flows freely, speech feels effortless, and tone resonates naturally. The voice carries warmth, clarity, and presence.

Tension in the jaw, neck, or shoulders often mirrors withheld emotion or unspoken truth.
Every unsaid word lingers as a muscular contraction; every repressed feeling echoes as tightness.

Relaxing and toning the throat through humming, chanting, or gentle sound vibration releases these energetic knots.

Your body is an instrument — and Vishuddha is its tuning fork. When tuned through conscious sound, the entire system resonates in harmony.

THYROID AND PARATHYROID: THE REGULATORS OF BALANCE

The thyroid and parathyroid glands sit at the center of Vishuddha's energetic field, governing metabolism, temperature, and cellular communication.
Energetically, they represent rhythm and expression — the body's capacity to translate thought into action and maintain equilibrium.

A balanced thyroid mirrors balanced communication: responsive, adaptable, and attuned to the needs of the moment. When overactive, energy races ahead of rest — speech may become rapid, anxious, or scattered.
When underactive, vitality slows — expression feels muted, the voice quiet, the spirit weary.

Bringing awareness to the throat through breath, gentle neck stretches, or chanting stabilizes this system, restoring harmony between energy and expression.
As the glands regain rhythm, so too does the voice of the soul.

THE ELEMENT OF ETHER: THE SPACE WHERE SOUND BECOMES SPIRIT

Vishuddha's element, ether (ākāśa), is the subtlest of all — the spacious medium through which sound and consciousness travel.
It teaches that vitality does not always roar like fire or flow like water; sometimes it expands in silence, stillness, and vibration.

When you are attuned to ether, the body feels light yet grounded, alert yet calm.
You sense that your words ripple through the unseen — shaping reality through intention and resonance.
In this awareness, every breath, every sound, becomes sacred creation.

To live through the vitality of the Throat Chakra is to honor the breath as spirit, the voice as truth, and silence as divine listening.
Vishuddha reminds us: energy is not only what we do — it is what we express, what we allow, and what we choose to vibrate into the world.

The key is resonance — a clear, steady tone that expresses rather than suppresses.

THE ELEMENT OF ETHER

Ether (Ākāśa) is the essence of Vishuddha — expansive, subtle, and luminous.
It is the principle of transmission: turning vibration into sound, thought into expression, and truth into creation.
When balanced, ether carries voice without distortion and silence without emptiness.
A healthy Throat Chakra teaches us the sacred art of right communication — to speak with integrity, to listen with presence, and to live in harmony with the sound of truth.

Just as the sky holds every tone without resistance, Vishuddha expresses clarity that is spacious yet grounded,a stillness that resonates through every word, breath, and silence.

THE FEELING OF RESONANT PRESENCE

A balanced Throat Chakra brings a sense of open vitality — not through effort, but through ease.
You feel aligned in your voice, calm in your breathing, and expressive without fear.
The throat relaxes, the shoulders soften, and the breath flows freely — carrying awareness through the entire body like a wave of light.

Sound and silence begin to work together; communication feels authentic, gentle, and powerful.
Each word spoken vibrates with purpose, each pause nourishes peace.
You feel connected to life through both voice and listening — guided by the rhythm of truth rather than the noise of reaction.

Energy rises smoothly from the heart to the mind, creating coherence between emotion, expression, and understanding.
To live with a balanced Vishuddha is to become the song itself — a clear channel through which spirit speaks, where sound becomes healing, and truth becomes light.

Spiritual Qualities: Truth, Integrity, and Divine Expression

When Vishuddha is balanced, spirituality becomes the art of expression in alignment with truth.
It is the realization that divine will is spoken through the human voice — that every word, tone, and silence can carry the vibration of higher purpose.

The Throat Chakra reveals that spiritual power is not found in how loudly you speak, but in how clearly your expression reflects the soul.

It teaches that enlightenment is not silence alone, but truthful sound — the courage to speak love into a world that has forgotten how to listen.

TRUTH AS DIVINE RESONANCE

Vishuddha transforms perception into expression — it is where understanding becomes voice.
When balanced, this chakra turns truth into vibration, allowing spirit to move through sound and word.
Speaking truth becomes prayer; listening becomes meditation.

You begin to recognize that your words shape energy — each one either heals or divides, uplifts or obscures.
When expression flows from divine awareness, communication becomes creation itself.
In that state, your voice is not merely personal — it is the voice of the soul remembering itself.

INTEGRITY AS SACRED SOUND

At the level of the Throat Chakra, integrity is lived as vibrational honesty — your inner tone matching your outer words.
It is not only *what* you say, but *how* your energy resonates behind it.

When Vishuddha is balanced, you speak without fear, and your silence holds peace rather than suppression.
Integrity purifies the sound current — dissolving deceit, gossip, and self-doubt into pure resonance.
Your words carry coherence because your being does.
This is truth embodied: sound and soul in harmony.

Integrity here becomes an act of reverence — a willingness to let every vibration you emit honor the divine within you and around you.

DIVINE EXPRESSION AS SPIRITUAL SERVICE

The Throat Chakra is where individuality meets divinity —
where your unique voice becomes an instrument of universal
consciousness.
When Vishuddha is open, creativity, teaching, and
communication flow effortlessly, not as egoic performance, but
as sacred service.

You recognize that your voice, your message, and your art are
not yours alone — they are channels through which spirit is
heard and felt. Every poem, prayer, or conversation becomes a
bridge between heaven and earth.

In this way, expression itself becomes devotion — your life
becomes a mantra of authenticity, each word and action
resonating with the music of divine intention.

THE ETHER OF TRANSCENDENCE

Spiritually, Vishuddha represents the purification of expression
— the moment sound turns into silence and silence becomes
infinite awareness.
It is the etheric temple through which truth ascends beyond
language.

Here, communication becomes communion.
You no longer need to convince or prove; your vibration speaks
for you.
The voice becomes light, the word becomes creation, and every
breath carries divine intelligence into form.

To live with a balanced Throat Chakra is to embody *divine
expression*: truth spoken with love, silence held with grace, and
presence resonating as pure, living sound.

CONNECTION TO DIVINE WILL

The highest spiritual expression of Vishuddha is surrender —
not through silence, but through resonance.
It is the moment when the personal voice becomes an
instrument of divine sound, when truth no longer belongs to
"me," but flows as the language of Spirit itself.

Here, you do not force expression — you allow truth to sing
through you.
Words arise naturally from stillness, guided by clarity rather
than control.
Listening and speaking become one act — a sacred exchange
between heaven and heart.

In this communion, the breath carries divine rhythm, and sound
becomes light.
You no longer speak to be heard; you speak to transmit truth.
You no longer seek to be understood; you *become*
understanding itself.

This is the spiritual radiance of the Throat Chakra:
to express with honesty, to listen with reverence, and to live as
the echo of divine harmony — not as separate from the Source,
but as its living voice.

The Experience of a Balanced Throat Chakra

When the Throat Chakra (Vishuddha) is in harmony, life feels
clear, expressive, and aligned with truth.
You move through the world with authenticity and ease —
neither withholding nor overexplaining, but communicating
from a place of inner resonance and faith.
Energy flows upward effortlessly; words and silence both arise

from wisdom rather than fear.
You feel transparent yet strong — a clear channel through which the voice of the soul flows freely into the world.

PHYSICAL EXPERIENCE

The throat feels open, relaxed, and spacious.
Breath moves easily through the body, carrying vitality and calm in equal measure.
The voice resonates with warmth and steadiness — not forced, but naturally strong.
The neck and shoulders release their habitual tension, allowing posture to lengthen and the chest to expand.
You feel connected to the rhythm of your own breath — balanced between expression and rest.
The body becomes an instrument of harmony, each inhale and exhale part of the sacred song of life.

EMOTIONAL EXPERIENCE

Emotionally, a balanced Vishuddha brings serenity and authenticity.
You express feelings clearly and compassionately, without repression or overreaction.
There is no longer fear in being seen or heard — only peace in standing in your truth.
Words arise as extensions of love rather than defense; silence becomes a refuge, not a prison.
You communicate with grace, knowing that honesty and kindness can coexist.
The emotional body hums like a finely tuned instrument — each tone pure, steady, and true.

MENTAL EXPERIENCE

The mind of a balanced Throat Chakra is perceptive, creative, and inspired.
Thoughts flow with clarity and coherence; ideas are easily articulated and translated into meaningful expression.
You listen deeply — not to respond, but to understand.
Communication becomes sacred exchange, and inner dialogue turns supportive rather than critical.
Mental tension dissolves as truth takes precedence over perfection.
You no longer seek to persuade or please — you seek to convey what is real.

SPIRITUAL EXPERIENCE

Spiritually, Vishuddha awakens the understanding that truth itself is divine.
You experience the word as creation — sound as vibration, vibration as life.
Speaking becomes prayer, and listening becomes communion with the Infinite.
Your voice feels guided — not by ego, but by the flow of divine will.
Through this awareness, you embody right speech, right listening, and right silence — the trinity of sacred communication.
You recognize that your voice is not separate from Spirit, but its echo moving through you.

OVERALL EXPERIENCE

To live with a balanced Throat Chakra is to live in vibrational harmony.
You feel calm yet expressive, honest yet gentle, powerful yet peaceful.
Your communication carries integrity, your presence radiates

authenticity, and your silence holds wisdom.
You no longer fear being misunderstood, for your essence
speaks louder than your words.
In this state, the light of Vishuddha shines clear and blue — the
radiant ether of truth, expression, and divine resonance flowing
through every breath and every word.

The Connection: From the Body Trinity to the Temple of Light

1. THE THREEFOLD FOUNDATION: EARTH · WATER · FIRE

The Root, Sacral, and Solar Plexus chakras form **the sacred triangle of embodiment** — the forces that root spirit into human experience.
They are the densest frequencies of consciousness:

- **Earth (Root)** gives stability and belonging.
- **Water (Sacral)** gives emotion and creativity.
- **Fire (Solar Plexus)** gives will and transformation.

Together they forge the human vessel — **the temple of form**.
Once this temple is strong, love (Air) can safely awaken in the
Heart.

2. THE BRIDGE OF AIR: HEART AND THROAT

When Fire has burned through illusion and purified the will, its
flame rises into Air — the element of **breath, love, and
communication.**
This is where your next trilogy begins:
**Heart (Anahata), Throat (Vishuddha), and Third Eye
(Ajna)** — the **Trinity of Light** or **the Temple of Spirit.**

- **The Heart** opens the sacred current of love and compassion — the alchemical air that unites above and below.
- **The Throat** refines that love into vibration — translating emotion into sound, truth, and creative expression.
- **The Third Eye** receives the resonance of truth as vision — perceiving through the clarity of awakened consciousness.

Thus, the Throat is not merely "after" the Heart — it is **Love expressed**, the sound of Spirit made audible through form.

3. VISHUDDHA: THE ELEMENT OF ETHER — THE FIRST LIGHT

After the dense alchemy of Earth, Water, and Fire,
and the breath of Air in the Heart,
Vishuddha introduces **Ether** — the subtlest element, the field of vibration through which sound and light move.

Where the lower chakras build and transform, and the Heart unifies, the Throat **transmits**. It is where energy becomes *frequency*, and frequency becomes *creation*.

- Fire (Solar Plexus) gives you the power to act.
- Air (Heart) gives you the reason to act — love.
- Ether (Throat) gives you the way to act — expression.

Vishuddha therefore is **the alchemical voice of the soul**,
where love becomes sound, truth becomes resonance,
and the inner and outer worlds finally meet in harmony.

4. THE SPIRITUAL ARCHITECTURE OF YOUR SERIES

Chakra	Element	Function	Triad	Theme
Root	Earth	Stability	Body Trinity	Foundation of Life
Sacral	Water	Flow & Creation	Body Trinity	Emotional Fluidity
Solar Plexus	Fire	Will & Transformation	Body Trinity	Empowered Action
Heart	**Air**	**Love & Integration**	**Temple of Light**	**Bridge Between Worlds**
Throat	**Ether**	**Truth & Expression**	**Temple of Light**	**Divine Communication**
Third Eye	Light	Vision & Perception	Temple of Light	Insight & Intuition
Crown	Consciousness	Unity	Final Illumination	Divine Connection

5. THE EVOLUTION OF ENERGY

Each chakra in your series teaches how energy ascends and refines:

1. **Root** — Be here.
2. **Sacral** — Feel deeply.
3. **Solar Plexus** — Act with purpose.
4. **Heart** — Love without condition.
5. **Throat** — Speak truth into existence.
6. **Third Eye** — See beyond illusion.
7. **Crown** — Surrender to unity.

The **Throat Chakra** is therefore **the sacred bridge** —
the translator between the emotional heart and the intuitive mind,
between human love and divine wisdom.
It is the **voice of the awakened heart**,
where matter learns to speak light.

Chapter 7 – Hidden Secrets & Esoteric Wisdom

Tantra and the Throat Chakra

In Tantric philosophy, **Vishuddha — the Throat Chakra —** is the chamber of purification, the alchemical ether where vibration becomes expression, sound becomes truth, and individuality becomes divine resonance.
If the Heart opens the breath of love, then the Throat gives that love a voice — translating the invisible into vibration and the subtle into sound.

Here, **Kundalini Shakti** rises from the fires of Manipura and enters the luminous field of **Akasha — the ether element —** where her radiance no longer burns but *resonates*.
Energy, once solid and defined, becomes a wave and frequency.
It is the moment when awareness begins to sing itself into existence.

Vishuddha is the sacred portal of communication between worlds — the bridge through which divine truth moves from the subtle to the spoken, from consciousness to creation.
It is here that silence becomes sacred sound, and expression becomes worship.

KUNDALINI'S ASCENT THROUGH SOUND

When **Kundalini** reaches the Throat, she becomes vibration —
Nada, the primal sound of the universe.
She is no longer fire but *resonant light*, the current of
consciousness made audible.
This is where the initiate begins to perceive truth not only
through thought but through tone, rhythm, and frequency.

Tantric scriptures describe Vishuddha as *the pure lotus of
sixteen petals*, shimmering like the blue of infinite sky.
Each petal corresponds to a Sanskrit vowel sound — the
building blocks of creation itself.
For in the Tantric view, **sound is not symbolic — it is causal.**
The universe, and every soul within it, was sung into being.

Through the Throat Chakra, Kundalini learns the art of divine
expression — the mastery of vibration as a creative force.
Every word becomes a spell, every tone a prayer, every silence
a return to source.

This marks the third great transformation on the Tantric path:
from action to expression, from power to purpose, from doing
to *being the voice of the Divine.*

THE ETHER OF CONSCIOUS COMMUNICATION

In the alchemy of Tantra, **ether (akasha)** is the field of subtle
vibration — the infinite expanse that holds all sound, light, and
memory.
It is the element of space, allowing all others to move and
interact.
Through it, communication between matter and spirit becomes
possible.

Just as air carries breath, ether carries awareness.
It is through this sacred medium that truth travels — not as

noise, but as resonance.

When the Throat Chakra is awakened, you begin to hear the world as vibration and feel the cosmos as sound.

Your words gain power because they are aligned with reality; your silence gains depth because it vibrates with understanding.

This is the esoteric secret of Vishuddha: **to speak is to create; to listen is to align.** The wise practitioner learns that mastery of sound begins not with volume, but with purity — of heart, of intention, and of tone.

THE VOICE AS A VESSEL OF LIGHT

Through Tantric practice, the Throat Chakra becomes a **luminous temple of sacred sound.**

Chanting, mantra, and breathwork refine the vibration of thought until it matches the frequency of truth.

The voice becomes an instrument of healing — carrying not just words, but *energy.*

When spoken from this purified center, speech becomes medicine, and silence becomes communion.

The initiate no longer seeks to be heard; they seek to transmit.

No longer to persuade; but to reveal.

Every utterance becomes a bridge between heaven and earth — a note in the symphony of divine order.

The **mantra of Vishuddha** echoes the vow of spiritual integrity:

"May my voice be pure.
May my truth serve light.
May my words carry the sound of peace."

At the deepest level of Tantric understanding, Vishuddha is not merely the center of speech — it is the doorway to the **Soundless Sound (Anahata Nada)**, the vibration beyond vibration.
This is the hum of the universe before sound takes form — the silence that sings within every atom.
To enter this space is to merge back into the eternal resonance of creation.

Here, **Kundalini no longer ascends — she dissolves.**
Sound returns to silence, expression to source, and the voice of the individual becomes one with the Voice of God.
In this state, you do not speak to the Divine — you *are* the Divine speaking.

The Body as the Temple of Resonance

Tantra honors **Vishuddha** as the seat of divine expression within the body — the sacred chamber where vibration, truth, and consciousness merge into sound.
Located at the throat, it is the **gateway between the heart and the mind**, where love becomes word and thought becomes song.
Here, the body is not only the vessel of breath — it is the **instrument of Spirit**.
Every cell vibrates, every breath hums with subtle resonance, every sound becomes a bridge between heaven and earth.

When Vishuddha is balanced, the voice carries purity and presence; speech becomes an act of creation, and silence becomes luminous awareness.
When blocked, words distort truth and the melody of life grows faint — the harmony between the seen and unseen disrupted.
In the awakened Throat Chakra, the body itself becomes a

temple of sound, vibrating with the cosmic rhythm known in Tantra as **Nada Brahma** — **"the world is sound."**

SHAKTI AND SHIVA IN VIBRATIONAL UNION

In Vishuddha, **Shakti's radiant ascent** transforms from the flame of Manipura into the vibration of Ether — pure frequency without form.
She becomes **Nada Shakti**, the Goddess of Sound, dancing as tone, mantra, and resonance.
Shiva, as eternal Silence, receives her vibration as awareness itself.
Their union here is not of movement and stillness, but of **sound and silence**, **voice and listening** — the divine conversation of creation.

Where in Manipura Shakti burned with will, in Vishuddha she sings with wisdom.
Where Shiva once observed her dance as light, now he vibrates as space, echoing her music through the cosmos.
This union gives rise to *clarity beyond speech* — the sacred truth that creation is not noise, but divine harmony unfolding through vibration.

Tantra teaches that this marriage of sound and silence births enlightenment: speech purified by awareness, expression refined by stillness, and vibration guided by truth.
Here, power no longer seeks to act — it seeks to **resonate**.

TANTRIC PRACTICES FOR VISHUDDHA

Traditional Tantric disciplines to awaken and harmonize the Throat Chakra focus on refining vibration, purifying sound, and aligning communication with higher consciousness:

• **Bija Mantra — HAM:**
Chant **HAM**, feeling the sound resonate through your throat and

skull.
Let the vibration expand into the Ether, cleansing confusion and aligning you with truth.

• Nada Meditation (Listening to the Inner Sound):
In deep silence, turn awareness inward to hear the subtle hum
— the *Anahata Nada*, the unstruck sound.
This vibration is the voice of consciousness itself.

• Bhramari Pranayama (Humming Breath):
Inhale deeply, then exhale with a gentle humming sound.
Feel the vibration soothe your nervous system and awaken inner clarity.
Each hum reconnects you to the cosmic frequency of balance and peace.

• Mantra Japa (Sacred Repetition):
Repeat a mantra that aligns with your soul's truth — not mechanically, but with awareness of vibration.
Let sound shape silence into devotion and silence refine sound into wisdom.

• Rituals of Purity and Expression:
Wear or visualize the color **sky blue** to invoke serenity.
Burn frankincense or sandalwood to cleanse the atmosphere.
Speak affirmations of clarity, honesty, and divine resonance.
Honor your voice as sacred — not for its volume, but for its truth.

THE DEEPER TANTRIC LESSON

Tantra teaches that **Vishuddha** is not merely the center of speech — it is the **gateway of resonance** where energy becomes frequency and truth becomes vibration.
Here, communication ceases to be a human act; it becomes *a cosmic event*.

When the Throat Chakra awakens, you realize that words carry power equal to prayer — they shape energy, alter matter, and bridge the visible and invisible worlds.
Expression becomes sacred when guided by integrity; silence becomes holy when infused with awareness.

At Vishuddha, individuality merges with the universal song.
You no longer speak to the Divine — you *speak as* the Divine, allowing wisdom to flow through you as tone and light.
The energy that once sought to control now seeks to communicate.
The voice becomes clear, humble, and radiant — a vessel for divine truth.

This is the secret of Vishuddha in Tantra: that **sound is light slowed into time**, that **truth is vibration made visible**, and that the **voice is the living bridge** between form and infinity.

To awaken the Throat Chakra is to remember that your very breath is sacred, your sound is creation, and your silence — the echo of God.

The Secret Wisdom Of The Throat Chakra

The hidden Tantric teaching of **Vishuddha** is that truth becomes divine when it is *vibrationally pure.*
It is not noise, but resonance — an acknowledgment that sound, word, and expression are not merely communication, but *creation itself.*

Where the Heart teaches love and compassion, and the Solar Plexus teaches mastery and will, the Throat reveals **illumination through sound** — the transmutation of fire into frequency, and of purpose into divine expression.
Here, power no longer acts through force, but through vibration.

The word becomes a bridge between the visible and invisible worlds — the breath of God spoken through the human form.

Vishuddha is the **etheric temple of purification**, where all the elements of the lower chakras are refined into clarity.
It is the chamber where Kundalini's radiant fire becomes song, and consciousness begins to hear itself.
Where the Solar Plexus proclaimed, *"I act, I choose, I shine,"* Vishuddha whispers with clarity and grace,
"I speak, I express, I become sound."

Here, the path to enlightenment is not silence alone, but **conscious resonance** — the transformation of vibration into wisdom, and speech into sacred service.
Through the Throat Chakra, the light that once burned now sings — radiant, clear, and free.

KUNDALINI: AWAKENING THROUGH THE SOUND OF THE THROAT CHAKRA
The Serpent Resonates

At the Solar Plexus, Kundalini burned with golden light — the fire of transformation.
As she rises into Vishuddha, that fire refines into *sound*.
The serpent no longer dances as flame but moves as **vibration**, shimmering blue and silver through the ether of the throat.

This is the initiation into **Nada — the divine current of sound.**
Here, Kundalini becomes *voice*, the cosmic hum that gave birth to creation.
The ancient Tantras call this the "Gate of Ether," where the soul awakens to its own resonance.

Where she once burned, she now vibrates.
Where she once consumed, she now harmonizes.
It is the sacred transmutation of energy into frequency — the passage from doing to being, from will to wisdom.

Kundalini no longer seeks to conquer the body; she begins to communicate through it.
Your voice, breath, and presence become instruments of her divine resonance.

THE DANCE OF SOUND

As Kundalini rises through the Throat Chakra, her rhythm changes again.
The roaring fire of Manipura softens into the luminous hum of Vishuddha — a *celestial song* pulsing through the ether.
This is the **alchemy of vibration**, where thought becomes tone and consciousness reveals its musical nature.

Each sound, each word, each breath carries power.
When expressed with awareness, it purifies; when distorted by ego, it clouds the air.
Tantra teaches that the key to this sacred sound is **listening** — to feel the resonance before you speak, to allow silence to shape sound, and to let truth emerge naturally from the heart.

In this sacred dance, **Shakti** vibrates as sound, and **Shiva** receives as silence.
Their union becomes *Nada Brahma* — "the world is sound."
Every vibration, every whisper of wind, every heartbeat in the cosmos sings this eternal mantra.

SIGNS OF AWAKENING

When Kundalini activates the Throat Chakra, her presence reveals itself as a refined and luminous vibration:
• Spontaneous humming, chanting, or hearing inner tones
• Heightened sensitivity to sound and vibration
• Clarity and calmness in speech
• A sense of weightlessness or expansiveness around the neck and shoulders
• Vivid dreams of sky, flight, or sacred symbols of sound

• Sudden inspiration to write, sing, teach, or speak truth
• Profound peace arising from silence itself

These are the harmonics of awakening — the ether vibrating in resonance with consciousness.
You may feel as though your body itself is singing, your breath humming with the voice of the universe.
This is Shakti awakening through sound — turning silence into song, and expression into illumination.

BALANCING THE ETHER

Just as fire must be tended, sound must be tuned.
An awakened Vishuddha shines with clarity when expression flows from truth — but it becomes distorted when energy is blocked or misused.
When overactive, the Throat may express through dominance, gossip, or restlessness; when underactive, through silence born of fear.

The Tantric path teaches the **middle resonance** — speech aligned with love, truth, and service.

• **Ground through the Root:** Let silence draw from stability, not fear.
• **Flow through the Sacral:** Allow emotion to soften tone and expression.
• **Burn through the Solar Plexus:** Speak with confidence, not control.
• **Open through the Heart:** Let love guide your words.

Through this alignment, the voice becomes clear — not merely to be heard, but to heal.

THE SACRED SOUND WITHIN

Tantra teaches:

"To know sound is to know vibration; to master vibration is to touch the Divine."

At Vishuddha, **Kundalini becomes Nada Shakti** — the Sound Goddess who sings the universe into being.
Her song is the hum of stars, the pulse of breath, the resonance that unites all things.
When you surrender to her current, your voice becomes the prayer of existence itself.

The same energy that once sought expression through action now reveals its truest power through *resonance*.
Your words no longer seek to persuade; they seek to reveal.
Your silence no longer hides; it radiates peace.

When sound flows through the Throat in alignment with truth, life itself becomes mantra — a continuous vibration of awareness unfolding in sacred harmony.

This is the secret of the Throat Chakra in Tantra:
that creation is vibration, that truth is sound, and **that the Divine forever speaks through those who listen deeply.**

Tantric Secrets Of The Resonant Sky

THE ELEMENT OF ETHER AND THE SOUND WITHIN IT

The **Throat Chakra (Vishuddha)** is the realm of **Ether — Akasha** — infinite, spacious, and luminous.
It is the sacred expanse where vibration becomes expression and silence becomes sound.
If the Solar Plexus taught transformation through fire, Vishuddha teaches **transcendence through resonance.**

Ether is the subtlest of the elements — it neither burns nor flows; it *contains and conveys.*
It is the field through which all sound travels, all light moves, and all consciousness communicates.
In Tantra, Akasha is the temple of truth — the inner sky where awareness vibrates as voice, where stillness speaks.

When **Kundalini** rises into the Throat Chakra, the inner fire of Manipura dissolves into radiant sound.
The light that once shone now hums; the flame that once transformed now sings.
The energy of will becomes frequency — the vibration of truth moving through the space of being.

Here, awareness is not seen or touched — it is *heard.*
Consciousness reveals itself as resonance, and the body becomes an instrument of divine sound.

POWER AS RESONANCE

In Tantra, **power is vibration in harmony with truth.**
It is not loudness, but clarity; not assertion, but alignment.
True mastery of Vishuddha lies not in speaking more, but in

speaking *from silence* — the silence that listens deeply before sound is born.

When sound is unconscious, it fragments.
When guided by awareness, it unites.

The adept learns to tune their vibration as a musician tunes a string — not too tight, not too loose.
The voice becomes a sacred current of energy, carrying not opinion but *frequency*.
Every word becomes a ripple in the cosmic field.
Every silence becomes a doorway to infinity.

Power through Vishuddha is not the power *to persuade*, but the power *to harmonize*.
It is the radiance of authenticity vibrating so purely that falsehood dissolves in its presence.

PURPOSE AS EXPRESSION

In Vishuddha, purpose transforms into **pure expression** — action refined into resonance.
Here, the ego no longer seeks to achieve; it seeks to *articulate the Divine*.
Every sound becomes sacred when it flows through awareness.

Tantra teaches that **to speak truth is the highest yoga.**
When you express from the soul rather than the self, vibration aligns with creation itself. Each word becomes mantra — sound shaped by consciousness. Each breath becomes a bridge between heaven and earth.

To live from Vishuddha is to understand that purpose is not doing — it is *resonating*. Work becomes transmission; creation becomes communication; and the voice becomes a vessel for light.

THE INNER MARRIAGE OF SHIVA AND SHAKTI

Within the Throat Chakra, **Shakti** dances as vibration, and
Shiva listens as infinite silence.
Their union is the cosmic symphony of **Nada Brahma — "The
world is sound."**

Shakti, the sound, moves in spirals of blue light — the
resonance of being made visible.
Shiva, the silence, receives her endlessly, holding her tones in
boundless space.
This is the **inner marriage of sound and stillness**, of speech
and understanding, of expression and awareness.

When sound arises from silence, it carries the truth of heaven.
When silence follows sound, it carries the wisdom of the earth.
Together they create the sacred rhythm of Vishuddha — the
pulse of divine communication through form and formlessness
alike.

Tantra teaches: *"When speech and stillness are one, the Divine
speaks through you."*

THE DEEPER TANTRIC REVELATION

The hidden teaching of Vishuddha is this:
Resonance itself is consciousness.
Every sound you utter, every breath you take, every silence you
hold is a wave in the infinite field of being.

The voice is not separate from the universe — it *is* the universe
speaking through you.
When you attune your vibration to truth, the entire cosmos
responds.
To sing is to remember, to listen is to awaken, and to speak
truth is to liberate energy bound by illusion.

In the deepest Tantric understanding, awakening is not only through stillness — it is through sound made conscious.

When you speak from the still point within the breath, your every word becomes mantra, your silence becomes music, and your presence becomes the echo of creation itself.

KUNDALINI AND THE ALCHEMY OF SOUND
Emotion as the Voice of the Soul

Emotion is vibration in motion — the inner music of being.
It is how consciousness resonates through form, how the infinite expresses its feeling through tone.
When **Kundalini** rises into the Throat Chakra, emotion finds its highest octave — no longer reactive, but *revelatory.*

The energy that once surged as feeling through the Sacral, and burned as purpose in the Solar Plexus, now flows as sound — the voice of the soul made audible.
Tears become release, laughter becomes prayer, words become creation.
Emotion here is no longer to be silenced or controlled — it is to be *sung.*

Vibration as Energy Transformed

At Vishuddha, the fires of Manipura turn into **frequency** — refined energy that heals rather than burns.
Old emotions vibrate loose from the body through voice, chant, and breath.
Each exhale becomes an act of purification, each tone a beam of light through shadow.

The Tantric sages taught:

"That which vibrates you also awakens you — if you listen with awareness."

When Kundalini sings through Vishuddha, she clears the channels of expression, releasing the residue of silence, shame, or suppression.
This is not noise — it is liberation.
Through this alchemy, emotion becomes communication, and communication becomes communion.
It is through this process that vibration gains consciousness, and sound becomes divine.

THE SOUND OF TRANSMUTATION
Where Fire Clarifies, Sound Reveals

If fire clarifies, **sound reveals**.
The flames of Manipura have purified; now, in Vishuddha, their light learns to *speak*.
This is where the brilliance of inner power becomes vibration — where the energy once burning in the belly now resounds as the voice of the soul.

The Throat Chakra does not reject expression; it refines it.
Here, the purified emotions of the Solar Plexus rise as a clear tone, shaped by awareness, carried by breath.
Anger becomes assertion with compassion.
Fear becomes the steady voice of truth.
Desire becomes prayer.
Grief becomes song.

This is the alchemy of Vishuddha — the conversion of *power into resonance*, of *light into sound.*
Each vibration, when expressed consciously, liberates the energy that was once bound to it.
Through sound, what was once hidden becomes seen — for vibration is light unfolding in time.

THE DANCE OF THE INNER SKY

When the Throat Chakra awakens, it moves through the being like a sky filled with song.
You may sense subtle pulsations around the neck, feel energy spiraling up the spine into the head, or hear an inner hum vibrating behind every breath.
This is **Shakti as sound** — not word, but wave; not noise, but knowing.

She no longer dances as flame; she ripples as resonance.
Each exhale carries light made audible, and each inhale drinks silence made luminous.
You begin to *speak from stillness, breathe from wisdom, and move from rhythm.*
The body becomes a tuning fork of awareness.
The mind quiets as sound becomes teacher — revealing that silence was never absence, only the space where all sound begins.

This is the dance of the inner sky — the awakening of the luminous voice through consciousness.
In this state, speech no longer reacts; it *reveals.*
Each word becomes a thread of light, weaving your inner and outer worlds into harmony.

THE LIGHT WITHIN THE SOUND

Every vibration carries hidden radiance.
Within every tone lies wisdom waiting to be heard.
When you meet your voice in the space of awareness, its secret alchemy unfolds:

• Anger becomes clarity.
• Fear becomes resonance.
• Shame becomes authenticity.

• Doubt becomes discernment.
• Silence becomes sanctuary.

This is the **blue purification of Vishuddha** — where sound itself heals, not by force, but by truth.
The voice does not need to be powerful to be sacred; it needs only to be aligned.
Each breath releases another layer of distortion, and what remains is purity — the clear tone of the soul.

Sound burns without smoke, purifies without flame, and reveals without destruction.
It carries the wisdom that fire once forged, and spreads it through vibration — effortlessly, endlessly.

THE HIDDEN TANTRIC TRUTH

Kundalini does not awaken by suppressing sound — she awakens by *becoming it.*
Each vibration, each mantra, each breath is her unfolding expression.
Where the fire of Manipura transformed emotion into power, the ether of Vishuddha transforms that power into *truth.*

When silence turns to sound without distortion, you witness the divine alchemy of Ether — where awareness speaks and vibration becomes illumination.
When the voice aligns with the heart and will, you become a vessel of sacred resonance — steady, luminous, and free.

Tantra teaches that enlightenment is not the absence of sound, but its transparency — the clear song of consciousness vibrating through form.
To sound is to become light in motion.
To speak truth with awareness is to allow **Shakti to sing** — no longer as fire consuming, but as sound revealing.

Through this alchemy, you become both **tone and silence** — the resonant expression of divine wisdom awakened within.

Secret Uses Of The Throat Chakra: Celestial Mysteries, Sound Trance, And The Alchemy Of Voice

Beyond its link to communication and truth, the **Throat Chakra (Vishuddha)** conceals the ancient teachings of **transformation through vibration, silence, and resonance.** In esoteric lineages, this etheric center was revered as **the inner sky** — the living temple where light becomes sound and consciousness speaks its own name.

Here, sound is not communication but *creation*. Vishuddha holds the mysteries of frequency — how vibration becomes form, and how awareness, love, and intention fuse to generate harmony in the soul.

CELESTIAL MYSTERIES: THE SKY WITHIN

In Tantric cosmology, Vishuddha is ruled by **Akasha**, the element of ether — infinite, weightless, radiant.
It is the dimension in which all sounds are born and into which all return.
Its rhythm mirrors the cycles of vibration:
Silence (potential), Sound (expression), Stillness (absorption).

Ancient adepts practiced *Nada Yoga* at dawn and dusk, attuning to the subtle hum of creation known as the **Anahata Nada** — the "unstruck sound" that echoes in the silence of meditation. Through deep listening, they entered communion with the universal current — hearing the resonance of spirit itself.

To work with Vishuddha is to learn the art of **attunement** —
knowing when to express outward, when to listen inward, and
when to rest in silence.
This celestial rhythm restores balance between speaking and
hearing, teaching that truth is not shouted — it *resonates.*
When aligned with the pulse of universal sound, the voice
becomes luminous rather than forceful — a gentle vibration that
heals, unifies, and reveals.

SOUND TRANCE AND THE STATE OF RESONANT AWARENESS

Where the Solar trance moves through stillness and flame, the
Throat trance moves through breath and tone — the luminous
awareness of sound.
In ancient temples, initiates chanted bija mantras or sang the
sacred OM until the boundaries between breath, body, and
sound dissolved.
In this state, the practitioner became *the vibration itself* —
endless, spacious, and free.

Modern seekers touch this through creativity and flow — when
expression becomes effortless, when writing, singing, or
teaching flows like water illuminated by light.
It is the trance of resonance, where sound arises from stillness
and returns to silence, carrying awareness as its song.

Here, the voice is not the speaker — it is the universe
remembering itself.
This is the state of radiant expression — consciousness
vibrating as sound.

THE ALCHEMY OF VOICE: TURNING SOUND INTO LIGHT

Just as the alchemist of Manipura turns fire into gold, the initiate of Vishuddha turns **sound into illumination.**
Every vibration, once purified by awareness, becomes the language of the divine.

Judgment becomes discernment.
Fear becomes articulation.
Silence becomes wisdom.
Emotion becomes song.
Thought becomes mantra.

This is **etheric alchemy** — the art of refining personal expression into sacred resonance.
Through breath, mantra, and awareness, the dense frequencies of emotion rise as harmonics of healing.
The words we once spoke in pain are transmuted into tone and truth.

Nothing is wasted in this process.
The same vibration that once wounded can become a bridge for compassion — the echo of wisdom that awakens others.
Through this practice, the self begins to resound as **light in motion.**

SOUND BONDING: COMMUNION WITH THE VOICE OF CREATION

Just as the Solar's ritual was fire bonding, the Throat's sacred act is **sound bonding** — communion through vibration.
In ancient rites, practitioners sat before resonant bowls, conch shells, or the open sky, chanting until the sound vibrated through bone and breath alike.
Each note was an offering, each silence a prayer.

This practice continues whenever you hum to soothe, speak from love, or listen in reverence.
Sound bonding reconnects you to the element of ether — teaching the rhythm of resonance: when to sound, when to rest, and how to harmonize with the silence beyond sound.
Spiritually, it reminds us that the same vibration that creates the universe also speaks through our breath.

PRIMAL EXPRESSION AND THE SONG OF CREATION

Where the Root expresses primal instinct, the Sacral expresses primal emotion, and the Solar expresses primal will — the Throat expresses **primal revelation** — the power to name, to bless, and to call energy into form.

This is the realm of **Nada Shakti**, the divine sound-current that sustains creation.
It is the resonance that fuels not only communication but also inspiration, prophecy, and truth.
When channeled consciously, this vibration becomes the **Voice of the Divine** — capable of healing through harmony without exhausting the self.

To awaken this current is to remember your birthright as a co-creator of worlds — one who shapes reality not through control, but through frequency.

THE HIDDEN WISDOM

The Throat Chakra reveals that truth is not spoken — it is *sounded.*
Its secret is not persuasion, but purity — the tone of authenticity that vibrates beyond words.
Just as the Root grounds, the Sacral flows, and the Solar transforms, the Throat reveals.
It turns thought into tone, intention into transmission, and consciousness into communication.

To honor Vishuddha is to remember that the sky within you is eternal — a space vast enough for all sound and silence to coexist.
When you live from this radiant etheric center, you no longer seek to be heard — you become harmony itself.
You do not force your truth upon the world — you let it *resonate until the world remembers its own.*

Western Mysticism: The Word Of Creation And The Temple Of Divine Truth

In Western esoteric and mystical traditions, **sound** has always been regarded as the primal act of creation — the vibration through which divine thought becomes form.
If Earth laid the foundation, Water gave movement, and Fire offered illumination, then **Ether** — the element of the Throat Chakra — reveals the *voice of the Creator* within creation itself.
Vishuddha is the **Temple of the Word**, the chamber of sacred resonance where the Divine speaks through vibration, rhythm, and truth.
Here, illumination expands into revelation; the light that Manipura kindled now takes shape as sound, meaning, and message.
It is the sphere of divine communication — where consciousness learns to *articulate light.*

THE LOGOS: THE WORD THAT WAS IN THE BEGINNING

"In the beginning was the Word, and the Word was with God, and the Word was God."
This verse from the Gospel of John expresses the Western understanding of what the yogis called *Nada Brahma* — the universe as sound.
In the cosmic temple, the Logos is the first vibration — the eternal tone of divine intelligence giving order to chaos.

Where Manipura's fire ignites awareness, the Throat expresses
that awareness as sound — the vibration that organizes creation
into pattern.
Mystics across ages have perceived the Logos not as speech, but
as *frequency* — the living breath that sustains all things.
The Hermetic philosophers taught that "God geometrizes by
sound" — that all form arises from divine vibration echoing
through the Ether.
Vishuddha, then, is the gateway where the unspoken becomes
spoken, the unseen becomes known, and the eternal becomes
audible.

THE TEMPLE OF DIVINE TRUTH

If Manipura lights the temple's altar, the Throat is the **archway
of resonance** through which that light is proclaimed.
This is the chamber where divine will finds its language —
where energy, purified by fire, becomes word, chant, and
invocation.

In Western mysticism, this principle is embodied in the sacred
breath — the *Spiritus Dei* — which animates and gives voice to
the divine spark within humanity.
To the Christian mystic, this is the *pneuma*, the Holy Spirit that
descended as tongues of flame — fire transformed into word.
In Kabbalah, the Throat corresponds with **Da'at**, the invisible
sefirah that bridges knowledge and manifestation — the hidden
door between wisdom above and understanding below.
Da'at is the sound of revelation — the knowing that comes
when truth vibrates through the soul.

To awaken Vishuddha is to open that same inner gate — to
speak not from personality, but from presence; not from
intellect, but from illumination.

THE ALCHEMY OF ETHER: FROM FLAME TO FREQUENCY

In Western alchemy, Ether — sometimes called the "quintessence" — was seen as the purest element, the essence that binds fire, air, water, and earth into harmony.
It is the philosopher's fifth element, the invisible thread linking spirit to matter.

Just as fire refines metal, sound refines light.
Through vibration, the raw brilliance of Manipura's fire becomes ordered harmony — the music of the spheres.
This is the **etheric alchemy** of Vishuddha: the transformation of force into frequency, and of light into language.

Where the alchemist sought the *Philosopher's Stone* through flame, the mystic found it through sound — the *Verbum Dimissum*, the lost word of divine creation.
To rediscover that word within oneself is to recover the soul's true tone — the vibration that restores harmony between heaven and earth.

MYSTERIES OF THE VOICE AND THE BREATH OF SPIRIT

In Western mysticism, **breath** was considered the first prayer — the silent word of life itself.
Each inhalation is a divine reception; each exhalation, divine expression.
The Hebrew *ruach*, the Greek *pneuma*, and the Latin *spiritus* all mean both "breath" and "spirit."
Thus, the act of breathing consciously is itself a sacrament — the living rhythm of God within man.

Mystics practiced breath as invocation: the breath that formed the *Tetragrammaton*, the ineffable Name of God.
Each syllable — inhaled and exhaled — echoed the vibration of

the divine essence.
When the Throat awakens to this mystery, speech becomes
sacred again.
Every word uttered in truth carries the light of creation; every
silence held in reverence becomes communion with Spirit.

THE CHRISTIC WORD AND THE VOICE OF REVELATION

For the Christian mystic, Christ represents the **Living Word** —
divine intelligence speaking through human form.
He is the personification of Vishuddha awakened — the perfect
harmony of truth, compassion, and expression.
When He spoke, His words healed; when He was silent, His
presence still resonated.

In this sense, the Throat Chakra embodies the same archetype:
the *Word made flesh*, truth made sound.
The mystic's prayer, "Thy will be done," echoes as the voice of
surrender — the merging of personal speech with divine
articulation.
Through this union, the human voice becomes a mirror of the
celestial chorus — a resonance of the eternal Word that began
all things.

THE SHARED WISDOM

Across Western mysticism, the message mirrors that of Eastern
Tantra:
Sound is sacred because it reveals.
It is the bridge between silence and form, spirit and matter,
heaven and earth.

Through the Word, the soul learns not only to know but to
communicate light.
Whether through Gregorian chant, the Kabbalist's divine
names, or the Hermetic magus's sacred utterance, all Western

traditions preserve the same revelation Tantra proclaims through Vishuddha:

The voice within you is the echo of the Divine.
When your words align with truth, God speaks through you.

To live from this etheric center is to live as both vessel and vibration — a resonant instrument of divine communication, a sky within the human temple, sounding not to be heard, but to harmonize.

Chapter 8 – Balancing & Healing Practices

Reiki Positions and Energy Protocols for the Throat Chakra

The **Throat Chakra (Vishuddha)** governs communication, self-expression, authenticity, and the resonance of truth.
In Reiki and subtle energy work, this center is treated after the Heart Chakra — once love and compassion flow freely — to help awareness rise into clear, conscious communication.
Balancing this chakra restores integrity between thought, word, and action, allowing one's voice to become a vessel for divine truth.

HAND POSITIONS FOR THE THROAT CHAKRA

Reiki placements for the Throat Chakra are located around the **neck, collarbones, and upper shoulders**, encompassing the thyroid gland, vocal cords, and etheric communication field.
This region stores energetic imprints related to expression, boundaries, and the ability to speak and live one's truth.
Always approach this area with gentleness and steady breath — the throat holds both power and vulnerability.

• **Front of Throat:**
Place both hands gently over the base of the throat or lightly on either side of the neck.
This calms communication, opens the vocal channel, and soothes tension caused by fear of judgment or suppression.

• **Jaw and Mouth Area:**
Positioning hands just below the chin or along the jawline supports the release of unspoken words, grief, or guilt related to past silence.
It invites honest yet compassionate expression.

• **Back of Neck (Cervical Spine):**
Hands placed on the back of the neck balance receptive and expressive flow.
This harmonizes listening (back) with speaking (front), aligning outer communication with inner knowing.

• **Front and Back Together:**
One hand on the throat and one behind the neck stabilizes the chakra's frequency.
It unites clarity (front) with wisdom (back), ensuring that speech arises from truth rather than reaction.

ENERGY PROTOCOLS

1. **The Blue Ray of Clarity**
   Invite Reiki to flow as a soft blue or turquoise light through the throat area.
   Feel it cool and clear the energy, dissolving tension, tightness, or hesitation.
   As the blue ray deepens, awareness expands — each breath becomes an act of calm presence.
   Affirm silently: *"I speak my truth with grace and clarity."*

2. **Releasing the Knot of Silence**
   Unspoken emotion often gathers like a "knot" at the throat.
   Gently move your hands in small, counterclockwise circles over the neck and collarbones to release constricted energy.
   Visualize the knot unraveling into light, freeing your ability to express without fear or force.

3. **Balancing Expression and Listening**
   Alternate placements between the throat and heart centers.
   This links voice with compassion and communication with empathy.
   As energy flows, visualize a current of pale blue light moving between the two chakras — expressing truth that uplifts, not wounds.

4. **Resonance Breath Practice**
   Place your hands lightly on the throat and breathe in rhythm with the Reiki flow.
   Imagine each inhalation filling the throat with silver-blue light and each exhalation releasing old words, lies, or guilt.
   Feel the soundless vibration of truth expanding through your entire auric field.

5. **Sealing the Voice of Light**
   Conclude by resting both hands gently over the throat.
   Allow Reiki to seal the energy field with harmony and integrity.
   Whisper or affirm aloud: *"My voice is a channel of divine truth. I speak with love, listen with peace, and live with authenticity."*

SYMBOLIC SUPPORT

Advanced Reiki practitioners may use symbols to enhance Vishuddha's purification and resonance:

• **Cho Ku Rei (Power Symbol):**
Amplifies the clarity and projection of the voice; strengthens energetic boundaries during communication; dispels fear of self-expression.

• **Sei He Ki (Harmony Symbol):**
Balances emotional tone within speech; transforms reactive or harsh communication into understanding and compassion.

• **Hon Sha Ze Sho Nen (Distance Symbol):**
Heals communication blocks rooted in the past — unspoken truths, vows of silence, or ancestral suppression of voice.
Use to send healing through timelines of expression.

• **Dai Ko Myo (Master Symbol):**
Awakens the divine word within — aligning personal truth with universal wisdom.
It transforms speech into sacred sound, allowing the practitioner's voice to carry light itself.

INTEGRATIVE PRACTICE

When working with the Throat Chakra, remember:
Expression and silence are two notes of the same sacred song.
Healing occurs not only in what is said, but in the awareness behind the words.

To harmonize Vishuddha fully, pair energy work with sound:

- Chant **HAM**, the bija mantra of the Throat Chakra.
- Tone softly or hum to feel vibration resonate through the neck and skull.
- Practice mindful speech and deep listening in daily life.

As this chakra awakens, the voice no longer seeks approval — it speaks to awaken truth.
Each word becomes a prayer, each silence a temple.
Through Reiki, you learn that the truest healing sound is authenticity itself.

THE PRACTITIONER'S ROLE

Working with the **Throat Chakra (Vishuddha)** requires presence, patience, and integrity.
Because this center governs truth, communication, and resonance, the practitioner must embody *authentic neutrality* — speaking and listening from stillness rather than opinion.
Through tone, breath, and compassionate awareness, the healer creates a space where the client's true voice can emerge — not by giving words, but by helping silence reveal them.

Reiki for Vishuddha is not about expression for its own sake; it is about restoring harmony between *sound and silence, truth and peace.*
The practitioner becomes a tuning fork — resonating calm clarity so that the client's own vibration may return to its natural frequency.
When this occurs, expression flows without effort, communication becomes honest, and the individual remembers how to speak and live from the soul.

HEALING REMINDER

Reiki at the Throat Chakra teaches one of the great spiritual paradoxes:
Silence and speech are not opposites — they are one when guided by truth.

As Vishuddha's ether is purified, life begins to resonate with transparency and grace.
Words align with wisdom, and listening becomes an act of devotion.
The voice softens into honesty, and silence deepens into peace.

Through this resonance, the soul remembers:
"I speak truth. I listen with love. I live in harmony with all that is."

Bridging the Heart Chakra to the Crown Chakra Through the Throat

The chakras are not isolated centers of energy, but a single, ascending symphony — a spiral of consciousness rising from the grounded self to the divine.
Between the open compassion of the **Heart** and the pure illumination of the **Crown** lies the **Throat Chakra (Vishuddha)** — the etheric bridge where love becomes expression and wisdom becomes sound.

This is the passage from *feeling to knowing, from compassion to communication, from silence to sacred speech.*
It is the stage where the heart's truth seeks its voice, and the mind's wisdom learns to listen.

THE PATH FROM HEART TO CROWN

As energy rises through these upper chakras, it refines vibration into subtler forms of consciousness:

• **Heart (Anahata):** The center of love, empathy, and connection — where self and other merge in compassion.
• **Throat (Vishuddha):** The chamber of expression and truth — where love gains language and wisdom finds resonance.
• **Third Eye (Ajna):** The eye of perception and intuition — where sound becomes insight, and expression transforms into understanding.
• **Crown (Sahasrara):** The seat of divine consciousness — where the individual merges with the infinite, becoming silence once again.

Through this continuum, Vishuddha serves as the *transmission point* — converting the heart's emotional current into articulate energy and preparing the mind to receive intuitive light.

It is the harmonizing tone between love and illumination, emotion and realization.

THE ROLE OF THE THROAT CHAKRA IN THE BRIDGE

The Throat is the *vibrational portal* between feeling and knowing. It translates the language of the heart into vibration — sound, word, song, or silence — and carries that resonance upward toward higher awareness. When energy reaches Vishuddha, it no longer burns or flows; it *resonates.* It becomes pure frequency — the breath of truth, the tone of being.

Without this bridge, the energy of the heart cannot rise to wisdom, nor can the insight of the higher mind be embodied through compassionate communication.
When Vishuddha is balanced, love finds its voice and wisdom finds its tone. But when blocked, the flow between heart and crown becomes distorted — either speech without empathy or silence without clarity.

Thus, the Throat Chakra teaches alignment through vibration: to speak only when the heart is present, to listen only when the mind is open, and to let silence be the space where both meet.

THE ENERGETIC ASCENT: FROM COMPASSION TO COMMUNION

Each chakra along this bridge represents a stage of divine communication:

• **Heart:** "I love."
• **Throat:** "I speak."
• **Third Eye:** "I see."
• **Crown:** "I am."

Together, these affirmations trace the awakening of higher consciousness — from love as emotion to love as knowing, from individuality to unity.

When energy flows freely through this bridge, compassion becomes understanding, and wisdom becomes gentle expression. Truth is no longer merely spoken; it is *lived* as vibration, radiating peace and coherence.

But when Vishuddha is clouded by fear, guilt, or self-doubt, truth constricts.
The voice trembles, the words distort, and wisdom becomes trapped in silence.
Healing this center liberates the breath of spirit — transforming the act of speaking into prayer and the act of listening into communion.

LIVING THE BRIDGE

To bridge Heart and Crown through the Throat is to embody the sacred art of resonance — living as both sound and silence.
It means expressing truth without judgment, listening without defense, and allowing each word to serve love rather than ego.
Here, communication becomes a spiritual practice, and every conversation becomes an opportunity to transmit light.

When the Heart is open, the Throat clear, and the Crown receptive, energy flows as divine dialogue — the human voice echoing the cosmic Word.
This is the moment when life itself becomes mantra:
Every breath a prayer, every word a vibration of truth, every silence a return to God.

In this state, the soul speaks and listens through you.
You become a vessel of harmony — a voice for the infinite, a bridge between heaven and earth, where **love learns to speak and light learns to sing.**

Bridging Heart to Crown Across Cultures

Across mystical traditions, the journey from the center of the chest to the crown of the head has been revered as the *ascent of illumination* — the transformation from love to wisdom, from compassion to communion with the Divine. In yogic philosophy, this higher passage flows through the upper chakras — **Heart (Anahata), Throat (Vishuddha), Third Eye (Ajna),** and **Crown (Sahasrara)** — forming the bridge between emotion and enlightenment.

While the Heart opens us to love and empathy, the Crown unites us with pure consciousness.
Between them, the Throat and Third Eye refine energy into expression and perception — the vibration of truth and the vision of understanding.
Across cultures, this ascending current is the movement of *breath becoming sound, sound becoming light, and light returning to silence.*

EASTERN TRADITIONS: THE PATH OF ETHER AND LIGHT

In Tantric and yogic systems, the upper chakras represent the subtle etheric realms — the transformation of dense prana into consciousness itself:
• **Anahata (Heart)** — *Vayu Tattva (Air):* Compassion, connection, balance.
• **Vishuddha (Throat)** — *Akasha Tattva (Ether):* Expression, resonance, truth.
• **Ajna (Third Eye)** — *Mahat Tattva (Light/Mind):* Intuition, perception, wisdom.
• **Sahasrara (Crown)** — *Pure Consciousness:* Unity, transcendence, divine realization.

This progression — Air → Ether → Light → Spirit — reflects the refinement of love into vibration, vibration into insight, and insight into pure awareness.

The Throat serves as the sacred resonance point — where the breath of the Heart becomes the mantra of the soul.

Here, sound is not merely spoken; it is *remembered* — the primordial Word (Nada) from which creation emerged.

In yogic terms, this is *Nada Yoga*, the yoga of sound — where silence becomes the seed of every sacred utterance and vibration itself becomes prayer.

INDIGENOUS AND SHAMANIC WISDOM: THE VOICE OF THE SKY

In Indigenous and shamanic cosmologies, the upper centers are the domain of the *sky realms* — the world of wind, bird, and song.

The Heart is the drumbeat of Earth; the Throat is the wind that carries the song; the Crown is the great sky into which that song dissolves.

Voice is seen as spirit in motion — the breath of the Creator moving through creation.

The shaman's chant, the healer's breath, the storyteller's voice — all are expressions of Vishuddha's sacred function: to weave worlds with sound.

When the heart's compassion guides the voice, words become medicine.

When the mind listens through silence, wisdom descends as song.

Thus, the bridge between Heart and Crown is the *songline of the soul* — where love rises as vibration and descends again as blessing.

TAOIST PHILOSOPHY: THE BREATH OF HEAVEN

In Taoist internal alchemy, the upper field — encompassing the chest, throat, head, and crown — is known as the *Palace of Spirit (Shen)*.
It is here that the refined qi ascends and transforms into light.
The Throat corresponds to the **Middle Heaven**, where the breath bridges Earth and Sky.

The Taoists teach that *when the breath becomes silent, it becomes spirit.*
Vishuddha parallels this truth — it is the energetic space where breath turns to tone, tone turns to vibration, and vibration returns to stillness.
This process is called **Lian Shen**, the "refinement of spirit," mirroring the chakra system's teaching that expression (Throat) must dissolve into perception (Third Eye) to open to enlightenment (Crown).

WESTERN MYSTICISM: THE WORD AND THE LIGHT

In the Western mystery schools, this bridge was understood through the sacred Logos — the Divine Word that creates reality through sound and intention.
"In the beginning was the Word, and the Word was with God, and the Word was God."
This line from *John 1:1* echoes Vishuddha's essence: sound as creation, speech as manifestation.

Medieval Christian mystics viewed this ascent as the path from *caritas* (love) to *sapientia* (wisdom) — the transformation of the heart's devotion into divine understanding.
Hermetic philosophers described it as the "Ladder of Light," where the voice of the soul rises through successive spheres of sound until it merges with the ineffable silence of the Divine.
In Kabbalistic teaching, it corresponds to the movement from **Tiferet (Beauty, the Heart)** through **Da'at (Knowledge, the**

Throat Gate) toward **Keter (Crown, Divine Unity)** — the sacred channel where knowledge and love ascend into wisdom and light.

THE SHARED WISDOM

Across cultures, the message remains the same:
Sound is the bridge between love and illumination.
The voice becomes the vehicle of spirit — transforming emotion into frequency, and frequency into understanding.

When the Throat is clear, the Heart's compassion can be spoken into the world, and the Crown's light can be expressed through human life.
Truth resonates, wisdom vibrates, and the Divine breathes through word, song, and silence alike.

To live through this bridge is to embody the eternal dialogue between heaven and earth —
the breath of God moving through the voice of the soul, the sound of love ascending into light, and the silence of light returning to love.

Western Mysticism and Alchemy: The Sacred Marriage of Air and Ether

In Western alchemy, the higher stages of transformation were known as *the Great Work* — the refinement of the soul from love into wisdom, from compassion into illumination.
While the lower mysteries united Earth, Water, and Fire within the heart, the higher mysteries joined **Air and Ether** — the elements of breath and spirit — within the realms of expression and revelation.

The classical alchemists described these upper stages as the
Sacred Marriage of Air and Light:

- **Air (Heart)** — love, balance, and communion.
- **Ether (Throat)** — vibration, resonance, and expression.
- **Light (Mind/Third Eye)** — perception, insight, and vision.
- **Spirit (Crown)** — unity, stillness, and divine consciousness.

Where the lower alchemy purified matter, the higher alchemy refined awareness itself.
The *inner fire* of the Solar Plexus became *the inner light* of consciousness, expressed through sound and truth.
In the language of Hermetic philosophy, this was the **sublimation of Sulphur into Spiritus Mercurii** — the transformation of fiery will into luminous speech, and speech into pure wisdom.

To the mystic, the Throat was the gateway where the soul learns to articulate divine truth — the "breath of God" passing through human form.
This was called *the Voice of the Logos*: the moment when word and light become one, and expression becomes creation.

PSYCHOLOGICAL PERSPECTIVES: FROM COMPASSION TO SELF-ACTUALIZATION

Modern psychology recognizes this ascent as the journey from emotional integration to authentic expression and insight:

- **Heart Chakra (Anahata):** Emotional maturity, empathy, and relational balance.
- **Throat Chakra (Vishuddha):** Communication, self-expression, and congruence between inner truth and outer voice.

- **Third Eye Chakra (Ajna):** Intuition, perception, and mental clarity.
- **Crown Chakra (Sahasrara):** Spiritual awareness, connection to higher purpose, and transcendence of ego.

If the lower chakras shape identity, the upper chakras refine awareness.
A blocked Throat manifests as silence, self-censorship, or inauthentic speech — signs of a soul that has learned love but not yet learned how to voice it.
Healing begins by restoring honest communication and emotional transparency, allowing the individual to express the heart's truth without fear of judgment.

In psychological language, this is the movement from *authentic self-expression* to *self-realization*: the ability to translate emotion into meaning and meaning into vision.
Vishuddha serves as the fulcrum of this transformation — the moment where consciousness learns to *speak its own awakening*.

THE UNIVERSAL BRIDGE

Across mystical and psychological systems alike, the message is consistent:
The path from the Heart to the Crown cannot bypass the Throat — the sacred chamber of resonance.

You must love before you can speak, speak before you can see, and see before you can know.

The Heart opens you to love.
The Throat teaches you to express that love with truth.
The Third Eye transforms truth into understanding.
The Crown dissolves understanding into unity.

Together, they form the celestial bridge of transcendence — the path where love becomes wisdom, sound becomes light, and light becomes silence.

To walk this bridge is to embody the divine dialogue itself — the eternal breath that speaks creation into being, the vibration through which heaven and earth remember their oneness.

Meditation & Visualization Exercises for the Throat Chakra

The Throat Chakra (Vishuddha) is the temple of sound — the etheric bridge where truth takes form through vibration.
It governs communication, self-expression, and the ability to live in harmony with one's authentic voice.
Meditation here awakens resonance, clears energetic constriction, and restores the flow between heart and mind.

These practices refine your inner vibration — helping you to listen deeply, speak clearly, and express the wisdom that moves through you.
As Vishuddha opens, sound becomes sacred once more — a prayer of truth rising through the breath of spirit.

1. THE BLUE LOTUS VISUALIZATION

Purpose: To purify and awaken the Throat Chakra through the vibration of calm truth.

1. Sit comfortably with your spine long and shoulders relaxed.
2. Bring your awareness to the base of your throat, the hollow above your collarbones.
3. Visualize a radiant **blue lotus** slowly blooming there, its petals luminous with soft, sky-colored light.

4. With each inhale, the flower draws in peace and clarity. With each exhale, it releases tension, guilt, or withheld words.
5. Whisper inwardly:
   "I speak my truth with peace. My words are gentle, clear, and true."
6. Continue until you feel lightness expanding through your neck and shoulders — the sense of openness that comes from honesty and trust.

2. THE SOUND CURRENT MEDITATION (NADA YOGA)

Purpose: To connect with the inner sound of the soul — the subtle vibration beyond words.

1. Sit quietly, close your eyes, and bring your attention to your hearing.
2. Instead of focusing outward, listen inward — as if tuning to the faint hum within your own being.
3. Allow your awareness to settle on any subtle tone, ringing, or silence.
4. As you rest here, realize that this vibration is eternal — the soundless sound (*Anahata Nada*) from which all creation arises.
5. With each breath, merge with this inner resonance until you feel your boundaries dissolve in stillness.
6. End with gratitude, affirming:
   "I am the sound of peace. My voice is the echo of truth."

3. THE BREATH OF SOUND (UJJAYI PRANAYAMA)

Purpose: To harmonize breath, voice, and energy — restoring calm focus and vocal strength.

1. Sit tall and relax your jaw and tongue.

2. Inhale deeply through the nose, gently constricting the throat so the breath sounds like a soft ocean wave.
3. Exhale with the same sound, letting the rhythm soothe your mind.
4. Continue for several minutes, feeling your breath caress your throat like wind over water.
5. Visualize this breath as shimmering blue light cleansing and cooling your vocal channel.
6. Finish by whispering:
"My breath carries peace. My words carry light."

4. THE BLUE FLAME MEDITATION

Purpose: To transmute fear of expression into radiant truth.

1. Sit or lie comfortably.
2. Imagine a **blue flame** glowing in your throat — gentle yet vibrant.
3. With each inhale, the flame brightens, filling you with courage and serenity.
4. With each exhale, it burns away self-doubt, fear of judgment, or the urge to please.
5. Whisper:
"I release fear. My truth shines clear."
6. Remain with this visualization until your voice, breath, and heartbeat feel like one steady rhythm — the rhythm of authenticity.

5. THE BRIDGE OF LIGHT MEDITATION

Purpose: To connect Heart, Throat, and Third Eye — aligning emotion, expression, and wisdom.

1. Focus first on your Heart Chakra — feel its green light expanding with compassion.

2. Now visualize a stream of turquoise-blue light rising from the heart to the throat, merging green and blue into a harmonious glow.
3. From the throat, allow this light to rise to your Third Eye, where it becomes indigo — the light of insight.
4. With each breath, feel this current flowing smoothly: **love → truth → vision.**
5. Whisper:
   "My words carry love. My voice reveals wisdom."
6. Rest in this bridge of light, sensing yourself as both listener and speaker — the voice of the heart made luminous through awareness.

6. THE BIJA MANTRA MEDITATION – HAM

Purpose: To activate Vishuddha through the sacred seed sound of purification.

1. Sit comfortably with a long spine.
2. Bring awareness to your throat.
3. Inhale deeply, and as you exhale, chant **HAM** (pronounced "hahm"), letting the *ah* vibrate through your throat and the *m* hum softly in your head.
4. Feel the vibration clearing constriction, harmonizing your breath and voice.
5. Continue for several minutes, then rest in silence, sensing the afterglow of openness and ease.
6. Close with the affirmation:
   "I speak with clarity. I listen with love. My voice is the sound of my soul."

Each of these meditations refines the sacred current of sound within you — the bridge between thought and creation, heart and mind, silence and song.
When practiced with devotion, Vishuddha becomes the bell of the soul — ringing truth through every word, breath, and act of presence.

Through the Throat Chakra, speech becomes prayer, and silence becomes divine listening.

To live from this center is to embody the pure resonance of spirit — **the voice of love made audible, the silence of wisdom made visible.**

Crystals for the Throat Chakra

Crystals connected to the Throat Chakra resonate with the pure vibration of **truth, communication, and resonance.**
Their energy clarifies self-expression, promotes honesty, and encourages calm, authentic speech.
These stones open the voice of the soul — helping you speak from love rather than fear, listen with compassion, and share your truth with grace and confidence.
By working with Throat Chakra crystals, you awaken the power of sound and intention — where every word becomes vibration, and every vibration becomes creation.

Blue Lace Agate

- **Qualities:** Calm communication, emotional clarity, serenity.
- Known as the *Stone of the Peacemaker*, Blue Lace Agate soothes the voice and mind, releasing tension and fear around speaking one's truth. Its gentle frequency brings harmony to communication and peace to conflict.
- **Use:** Place over the throat during meditation to release blocked expression or wear as a pendant to promote gentle, heartfelt speech throughout the day.

Aquamarine

- **Qualities:** Courage, clarity, self-expression.
- Aquamarine, the *stone of the sea*, carries the energy of clear waters — calm yet powerful. It helps dissolve fear of judgment and encourages authentic, honest communication.
- **Use:** Hold while journaling or before public speaking to calm nerves and express truth with confidence. It also supports emotional release through the voice and breath.

Lapis Lazuli

- **Qualities:** Wisdom, truth, higher communication.
- Revered by ancient civilizations as a stone of divine insight, Lapis Lazuli bridges the Throat and Third Eye Chakras — uniting speech with higher wisdom. It supports visionary expression, intellectual clarity, and truthful leadership.
- **Use:** Wear near the throat or meditate with Lapis between the throat and brow to align communication with intuition and spiritual purpose.

Turquoise

- **Qualities:** Protection, authenticity, creative expression.
- Turquoise unites the elements of sky and earth, promoting balance between speaking and listening, giving and receiving. It protects the voice from exhaustion and clears the pathway for creative inspiration.
- **Use:** Singers, teachers, and healers can wear Turquoise at the throat for sustained clarity, or place it under the pillow to encourage honest dreams and inner truth.

Celestite

- **Qualities:** Angelic communication, purity, elevated resonance.
- Celestite carries the vibration of the heavens — soft blue light that clears the aura and lifts communication to its spiritual octave. It encourages divine dialogue, prayer, and inspired speech.
- **Use:** Meditate with Celestite at the throat or crown to connect with guidance from higher realms, or keep near your workspace to infuse your voice with peace and grace.

Blue Kyanite

- **Qualities:** Alignment, truth, energetic flow.
- Blue Kyanite is the great equalizer of the energy body — aligning all chakras through resonance. It clears blockages in the throat, helping energy move freely from heart to voice.
- **Use:** Hold during deep breathing or affirmation practice to restore energetic balance and enhance authentic self-expression. It is also powerful for healers and teachers who communicate energy through words and tone.

THROAT CHAKRA CRYSTAL AFFIRMATION

"My voice is clear and true.
I speak from love and listen with wisdom.
My words flow in harmony with the light of my soul."

HOW TO WORK WITH THROAT CHAKRA CRYSTALS

Crystals connected to the Throat Chakra harmonize vibration, voice, and truth.
They clear the energy pathways between the heart and the mind, allowing you to express your authentic self with clarity and compassion.
Working with these stones strengthens communication, deepens listening, and restores confidence in the power of your voice.
Through them, your words regain sacred purpose — sound becomes vibration, and vibration becomes creation.

• Placement

Lay stones directly over the throat or upper chest during meditation to balance Vishuddha's energy and release tension.
You may also place them in a triangular formation between the heart, throat, and third eye to harmonize emotion, expression, and intuition.

• Sound Charging

Because the Throat Chakra vibrates to the element of sound, chanting, singing, or humming with your crystals amplifies their frequency.
Hold your chosen stone (Aquamarine, Lapis Lazuli, or Blue Lace Agate) at your throat as you softly vocalize or tone the mantra **HAM**.
Allow the resonance to pass through both crystal and body, clearing stagnant energy and aligning your voice with truth.

• Communication Spaces

Keep Throat Chakra crystals in areas associated with communication — your desk, studio, or bedside — to encourage calm expression and authentic connection.

They are ideal companions for teachers, writers, speakers, and healers whose voices carry light and intention.

• **Affirmation**

While holding your crystal, speak slowly and clearly:
"My voice is clear. My truth flows with ease.
I speak, listen, and live in harmony."

CHARGING CRYSTALS WITH THE ELEMENT OF ETHER AND SOUND

The Throat Chakra is governed by Ether — the subtle element of vibration and resonance.
To charge these crystals is to tune them, much like an instrument, to the frequency of truth and clarity.
Ether purifies through sound and breath rather than fire or water.
It expands energy, clears distortion, and restores coherence between your inner and outer expression.

1. SOUND BATH CHARGING

Sound is the natural purifier of Vishuddha.

- Use a **singing bowl**, **tuning fork**, or **chanting voice** to immerse your stones in vibrational frequency.
- As you tone the mantra **HAM** or hum softly, visualize ripples of blue light washing through your crystals.
- Whisper:
  "Through sound I cleanse, through silence I align.
  May these stones resonate with truth and peace."

2. BREATH CHARGING

Breath is the carrier of Ether — the bridge between silence and sound.

1. Hold your crystal at your throat or lips.
2. Inhale deeply through the nose, and as you exhale, gently breathe over the stone.
3. Imagine your breath as cool blue light, cleansing the crystal of stagnation and infusing it with calm clarity.
4. End by affirming:
   "With every breath, my truth flows freely."

3. MOONLIGHT CHARGING

Moonlight carries the serene frequency of reflection and expression — perfect for Throat Chakra attunement.

- Place your crystals on a windowsill during a waxing or full moon.
- As they bathe in lunar glow, visualize soft silver-blue light filling them with serenity and clear communication.
- Speak the intention:
  "By the light of truth and the calm of night, these stones awaken my voice to divine insight."

4. WIND AND WHISPER CHARGING

The element of air also nourishes Vishuddha.

- Take your crystals outdoors on a breezy day.
- Hold them where they can feel the wind's movement — or gently blow across them with conscious breath.
- Imagine the wind carrying away energetic heaviness and whispering new inspiration into them.
- Say:
  "Air of clarity, breath of life — cleanse and awaken these crystals of light."

5. VOCAL BLESSING

Because sound is the language of spirit, your voice is the purest way to charge Throat Chakra stones.

- Sit in quiet meditation with your chosen crystal in your hands.
- Speak a truth, prayer, or poem aloud — not for perfection, but for resonance.
- Feel the vibration move through your words into the stone, filling it with intention and love.
- Finish with the affirmation:
  "My words carry light. My truth flows through sound."

CHARGING AFFIRMATION

"Through sound and silence, I align.
My crystals sing with clarity and peace.
Their vibration amplifies the voice of my soul."

Crystals of the Throat Chakra are sacred instruments — amplifiers of truth, harmony, and resonance.
Through them, the soul learns to sing its own name again — to express love as vibration and to honor silence as the birthplace of creation.
When charged through sound, breath, and light, they awaken the pure current of Vishuddha —
the eternal song of the spirit made visible through voice.

Essential Oils for the Throat Chakra

The Throat Chakra (Vishuddha) responds to cool, clarifying, and expansive aromas that open the breath, calm the mind, and encourage authentic expression.

These soothing yet powerful oils clear energetic congestion, dissolve fear of judgment, and harmonize communication between heart and mind.

Essential oils for the Throat Chakra nurture truth, creativity, and self-trust — supporting the ability to speak with honesty, listen with compassion, and express from the soul.

They open the energetic channel of resonance, where thought becomes sound and sound becomes vibration — the living language of spirit.

Eucalyptus

- **Qualities:** Clarity, release, breath.
- Eucalyptus clears energetic and physical blockages, opening the throat and lungs to the flow of air and expression. Its refreshing scent dissolves stagnation and fear, restoring fluidity and focus to communication.
- **Use:** Diffuse to clear the mind before writing or speaking, or inhale deeply to expand breath and calm nerves before conversations that require honesty.

Chamomile (Roman or German)

- **Qualities:** Peace, patience, truthful calm.
- Chamomile's gentle floral aroma soothes the nervous system and softens harsh communication patterns. It encourages speaking with kindness and listening with understanding.

- **Use:** Apply (diluted) to the throat area before meditation or difficult conversations, or diffuse in shared spaces to foster harmony and emotional balance.

Sandalwood

- **Qualities:** Sacred expression, inner stillness, divine connection.
- Sandalwood opens the Throat Chakra to higher resonance, helping you communicate from the soul rather than the ego. Its grounding, meditative scent connects voice to spirit, merging human expression with divine wisdom.
- **Use:** Diffuse during meditation or chant practice to align breath, sound, and intention. Apply (diluted) to the throat and heart to balance spiritual and emotional truth.

Lavender

- **Qualities:** Balance, relaxation, self-trust.
- Lavender's tranquil scent cools the energetic "heat" of suppressed or overactive speech. It promotes gentle confidence, allowing you to express feelings without fear.
- **Use:** Inhale or diffuse before public speaking, journaling, or vocal work. Blend with chamomile for a calming ritual that restores balance between silence and sound.

Peppermint

- **Qualities:** Clarity, freshness, mental flow.
- Peppermint awakens the mind and clears the pathway of communication. Its crisp energy supports truthfulness, creative inspiration, and mental precision.
- **Use:** Diffuse to refresh the atmosphere when brainstorming, teaching, or engaging in open dialogue.

Inhale before expressing complex ideas to enhance articulation and flow.

Frankincense

- **Qualities:** Integration, higher will, sacred speech.
- Frankincense bridges the lower and higher chakras, guiding words from the heart through the clarity of the mind. It enhances meditative focus, truthfulness, and spiritual presence in communication.
- **Use:** Inhale during prayer, chanting, or reflective writing. Add to a carrier oil and anoint the throat and temples to align your voice with divine guidance.

How to Use Throat Chakra Oils

- **Diffusion:** Add a few drops to a diffuser during journaling, singing, or creative work to open expression and clear mental tension.
- **Massage:** Blend with a carrier oil and gently massage the neck, shoulders, or upper chest to relax tension and restore vocal ease.
- **Inhalation Ritual:** Cup your hands over the nose and mouth, inhale deeply, and exhale through the throat. Imagine sound and breath moving freely through you.
- **Chanting Meditation:** Apply a drop (diluted) of sandalwood or frankincense to the throat before chanting the mantra **HAM**, enhancing resonance and clarity of tone.

AFFIRMATION TO PAIR WITH AROMATHERAPY

"With each breath, my voice awakens.
I speak truth with love,
I listen with peace, and my words become light."

ENERGETIC INSIGHT

Essential oils for the Throat Chakra are not merely fragrances
— they are the breath of truth itself.
Each aroma carries a vibration that refines the voice and calms
the mind, reminding the spirit that words are sacred vessels of
creation.
Through the power of scent and sound, these oils teach the art
of resonance — to speak without harm, to express without fear,
and to let silence hold as much truth as speech.

When the breath and fragrance unite, Vishuddha blossoms —
the voice becomes clear, the mind quiet, and every word
becomes an offering of harmony to the world.

Blending for Expression: Essential Oil Combinations for the Throat Chakra

Blending essential oils for the Throat Chakra (Vishuddha) is the
art of sacred resonance — merging aroma, breath, and intention
into a clear, harmonious vibration.
Each blend becomes a song of authenticity, helping you express
truth with grace, listen with empathy, and communicate from
the heart.

Because Vishuddha is governed by the element of **Ether** (sound
and vibration), blends for this chakra should feel **cool,
expansive, and clarifying** — opening the throat, soothing
tension, and aligning the voice with higher truth.

When creating your blend, let your **intention guide your
selection** — your reason for blending becomes the frequency
that shapes its power.
Combine up to three essential oils in a carrier such as jojoba,
sweet almond, or fractionated coconut oil.

Shake gently and charge your blend with conscious breath or mantra before use.

1. Clear Communication

Purpose: To enhance honest expression and calm the voice.
Blend:

- 2 drops Lavender
- 2 drops Eucalyptus
- 1 drop Frankincense
  Use: Apply (diluted) to the throat and upper chest before speaking, teaching, or singing. Diffuse to promote open dialogue and ease of communication.
  Affirmation: *"My words flow with truth, clarity, and calm."*

2. Authentic Voice

Purpose: To release fear of judgment and encourage heartfelt expression.
Blend:

- 2 drops Chamomile (Roman or German)
- 2 drops Sandalwood
- 1 drop Peppermint
  Use: Inhale deeply before important conversations, recording, or creative work. Apply to the back of the neck or diffuse while journaling.
  Affirmation: *"I express my truth with confidence and compassion."*

3. Peaceful Listening

Purpose: To open space for intuitive and empathic communication.
Blend:

- 2 drops Frankincense
- 2 drops Lavender
- 1 drop Geranium
  Use: Diffuse during meditation, counseling, or conflict resolution to encourage understanding and calm.
  Affirmation: *"I listen with presence. My heart hears what words cannot say."*

4. Creative Expression

Purpose: To inspire artistic and verbal flow — writing, singing, or storytelling.
Blend:

- 2 drops Lemon
- 1 drop Eucalyptus
- 1 drop Clary Sage
  Use: Diffuse or apply (diluted) to the throat and temples while creating. Inhale before journaling or public presentations to awaken inspiration.
  Affirmation: *"My creativity flows freely. My voice is my art."*

5. Truth & Serenity Ritual Blend

Purpose: To align speech with spiritual truth and inner peace.
Blend:

- 1 drop Sandalwood
- 1 drop Frankincense
- 1 drop Blue Chamomile (or Myrrh for depth)
  Use: Anoint the throat and heart before meditation, chanting, or moonlight reflection. As you breathe in, visualize soft blue light radiating from your throat, filling your aura with calm truth.
  Affirmation: *"I speak the language of light. My truth is peace."*

CHARGING YOUR BLENDS WITH THE ELEMENT OF ETHER AND SOUND

Because the Throat Chakra is ruled by Ether, **sound and breath** are its natural activators.
Charging your blends through vibration — chanting, breathwork, or music — infuses them with clarity and resonance.
Ether expands energy through frequency, attuning your oils to harmony and divine expression.

1. Sound Infusion

- Chant the bija mantra **"HAM"** seven times over your blend.
- Feel the vibration ripple through your throat and into the oils.
- Visualize blue light spiraling into the bottle as you speak.
- Whisper:
  "Sound of truth, awaken within this blend.
  Let every word be an echo of love."

2. Breath Activation

- Cup your blend in both hands at your throat.
- Inhale deeply through the nose, exhale gently over the bottle.
- Imagine your breath as blue mist, filling the oils with calm and clarity.
- Repeat: *"With each breath, my truth awakens."*

3. Moonlight Charging

- Place your blend under the soft glow of the full or waxing moon.

- The moon's cool light aligns with Vishuddha's receptive nature, awakening intuition and serenity.
- As it charges, visualize a halo of silver-blue radiance infusing your blend with peace and truth.

4. Singing Bowl Resonance

- Set your blend near a singing bowl tuned to the note **G** (the frequency of the Throat Chakra).
- Strike the bowl gently and let its vibration pass through the oils.
- Imagine sound waves purifying and harmonizing the blend's energy.

5. Prayer of Resonance

Hold your blend to your heart and speak:
"May this creation carry the vibration of truth,
the peace of silence,
and the light of understanding."

ENERGETIC INSIGHT

Throat Chakra blends are not merely fragrances — they are **frequencies of truth** made tangible.
Each scent carries the whisper of divine resonance, teaching the balance between speech and silence, action and stillness.
Through them, the voice becomes sacred again — a bridge between human heart and higher consciousness.

These blends awaken Vishuddha's essence — the courage to speak, the humility to listen, and the grace to let sound become light.

Crystal + Aroma Activation For Sacred Voice

(Throat Chakra – Vishuddha)

The Throat Chakra awakens not through effort, but through resonance.
It opens when breath, vibration, scent, and awareness move together — when the voice remembers that expression is not performance, but truth revealed.
This ritual unites two sacred allies — **crystals and essential oils** — to clear the channel of communication, awaken creative flow, and align your voice with the higher harmony of spirit.

PREPARATION

Set aside 10–15 minutes in a calm, open space.
Soft lighting, gentle music, or the flicker of candlelight is ideal.
Sit comfortably with your spine tall, shoulders relaxed, and jaw unstrained.
Have these items ready:
• One Throat Chakra Crystal: *Aquamarine, Blue Lace Agate, Lapis Lazuli,* or *Sodalite*
• Your Expression Blend: Any essential oil combination from the previous section (or simply *Chamomile and Sandalwood* diluted in a carrier oil)
• A singing bowl, chime, or soft instrumental sound (optional)

1. The Breath of Clarity

Take three deep breaths into your throat and upper chest.
Inhale through the nose, feeling cool air expand your lungs and soften your neck.
Exhale gently through the mouth, releasing tension and unspoken words.
With each breath, imagine a wave of blue light washing through

your throat — spacious, calm, and luminous.
Whisper:
"I breathe truth. I release resistance. I open to harmony."

2. Anointing the Channel of Voice

Warm a few drops of your oil blend between your palms.
Cup your hands over your nose and mouth, inhaling the
soothing aroma.
Then, with intention, anoint:
• The **Throat** (center of communication and resonance)
• The **Heart** (truth through compassion)
• The **Third Eye** (clarity and intuitive perception)

As you touch each point, breathe the mantra of openness into it.
Feel the fragrance diffusing through your breath — clearing
pathways of energy and aligning thought with voice.
Affirm softly:
*"My words flow from peace. I speak clearly, honestly, and with
love."*

3. Crystal Resonance

Hold your chosen crystal in your left hand — your receiving
hand.
Bring it to the base of your throat and close your eyes.
Visualize a soft blue light emanating from the stone, pulsing
with each breath.
Gently trace slow, clockwise circles over your throat as you
inhale.
With each movement, feel your voice becoming lighter, freer,
more authentic.
Whisper or tone the mantra:
"HAM"
Let it vibrate through your entire being — resonating like
ripples across still water.
This is the frequency of truth awakening within you.

4. The Voice Meditation

Place the crystal over your throat (or rest it gently in your open palms before you).

Imagine a luminous blue sphere spinning gently in your throat center — glowing with clear, radiant light.

With every inhale, it expands outward — clearing the channels of expression.

With every exhale, it radiates calm, confident sound.

Feel the subtle vibration of your own breath humming through your body.

Whisper or hum softly — not for words, but for vibration.

Let your sound become a thread of peace weaving through your entire field.

5. Integration

Bring one hand to your heart and one to your throat.

Feel the bridge between love and truth glowing in harmony.

You are both listener and speaker — calm and courageous, silent and expressive.

Whisper:

"My heart guides my voice. My voice carries my soul's truth. I speak with love, I listen with grace, I live in resonance."

Take several grounding breaths and open your eyes slowly.

Sit in the afterglow of your own stillness — serene, luminous, and free.

Aftercare

• Cleanse your crystal in moonlight or by sound (a chime, singing bowl, or mantra).

• Store your oil blend in a cool, sacred space infused with peaceful intention.

• Repeat this ritual weekly, during the **waxing moon** or **dawn hours**, to restore clarity, calm, and creative flow.

When practiced consistently, this ritual reminds you that your voice is sacred — not to persuade or perform, but to reveal. Through scent, sound, and crystal, you awaken the radiant resonance of Vishuddha — the truth of your being expressed as vibration, the peace within made audible.

Sound Ritual For Sacred Expression

A Throat Chakra Mantra & Candle Ceremony

Sound is the sacred element of Vishuddha — the vibration of creation, communication, and truth.
When we align with sound consciously, we awaken the voice of spirit — the resonance of clarity, authenticity, and divine harmony.
This ritual can be performed through mantra, humming, chanting, or even silent vibration within the breath.
Its purpose is to open the channel of communication, dissolve fear of expression, and awaken the voice of inner peace.

Preparation: Setting the Energy of Resonance

Choose a time of stillness — dawn, dusk, or any moment when you feel called to speak your truth or reclaim calm.
This ritual is especially potent during the waxing moon or when you feel unheard, creatively blocked, or energetically constricted.

Gather:
• One candle (blue or white)
• 1–2 drops of Sandalwood, Chamomile, or Frankincense essential oil
• A bowl of water (symbol of Ether's reflection and emotional clarity)
• One Throat Chakra crystal (Aquamarine, Blue Lace Agate, or

Lapis Lazuli)
• Optional: Singing bowl, chime, or soft instrumental sound

Take a moment to center yourself and light your candle, saying softly:
"I awaken the voice of truth. I speak with love and clarity."

Step 1: Blessing the Sound

Sit comfortably with your spine long and shoulders open.
Place one hand over your throat and one over your heart.
Close your eyes and breathe deeply, letting each inhale expand your chest and each exhale soften your jaw.

Visualize a sphere of soft blue light glowing in your throat.
As you breathe, this light begins to hum faintly, a sound only you can feel.
Whisper:
"As above, so within — as this breath flows, so too does my truth arise."

Step 2: Anointing with Sound and Scent

Place a drop or two of your essential oil blend on your palms.
Rub your hands together until warm, then cup them over your nose and inhale deeply.
Allow the aroma to open your breath and clear the mind.

Anoint these points with intention:
• **Throat:** Expression and communication
• **Heart:** Compassionate truth
• **Forehead (Third Eye):** Insight and understanding

As you anoint, affirm softly:
"My words are born from peace. My truth flows from clarity."

Step 3: Crystal Resonance

Hold your chosen crystal in your left hand — your receptive hand.
Bring it near your throat and visualize blue light spiraling from the crystal into your voice center.
With each breath, this light expands, clearing tension and illuminating the space between mind and heart.

Now begin to softly hum or chant the bija mantra:
"HAM."
Let the sound vibrate through your throat, chest, and skull.
Feel its resonance ripple through the body — calming, cleansing, expanding.
The vibration itself is the healing.

Whisper:
"I am sound. I am peace. I am truth made visible."

Step 4: The Sound Meditation

Sit quietly before your candle.
Gaze softly into the flame or close your eyes and visualize it within your throat — a steady blue-white flame of truth.
With every inhale, breathe in light.
With every exhale, release withheld words, judgments, or fears into the flame.

You may hum gently, tone softly, or remain in silence — whichever feels most natural.
Each breath becomes sound; each sound becomes prayer.
Stay here for several minutes, breathing the rhythm of truth.

Whisper:
"I am the resonance of harmony.
My voice is clear, my heart is kind, my words are light."

Step 5: Integration

When you feel complete, place one hand on your heart and one on your throat.
Feel the flow between love and truth — your heart guiding your voice, your voice expressing your heart.
Say aloud:
"My truth is gentle. My voice is strong.
I speak light into the world."

Take a final deep breath, then extinguish the candle (or bow to the sound that lingers in silence) in gratitude.
Visualize a halo of blue light remaining at your throat — peaceful, radiant, alive.

Aftercare

• Cleanse your crystal with water or by sound — a chime, bell, or singing bowl.
• Store your oil blend or ritual tools near your altar or a silver-blue cloth to preserve the vibration of calm communication.
• Repeat this ritual weekly or before important communication — speaking, teaching, or creative expression.

When practiced with awareness, this **Sound Ritual** awakens the luminous power of Vishuddha — the voice that heals through resonance and reveals through stillness.
You emerge not louder, but clearer —
a living instrument of truth,
a vessel of peace,
a voice in harmony with the divine.

Somatic Practices For The Throat Chakra

Reclaiming Expression Through Breath and Sound

Where the Solar Plexus ignites the fire of will, the Throat Chakra — *Vishuddha*, the seat of communication, creativity, and truth — releases it into the world through vibration.
This is the realm of sound and silence, where breath becomes voice, and expression becomes liberation.

The Throat thrives on openness and rhythm.
When constricted by fear, self-doubt, or repression, energy tightens around the neck and shoulders — silencing both the literal and spiritual voice.
Somatic awareness restores freedom, teaching you to *breathe from truth, move from resonance,* and express with calm strength.

The following practices reconnect breath and voice with the intelligence of the body, helping you speak, sing, and live from authenticity — the harmony between heart and word, thought and sound.

1. RESONANT BREATH: AWAKENING THE VOICE WITHIN

This breath activates the Throat Chakra through vibration and sound, awakening clear communication and inner calm.

Practice:

1. Sit or stand with your spine tall and shoulders relaxed.
2. Inhale through the nose, feeling your ribcage widen.
3. As you exhale, hum gently — a soft *mmm* that vibrates through the lips and throat.

4. Feel the resonance travel into your chest and skull, clearing stagnation and tension.
5. Continue for several rounds, letting the hum grow longer and smoother.
6. After a few breaths, close your eyes and listen to the echo of your own vibration.

Mantra:
"With each breath, I express peace. My voice vibrates with truth."

2. THE OPEN THROAT STRETCH: RELEASING SUPPRESSION

Physical tension in the neck, shoulders, and jaw often reflects withheld words or unspoken feelings.
This gentle release restores openness and flow.

Practice:

1. Sit or stand comfortably. Drop your chin to your chest and exhale.
2. Inhale and slowly roll your head to the right, stretching the side of the neck; exhale and roll left.
3. With each circle, imagine releasing stagnant energy and unspoken emotion.
4. Bring your shoulders up toward your ears, then exhale and drop them down with a sigh.
5. Place one hand lightly on your throat, the other on your heart, and breathe between them.

Mantra:
"I release what was withheld. I open to my natural voice."

3. THE BRIDGE OF BREATH: CONNECTING HEART AND VOICE

This exercise aligns emotional truth (Heart Chakra) with authentic expression (Throat Chakra).

Practice:

1. Sit tall and bring one hand to your heart, one to your throat.
2. Inhale into your heart; exhale through your throat with a gentle sigh or tone.
3. Feel the current of breath traveling between the two centers — compassion flowing upward, truth flowing outward.
4. Continue for 5–10 breaths, visualizing a turquoise light connecting heart and throat.

Mantra:
"My heart guides my words. My voice speaks with love."

4. THE SOUND WAVE FLOW: MOVING WITH VIBRATION

This mindful movement awakens the element of Ether — the vibrational field of Vishuddha — through sound, flow, and breath.

Practice:

1. Stand or sit in an open posture.
2. Inhale, lifting your arms out to the sides as though gathering energy.
3. Exhale and bring your palms together at your throat while toning softly — "Ahhh," "Ommm," or "Ham."
4. Feel your voice ripple through your body like a wave of sound.

5. Repeat several times, letting each tone lengthen and deepen.
6. Rest in stillness afterward, sensing the gentle hum that remains in your body.

Mantra:
"My voice is light in motion. My sound carries peace."

5. THE LISTENING POSE: FINDING STILLNESS IN SOUND

Expression and silence are two halves of the same sacred rhythm.
This practice restores receptivity, helping you listen not just with your ears, but with your entire being.

Practice:

1. Sit comfortably with eyes closed, spine tall.
2. Bring your awareness to the sounds around you — near, far, subtle, or rhythmic.
3. Instead of labeling them, allow each sound to move through you.
4. Feel the space between sounds — the vast silence that holds them all.
5. Let your breath synchronize with this rhythm of listening and stillness.

Mantra:
"I listen deeply. I am the space where sound becomes peace."

ENERGETIC INSIGHT

The body speaks before the voice ever forms a word.
When the shoulders open, the breath deepens, and the throat softens, energy flows upward freely — turning communication into communion.

Somatic awareness at the Throat teaches that *true expression begins in stillness*.
To move, hum, or speak from this center is to embody both presence and permission.

As Vishuddha awakens through sound and breath, expression becomes effortless — not to impress, but to connect; not to be heard, but to harmonize.

When the Throat Chakra is free, **your voice becomes medicine** — a vibration of peace, truth, and resonance moving through the world.

Yoga Poses For The Throat Chakra

Awakening Clarity, Expression, and the Voice of Truth

The Throat Chakra (*Vishuddha*) governs the flow of communication, creativity, and spiritual resonance.
Through gentle postures that open the neck, shoulders, and upper chest, you awaken the passage between heart and mind — clearing the channel for authentic expression.
These movements enhance breath flow, dissolve energetic constriction, and invite you to speak, listen, and live from inner truth.

1. Shoulderstand (Sarvangasana) – The Inverted Perspective

Lie on your back and slowly lift your legs overhead, supporting your lower back with both hands.
Keep the chin tucked slightly toward the chest and breathe deeply through the throat.
This inversion stimulates blood flow to the thyroid and opens the energetic passage between the heart and head.

Focus: Clarity, purification, and perspective.
Affirmation: *"I see truth from a higher view. My words flow with grace and awareness."*

2. Fish Pose (Matsyasana) – Opening the Channel of Voice

From a reclined position, slide your hands beneath your hips, press your elbows into the ground, and lift your chest toward the sky.
Let your head gently release backward, opening the throat and heart.
Breathe as though you are drinking in light through your neck and exhaling sound through your heart.

Focus: Vocal freedom, self-expression, and emotional release.
Affirmation: *"I open my throat and speak with love."*

3. Cat-Cow Flow (Marjaryasana–Bitilasana) – The Breath of Expression

Come onto hands and knees.
Inhale, arching your spine and lifting your chin (Cow Pose); exhale, rounding your spine and drawing your chin toward the chest (Cat Pose).
Synchronize each motion with slow, audible breath — letting sound vibrate softly through the throat.

Focus: Releasing tension, harmonizing breath and voice.
Affirmation: *"I move and breathe in rhythm with my truth."*

4. Supported Bridge Pose (Setu Bandhasana) – Expanding the Flow of Communication

Lie on your back with knees bent and feet flat on the mat.
Lift the hips gently and place a block or cushion beneath your sacrum for support.
Relax your throat, allowing the head to tilt slightly back and the

neck to lengthen.
With each breath, feel the space open from heart to jaw — the
current of truth awakening.

Focus: Heart-throat connection, emotional balance, and gentle
openness.
Affirmation: *"My heart supports my voice. I express with
compassion."*

5. Lion's Breath (Simhasana) – Releasing Fear of Expression

Kneel or sit cross-legged, placing your palms on your knees.
Inhale deeply through the nose, then open your mouth wide,
extend your tongue, and exhale forcefully while making a "ha"
sound.
Feel the release of held emotion and the awakening of confident
presence.

Focus: Clearing blocked expression and activating courage in
communication.
Affirmation: *"I release hesitation. I express boldly and
freely."*

6. Plow Pose (Halasana) – Turning Inward to Hear the Inner Voice

From Shoulderstand, slowly lower your legs overhead until
your toes touch (or near) the floor behind you.
Support your back with your hands if needed, keeping the
breath smooth and steady.
This inversion deepens inner listening and stills mental noise.

Focus: Introspection, purification, and surrender.
Affirmation: *"In silence, I hear the truth within."*

7. Corpse Pose with Sound Awareness (Savasana with Vishuddha Focus)

Lie flat with your arms relaxed by your sides.
Place one hand over your throat and one over your heart.
With every inhale, imagine soft blue light expanding through your neck and shoulders.
With every exhale, release tension and let your breath become a gentle hum of peace.

Focus: Integration, tranquility, and vibrational balance.
Affirmation: *"My voice is clear. My energy is calm. I rest in truth."*

ENERGETIC INSIGHT

Throat Chakra Yoga transforms silence into resonance and effort into ease.
Each posture becomes a conversation between breath and awareness — teaching that expression begins not in the mouth, but in the alignment of body and soul.

When Vishuddha flows freely, your words carry frequency, not force; presence, not persuasion.
You no longer strain to be heard — you *resonate.*
In this harmony of breath, movement, and vibration, your truth becomes light in motion — the voice of spirit expressing through you.

Healing Through Sound Rituals And Lunar Cycles

Honoring the Element of Ether and the Rhythms of Inner Expression

The Throat Chakra (*Vishuddha*) is ruled by the element of ether — the vast field of vibration that carries sound, truth, and communication.
Where the Solar Plexus burns with the sun's radiance, the Throat glows with the moon's reflection — calm, receptive, and luminous.

Just as the moon waxes and wanes, so too does your expression move in cycles of silence and sound, inspiration and rest.
To heal the Throat Chakra is to honor this rhythm — to know when to speak and when to listen, when to project and when to receive.

Through sacred sound, we return to harmony with our natural voice — the one that does not strive to be heard, but resonates in truth.

Sound As A Sacred Healer

Sound restores what silence reveals.
It bridges the unseen with the seen, transforming vibration into creation.

Across cultures, sacred sound has been used to purify, heal, and connect with the divine — from the Vedic chanting of *Om* to Gregorian hymns, to the Indigenous drumming that carries prayer through the air.
Where fire cleanses through flame, sound cleanses through resonance.

It clears stagnation, dissolves illusion, and aligns the frequency of the self with the harmony of the cosmos.

In Vishuddha's teaching, sound is not only expression — it is liberation.
Every breath, every hum, every word is an offering of energy into form.
Through awareness, you become both the singer and the silence between notes — the echo of divine truth moving through you.

Intention for Practice

"Like sound, I vibrate in harmony.
I release fear and speak with clarity and grace."

LUNAR RITUAL FOR RESONANCE AND RELEASE

A Ceremony for Truth, Expression, and Inner Peace

This ritual invites you to release the heaviness of silence and restore balance to your voice and breath.
It is best performed under the waxing or full moon — times when the Throat Chakra's reflective energy is most potent.

You'll Need:

• One candle (blue, silver, or white) to symbolize truth and illumination
• A bowl of water to reflect lunar energy
• A few drops of essential oils such as chamomile, sandalwood, or frankincense
• One Throat Chakra crystal (Aquamarine, Blue Lace Agate, or Lapis Lazuli)
• Optional: a singing bowl, bell, or your own voice

1. Prepare the Space

Choose a calm space where you can hear your own breath.
Light the candle and place the bowl of water beside it — the
meeting of light and reflection, action and awareness.

Take a slow, deep breath in through the nose and exhale gently
through the mouth, releasing any tension in your jaw or throat.
Say aloud:
"With this flame, I illuminate truth.
With this breath, I awaken my voice."

Add your chosen oils to the water or diffuser.
Let the aroma remind you of calm clarity — the essence of
speaking from peace.

2. Awaken the Voice

Hold your crystal in your hand or place it near your throat.
Inhale deeply, and on the exhale, hum softly — feeling the
vibration travel from your throat into your heart.
Continue this gentle hum for several breaths, letting the sound
smooth the edges of your mind.

Whisper or chant the bija mantra:
"HAM."
Allow the sound to resonate — not loud, but steady —
expanding through the air around you.

Visualize your Throat Chakra glowing in blue light, like a
luminous moon radiating truth and serenity.

3. Release Through Resonance

As you hum or speak softly, begin naming what you are ready
to release into sound — withheld words, self-judgment, or fears
of expression.

You may say:
"I release the fear of speaking my truth."
"I release the weight of silence."
"I release the need for approval."

With each phrase, imagine the vibration carrying these patterns into the water before you, where they dissolve like ripples fading into stillness.

4. Harmonize with Intention

Place both hands on your throat and take three deep breaths.
On each inhale, draw in peace.
On each exhale, release effort.

Whisper or sing softly:
"My words are light.
My voice is love.
My truth flows freely."

Now, gaze at the moon (or visualize it if indoors) and imagine its reflection shimmering in the bowl of water.
Sense that reflection within you — calm, receptive, and radiant.

5. Seal in Resonance

When you feel complete, close your eyes and sit in silence.
Listen — not to external sound, but to the vibration that lingers in your body.
This is the hum of alignment — the soundless sound (*Anahata Nada*) of divine connection.

When ready, extinguish the candle.
Touch the surface of the water and say:
"Sound purifies, silence restores, and I am whole in both."

Pour the water into the earth or down the drain with gratitude, releasing your intentions into the flow of creation.

Purpose

This ritual reminds you that healing the voice is not about speaking louder — it is about resonating deeper.
Sound does not force its way; it fills the space that is open to receive it.

By honoring your natural cycles of expression — like the moon's phases of illumination and rest — you come into harmony with your truth.
Each word becomes a prayer, each breath a vibration of love.

When you listen and speak in balance, you embody the sacred teaching of Vishuddha: **to express without attachment, to hear without defense, and to communicate as the living echo of divine sound.**

Affirmations, Mudras, And Daily Balancing Practices For The Throat Chakra

Awakening Expression, Authenticity, and Inner Harmony

The Throat Chakra (*Vishuddha*) is the sacred center of communication and resonance — the bridge between thought and truth, emotion and expression.
When balanced, it empowers you to speak clearly, listen deeply, and live authentically.
When blocked, words falter, creativity dims, and the inner voice grows quiet under the weight of doubt or judgment.

Through daily affirmations, sound vibration, and mindful mudras, the Throat Chakra opens like a clear sky — vast,

luminous, and free.
These practices harmonize breath, sound, and awareness,
allowing truth to move through you effortlessly and with grace.

AFFIRMATIONS FOR TRUTH AND CLARITY OF EXPRESSION

Words are the sacred current of Vishuddha.
When spoken with presence, they carry vibration — the power
to heal, inspire, and align you with authenticity.
Speak these affirmations aloud each day with one hand on your
throat and the other on your heart, letting your voice flow like
gentle waves of light.

MORNING ACTIVATION AFFIRMATIONS

• "I express my truth with clarity and compassion."
• "My voice is clear, confident, and aligned with love."
• "I speak with purpose and listen with presence."
• "My words carry wisdom and healing."
• "Each breath awakens my authentic voice."

EVENING INTEGRATION AFFIRMATIONS

• "I release unspoken words and rest in silence."
• "My voice and heart are in harmony."
• "I have communicated my truth with integrity today."
• "I listen to the stillness within me."
• "My words, like my breath, flow in peace."

MANTRA FOR MEDITATION

HAM — (pronounced "hahm")
The bija mantra of Vishuddha — the sound of Ether, resonance,
and purification.
Chant softly, feeling the vibration hum through your throat and
chest.

Each repetition dissolves fear and strengthens your connection to truth.

Focus: Visualize a soft blue light radiating through your neck and shoulders with every "HAM," expanding into an aura of calm, open communication.

MUDRAS FOR BALANCING THE THROAT CHAKRA

In yogic tradition, mudras are sacred seals that direct prana (life force) through specific pathways.
For Vishuddha, they enhance clarity, balance communication, and harmonize the energy of voice and silence.

1. Granthita Mudra — The Gesture of Unbinding

This mudra releases blockages in the throat and chest, freeing self-expression and restoring harmony between speaking and listening.

How to Practice:

1. Sit comfortably with your spine tall.
2. Interlace the fingers of both hands, palms facing inward.
3. Rest your hands lightly at the base of your throat.
4. Inhale through the nose; exhale slowly through the mouth with a soft hum.
5. Continue for 5–10 minutes, allowing energy to flow freely through the neck and shoulders.

Affirmation:
"I release all that constricts my voice. My words flow in freedom and peace."

2. Shankh Mudra — The Gesture of the Sacred Conch

Symbolizing the purity of sound and divine communication, this mudra balances the voice, calms anxiety, and opens intuitive listening.

How to Practice:

1. Wrap the fingers of the right hand around the thumb of the left hand.
2. Place the left index finger along the right thumb.
3. Hold the mudra before your throat or heart.
4. Inhale deeply, exhale with the sound of "OM" or "HAM."
5. Practice for several minutes, feeling the sound vibrate through your hands and throat.

Affirmation:
"My voice is sacred. I speak the truth with love."

3. Akasha Mudra — The Gesture of Spacious Awareness

Associated with the element of ether, this mudra expands inner space, clarity, and self-expression.
It opens the throat and ears to both inner and outer communication.

How to Practice:

1. Touch the tip of your middle finger to the tip of your thumb.
2. Keep the other fingers extended and relaxed.
3. Rest your hands on your thighs, palms upward.
4. Focus on your breath moving through your throat as a soft blue current of light.

Affirmation:
"I am open, clear, and connected to the wisdom of the universe."

Daily Balancing Practices

1. Morning Sound Activation:
Upon waking, sit quietly and hum softly for one minute, feeling the vibration clear your throat and calm your mind.
Whisper: *"Today, I will speak truthfully and listen with an open heart."*

2. Blue Light Breath:
Take three slow breaths, visualizing cool blue light flowing in through your nose and radiating from your throat.
Let it cleanse tension and create spacious calm.

3. Evening Reflection:
Before sleep, place your hand over your throat and ask:
"Did I express myself honestly and kindly today?"
Whether your answer is yes or no, breathe compassion into your voice and let silence renew you.

ENERGETIC INSIGHT

Vishuddha teaches that true expression arises not from speaking more, but from speaking consciously.
When the Throat Chakra is balanced, communication becomes sacred — an act of alignment rather than reaction.

Your words carry frequency; your silence holds space.
Together they form the language of wisdom.

When you live from this awareness, your voice no longer seeks to persuade or prove —
it becomes a clear channel for truth, peace, and divine resonance.

You are the echo of creation — the sound through which spirit speaks.

Food Therapy For The Throat Chakra

Nourishing Clarity, Communication, and Inner Calm

The Throat Chakra (*Vishuddha*) governs the voice, thyroid, and respiratory system — the subtle bridge between the mind and heart.
It is the body's center of resonance, where vibration becomes expression and nourishment becomes clarity.
To feed Vishuddha is to soothe, hydrate, and purify — supporting the flow of energy through breath, sound, and intention.

When balanced, you speak clearly, listen deeply, and digest life with calm awareness.
When imbalanced, you may experience throat tension, dryness, or thyroid imbalance, and communication may feel constricted or excessive. The goal is to cultivate harmony and spaciousness — cooling the fires of overexpression while warming the stillness of suppression — through foods that calm, cleanse, and open the channels of breath and sound.

Energetic Principles

• **Element:** Ether (Space)
• **Sense:** Hearing
• **Color:** Sky Blue
• **Location:** Throat, neck, jaw, and thyroid
• **Themes:** Communication, truth, expression, purification, spacious awareness

FOODS THAT HEAL AND BALANCE THE THROAT
CHAKRA
Blue and Cooling Foods: The Frequency of Calm Clarity

Blue and naturally cooling foods vibrate with Vishuddha's
frequency, helping soothe inflammation, ease tension, and
balance thyroid and respiratory function.
They also support mental clarity and emotional peace —
foundations of clear communication.

Examples:
• Blueberries, blackberries, plums, and figs
• Coconut water, pears, cucumber, and apples
• Seaweeds (nori, kelp, dulse) — rich in iodine for thyroid
balance
• Herbal infusions like chamomile, lavender, or lemon balm

How to Use:
Enjoy these foods fresh or lightly steamed to preserve hydration
and vitality.
Sip herbal tea slowly and mindfully, allowing each swallow to
cool and soothe the throat.

Hydrating and Purifying Foods

Because Vishuddha's element is Ether, hydration is essential for
resonance.
These foods and drinks keep your throat moist, your voice clear,
and your mind calm.

Examples:
• Fresh fruits high in water content — watermelon, melon,
grapes
• Soups and broths with light herbs and sea salt
• Leafy greens — spinach, kale, romaine
• Warm water with honey and lemon for throat cleansing

Ritual Practice:
Before drinking, pause and take one slow breath through your nose, exhale through your mouth, and whisper:
"May this water clear my voice and calm my mind."
Drink with awareness, feeling gratitude for the life-giving element of flow.

Soothing Spices and Herbs

While Solar Plexus foods ignite heat, Vishuddha thrives on gentle warmth and aromatic calm.
Spices that soothe the throat and open breath are ideal — balancing without overwhelming.

Examples:
• Fennel, cardamom, coriander, and mint
• Licorice root, slippery elm, and marshmallow root (for throat coating)
• Tulsi (holy basil) to purify energy and support breath
• A pinch of cinnamon or ginger for balanced warmth

How to Use:
Steep herbs into warm teas or infuse them into broths.
Avoid overuse of chili, garlic, or heavy spices, which can dry or irritate the throat.

Proteins and Nourishment for Voice and Nerves

A balanced nervous system supports steady speech and composure.
Choose light, easily digestible proteins and omega-rich foods that calm the body while sustaining vocal energy.

Examples:
• Almonds, walnuts, flaxseed, chia seeds
• Legumes, lentils, or tofu (prepared gently)

• White fish or light grains (quinoa, amaranth, basmati rice)
• Herbal ghee or coconut oil for subtle lubrication

Tip:
Eat slowly, with silence between bites.
This mindful eating honors the throat's dual role in nourishment and expression — teaching that how you eat is as vital as what you eat.

ENERGETIC INSIGHT

Balancing Vishuddha through food is an act of devotion to your voice — not only your spoken one, but the energetic vibration that radiates from every cell.
Cooling, soothing, and hydrating foods bring harmony to a chakra often overheated by words left unspoken or spoken too harshly.

As you nourish this center, remember: your throat is both the passage of truth and the temple of silence.
Feed it with clarity, respect, and calm awareness, and it will return to you a voice that heals — one that speaks not from fear, but from freedom.

Eat lightly. Drink deeply. Speak truthfully. Rest often.
This is the nourishment of Vishuddha — where sustenance becomes sound and silence becomes strength.

Water-Infused Fruits And Clarity-Enhancing Vegetables

Fruits and vegetables rich in water and air elements carry Vishuddha's frequency of fluidity, purity, and calm expression. They cool excess heat from the body and soothe the throat, nurturing both the physical and energetic voice.

Examples:
• Blueberries, blackberries, pears, and plums
• Cucumber, celery, fennel, and zucchini
• Coconut water, seaweed, or light leafy greens
• Steamed cauliflower or lotus root to calm and clarify

How to Use:
Enjoy fruits and vegetables raw or lightly steamed to preserve their cooling, hydrating essence.
Drink water infused with mint, cucumber, or lemon to refresh the voice and promote mental clarity.

FOODS TO BALANCE EXCESS ETHER ENERGY

When Vishuddha is overactive, one may feel scattered, anxious, or overly talkative — floating in ideas without grounding in action.
To restore equilibrium, eat warm, moist foods that anchor the body and bring energy downward.

Grounding and Nourishing Choices:
• Root vegetables such as carrots, yams, or beets
• Warm soups with miso, lentils, or barley
• Herbal teas made with ginger or licorice root
• Cooked grains like quinoa or basmati rice

Avoid:
Excess raw or frozen foods, carbonated drinks, and excessive caffeine, which may dry the throat or overstimulate the nervous system.

RITUAL OF MINDFUL DRINKING

Vishuddha thrives on hydration and awareness.
Turn each sip into a meditation — a moment of communion with the element of Ether.

Practice:
Before drinking, pause and observe the clarity of your water.
Breathe deeply, feeling the breath pass gently through your throat.
Whisper:
"May this water cleanse my voice and open my truth."
Drink slowly, with gratitude for the clarity that flows within and without.

Affirmation:

*"Each sip clears my voice.
Each breath opens my truth.
I speak with ease, purity, and grace."*

ENERGETIC INSIGHT

Eating for Vishuddha is an act of harmony — finding balance between nourishment and expression.
This is not a diet of restriction, but a rhythm of resonance: foods that calm the voice, center the breath, and purify the mind.

As you eat and drink with presence, your inner sound grows steady and luminous.
You learn to speak not from tension, but from tranquility.
Each meal becomes a reminder of divine communication — the way silence nourishes sound, and truth flows through balance.

HEALING RITUAL: THE SACRED WATER PRACTICE

Purifying the Voice Through Presence and Flow

1. Choose a moment each day to drink water in silence. Let it be the first sip of morning or the final sip before rest.
2. Before drinking, gaze into the glass as if into still water reflecting the sky.

Whisper:
"May my words be as clear as this water,
May my voice carry peace."

3. Drink slowly, imagining the water traveling through your throat — cleansing tension, washing away unsaid words, and opening space for calm truth.
4. Rest in the quiet after drinking.
   Listen — not for sound, but for stillness.

Each sip becomes a sacred offering to your inner voice — an act of devotion to truth, peace, and clear expression.

Affirmation for Nourishment and Expression

"Every drop restores my clarity.
Every breath carries my truth.
I honor the flow of life within me —
the voice of the soul made sound."

HERBAL AND TEA REMEDIES FOR THE THROAT CHAKRA

Supporting Communication, Clarity, and Serene Expression

The Throat Chakra (*Vishuddha*) is the etheric bridge between the heart and the mind — the sacred center of sound, resonance, and truth.
Just as air carries vibration, this chakra carries your voice, translating thought into expression and silence into wisdom.
When balanced, Vishuddha allows words to flow with grace, and silence to feel restful and alive.

Herbs and teas for the Throat Chakra soothe, lubricate, and open the channels of voice and breath.
They calm inflammation, clear stagnation, and nurture the rhythm of speaking and listening.
These plants teach gentleness — to express without strain, to

communicate with compassion, and to rest in the stillness between sounds.

Energetic Principles of Herbal Healing

- **Element:** Ether (Space)
- **Body Systems:** Throat, thyroid, respiratory, vocal cords
- **Color Frequency:** Blue
- **Core Actions:** Soothe, clarify, cool, harmonize
- **Spiritual Lesson:** Truth through conscious communication

KEY HERBS FOR THE THROAT CHAKRA
Licorice Root (Glycyrrhiza glabra)

Qualities: Moistening, soothing, harmonizing.
Licorice root is one of the most potent allies for the throat. It coats and calms irritated tissues, restores vocal strength, and balances both the physical and energetic voice.
It also supports adrenal energy, grounding overuse of the throat caused by stress or overtalking.

Use:
Sip as a warm tea to soothe dryness and clear the throat before speaking or singing.
Combine with slippery elm or marshmallow root for deeper lubrication.

Affirmation:
"My voice flows with ease and gentleness."

Peppermint (Mentha × piperita)

Qualities: Cooling, clarifying, refreshing.
Peppermint clears energetic congestion in the throat and chest, awakens mental clarity, and refreshes communication.
It is especially beneficial for those who struggle with speaking under pressure or holding their breath during stress.

Use:
Drink before important conversations or creative expression to open breath and refresh your voice.
Inhale the steam for respiratory clarity.

Affirmation:
"I breathe clearly. My words are calm and bright."

Chamomile (Matricaria recutita)

Qualities: Calming, harmonizing, anti-inflammatory.
Chamomile softens the emotional tone behind speech, easing anxiety or harshness in communication.
It also soothes the throat after strain, restoring gentle resonance and emotional balance.

Use:
Sip as a bedtime tea to relax the neck, shoulders, and voice after a long day.
Blend with lemon balm or lavender for peace and composure.

Affirmation:
"I speak with patience and kindness."

Lemon Balm (Melissa officinalis)

Qualities: Calming, uplifting, heart-centered.
Lemon balm bridges heart and voice, harmonizing emotional truth with expression.
It helps those who overthink their words, allowing communication to flow effortlessly and authentically.

Use:
Drink during writing, teaching, or public speaking to ease self-consciousness.
Blend with chamomile or peppermint for clarity and comfort.

Affirmation:
"My words reflect peace and harmony."

Slippery Elm (Ulmus rubra)

Qualities: Demulcent, restorative, healing.
Slippery elm soothes the mucous membranes of the throat and digestive tract.
It brings relief from dryness or irritation — perfect for singers, teachers, or anyone using their voice extensively.

Use:
Mix powdered bark with warm water and honey for a soothing tonic.
Sip slowly, allowing it to coat the throat and calm the voice.

Affirmation:
"I honor my voice with rest and care."

Blue Vervain (Verbena hastata)

Qualities: Relaxing, releasing, clearing.
Blue vervain clears tension from the neck and shoulders, where unspoken emotions often reside.
It releases repressed expression, easing the pressure to hold back truth or perfectionism.

Use:
Drink as a light infusion in the evening to dissolve tightness in the throat and jaw.
Blend with chamomile or lemon balm for emotional clarity.

Affirmation:
"I let go. My voice is free and honest."

VISHUDDHA TEA BLENDS
1. Voice of Clarity Blend

Purpose: To open and clear the throat before communication or creative work.
Blend: Peppermint, lemon balm, licorice root.
Use: Sip warm before teaching, writing, or singing.
Affirmation:
"My words are clear. My truth is kind."

2. Serenity of Sound Blend

Purpose: To calm tension, reduce anxiety, and harmonize breath and voice.
Blend: Chamomile, blue vervain, lavender, and honey.
Use: Drink during moments of overwhelm or before sleep.
Affirmation:
"I speak gently, and my voice rests in peace."

3. Truth and Harmony Elixir

Purpose: To align the voice with the heart and purify self-expression.
Blend: Lemon balm, slippery elm, peppermint, and rose petals.
Use: Sip slowly during journaling, prayer, or meditation.
Affirmation:
"I express my truth in harmony with love."

RITUAL USE OF HERBAL INFUSIONS
Morning Breath Ritual:

Hold your warm tea close to your lips.
Inhale its steam deeply and whisper:
"May my words today be pure and clear."
As you sip, feel the vapor awaken your throat and lungs,
preparing your voice for conscious communication.

Evening Silence Ritual:

Drink your tea in stillness.
With each sip, release words left unsaid, or thoughts that clutter the mind.
Place your hand gently over your throat and whisper:
"In silence, I restore my strength."

ENERGETIC INSIGHT

Herbs for Vishuddha are masters of resonance.
They teach the subtle balance between sound and stillness,
between speaking your truth and listening with an open heart.
Each sip becomes a vibration — a prayer in motion — clearing,
cooling, and aligning you with authenticity.

When you honor your voice as sacred, words regain their
power, silence regains its wisdom, and you remember: your
voice is not only for speaking — it is for healing, creating, and
becoming the echo of your soul.

COOLING AND CALMING HERBS FOR OVERACTIVE THROAT ENERGY

When the Throat Chakra flows too strongly, its energy can
manifest as excessive talking, nervous chatter, anxiety, or
scattered thought.
The voice that once carried truth may become restless or
strained — words rushing ahead of awareness.
In these moments, the element of Ether seeks grounding and
moisture; the body and mind call for calm, clarity, and spacious
silence.

Cooling, soothing herbs help restore the rhythm between sound
and stillness.
They ease throat tension, quiet mental overactivity, and bring
the voice back into resonance with peace.

These gentle plant allies teach the wisdom of listening — that expression, when guided by calm awareness, becomes healing rather than exhausting.

BALANCING HERBS FOR VISHUDDHA

• **Chamomile** – Calms emotional turbulence, soothes throat inflammation, and restores inner stillness.
• **Lemon Balm** – Softens anxious energy, quiets racing thoughts, and harmonizes communication between mind and heart.
• **Licorice Root** – Moistens and cools the throat; restores vocal strength and balances overused speech.
• **Peppermint** – Clears mental tension and refreshes breath; helps the voice express clarity instead of control.
• **Rose Petal** – Opens the heart and cools reactive energy, allowing words to flow with compassion and gentleness.
• **Blue Vervain** – Releases tension in the neck and shoulders, easing suppressed or excessive expression.

THROAT CHAKRA HARMONY TEA BLEND

Supports serenity, vocal balance, and mindful communication.

Ingredients:
• 1 tsp dried chamomile flowers
• 1 tsp lemon balm leaves
• ½ tsp licorice root (or slippery elm for added soothing)
• ½ tsp rose petals
• Optional: A few peppermint leaves or a drizzle of honey for gentle sweetness

Instructions:

1. Pour hot (not boiling) water over the herbs and steep for 7–10 minutes.

2. As the steam rises, inhale deeply — allowing the scent to move through your throat and clear your breath.
3. Sip slowly, feeling each swallow cool, cleanse, and soften your voice.

As you drink, imagine a soft blue light flowing through your throat, restoring peace and fluid communication.

Affirmation:

"My voice flows with calm and clarity.
My words carry peace, not pressure.
I listen, I speak, I rest in truth."

ENERGETIC INSIGHT

The cooling herbs of Vishuddha remind us that silence is not absence — it is space.
They teach the medicine of slowing down: that truth spoken softly carries more power than words spoken in haste.
Through their gentle wisdom, your throat finds balance — no longer a channel of strain, but a vessel of serenity, sound, and sacred stillness.

HERBAL BATH FOR CLARITY AND EXPRESSION

A ritual bath to soothe the voice, calm the mind, and harmonize Vishuddha's flow.
This practice helps release tightness in the throat, shoulders, and jaw — areas where words often go unspoken or emotions are held.
It invites stillness, cools excess energy, and restores the natural rhythm of breathing, listening, and expression.

Ingredients:

- 1 cup Epsom or sea salt (for purification and relaxation)
- 1 tbsp dried chamomile (for peace and softening tension)
- 1 tbsp rose petals (for emotional openness and self-kindness)
- 1 tsp peppermint leaves or lemon balm (for cooling and clarity)
- 3 drops lavender or eucalyptus essential oil (for calm breath and clear voice)

Instructions:

1. Add the salt and herbs to warm—not hot—bathwater, swirling gently counterclockwise to release tension and invite calm.
2. Step into the bath slowly, allowing the water to cradle your throat, shoulders, and upper chest.
3. Close your eyes and breathe deeply, feeling each inhale expand your throat with cool, spacious light.
4. Visualize a soft blue glow descending through your crown and settling at your throat — luminous, tranquil, and clear.
5. With each exhale, release the need to speak or be heard. With each inhale, welcome inner silence, peace, and the truth that rests within it.

Intention:

Let words unspoken dissolve in the water.
Let the voice within emerge — gentle, true, and free.
Emerge from the bath with serenity of mind, ease of expression, and clarity of purpose.

Affirmation for Herbal Healing

"My voice is calm and clear.
Like water, I flow with truth.

Like air, I breathe peace into my words.
Like silence, I listen and understand."

Nature Practices For The Throat Chakra

Reconnecting to the Breath of Life

Where the Heart Chakra opens us to love and the Third Eye awakens inner vision, the Throat Chakra (*Vishuddha*) invites us into resonance — the harmony of truth, vibration, and expression. Its element is **Ether**, the vast sky — still, spacious, and alive with sound. To heal and balance Vishuddha is to remember your connection to breath, to wind, to voice — to the sacred air that moves through all creation.

In nature, the Throat Chakra speaks through the whisper of leaves, the hush before dawn, the song of water, and the echo of your own breath against the open sky.
Vishuddha invites you to listen deeply — not just with your ears, but with your whole being — and to speak with intention, like the wind that shapes the world gently yet persistently.

1. SKY GAZING: EXPANDING INTO SILENCE

The Ether element connects you to the infinite — the spacious awareness beyond thought or speech.
Gazing at the sky opens the Throat Chakra, softening overthinking and expanding perception.

Practice:
• Find an open space outdoors where you can see the sky clearly.
• Sit or lie down comfortably, shoulders relaxed, and breathe deeply into your throat.
• As you gaze upward, feel the vastness above you mirrored within.

• With each inhale, draw in cool, spacious light; with each exhale, release tension in your neck, jaw, and shoulders.
• Whisper:
"I am the sky — open, clear, and free."

Insight:
Sky gazing teaches surrender — to be vast yet centered, silent yet full of sound.

2. BREEZE MEDITATION: LISTENING TO THE VOICE OF THE WIND

Air carries vibration — the same way your voice carries truth. Listening to the wind connects you with the natural language of breath and resonance.

Practice:
• Sit beneath a tree or near open water where the breeze can reach you.
• Close your eyes and breathe in rhythm with the wind.
• As it brushes your skin, imagine it clearing your throat and chest of unspoken words.
• When the breeze stills, rest in silence — the sacred pause between expressions.
• Whisper:
"With each breath, I speak in harmony with life."

3. FLOWING WATER CONTEMPLATION: CLEANSING THE VOICE

Water mirrors sound; it ripples when touched, much like the throat vibrates with words.
Flowing water reminds us that truth is fluid, not fixed — that authentic expression flows, never forces.

Practice:
• Sit beside a river, stream, or fountain.

• As the water flows, focus on the sound — its rhythm, its tones.
• Visualize your own words becoming like this — clear, calm, and graceful.
• If emotion arises, allow tears or sighs; they are the body's way of releasing old energy.
• Affirm softly:
"My words flow like water — gentle, clear, and true."

4. SINGING OR HUMMING IN NATURE: THE VOICE AS OFFERING

The Throat Chakra thrives through vibration.
Humming or toning harmonizes your voice with the sounds of the natural world, awakening Vishuddha's resonance.

Practice:
• Find a peaceful outdoor place — near trees, water, or mountains.
• Take three slow breaths, then begin to hum softly.
• Match your tone to the sounds around you — birds, wind, waves.
• Let your vibration merge with the world's symphony.
• Feel your throat open and vibrate with ease.
• Whisper:
"I am one note in the song of creation."

5. LISTENING WALK: THE SILENCE BETWEEN SOUNDS

Vishuddha is as much about listening as it is about speaking.
A mindful walk trains you to hear the subtle — to attune your awareness to the natural music of existence.

Practice:
• Walk slowly in nature, without devices or distractions.
• With each step, notice sound: wind, footsteps, distant birds, rustling leaves.

• Between sounds, feel the quiet — the space that holds all vibration.
• With every breath, whisper inwardly:
"In silence, I hear truth."

Insight:
When listening deepens, communication becomes effortless and sincere.

6. THE BRIDGE OF BREATH: CONNECTING HEART AND VOICE

The Throat Chakra connects what you feel (Heart) with what you express (Mind).
Breathing consciously through this bridge restores integrity between emotion and word.

Practice:
• Sit outdoors where you can feel the air move.
• Place one hand on your heart and the other on your throat.
• Inhale through the heart, exhale through the throat.
• Imagine blue light rising upward with each breath, carrying compassion into communication.
• Whisper:
"My heart speaks through my voice. My voice carries love into the world."

Affirmation for Nature Connection

"The wind within me mirrors the wind around me.
My voice flows like the sky — vast, open, and true.
I speak with peace. I listen with grace.
I am the harmony between silence and sound."

Chapter 9 – Advanced Practitioner Applications

Energetic Sound, Vibrational Transmutation, and Empowered Resonance

For the advanced practitioner, the **Throat Chakra (Vishuddha)** represents the bridge between the manifest and the unseen — the sacred threshold where thought becomes vibration and vibration becomes creation.
Where the Heart teaches compassion and the Third Eye reveals insight, the Throat transforms both into *resonance* — the expression of truth through sound, frequency, and alignment.

To master this energy is to become an instrument of Divine vibration — one who can listen, receive, and transmit the subtle harmonics of spirit through voice, presence, and silence.
At this level, the work moves beyond communication into *frequency mastery*: refining tone, purifying intent, and allowing sound to become the vehicle for healing and transformation.

To work with Vishuddha is to become a keeper of sacred resonance — one who knows when to speak, when to sing, and when to let silence do the healing.

ENERGETIC DYNAMICS OF THE THROAT FIELD

The energy of Vishuddha moves like waves in an infinite sky — oscillating gently, transmitting truth, and carrying the

intelligence of vibration through the etheric field.
Where Manipura burns, Vishuddha hums.
Its essence is resonance — neither heat nor motion, but sound
that permeates space.

In a client's field, this may be perceived as:
• A subtle ringing or hum surrounding the neck and upper chest.
• Vibrational ripples felt across the shoulders, jaw, or ears.
• Shifts in tone, voice, or emotional release through breath or
sighing.
• Expansive blue or silvery light radiating around the throat and
upper aura.

When **balanced**, the energy feels open, cool, and luminous —
communication flows effortlessly, the breath is steady, and
silence feels nurturing rather than empty.
When **blocked**, it may feel constricted, heavy, or dry —
accompanied by suppressed emotion, tightness in the jaw or
neck, or difficulty expressing truth.
When **overactive**, it may feel overstimulated or erratic —
manifesting as excessive talking, scattered focus, or vocal strain
from forcing expression rather than allowing it.

Advanced practice requires the practitioner to listen — not only
to words, but to frequencies behind them.
You are not forcing resonance; you are *tuning* it — aligning
vibration until truth and energy flow as one harmonic field.

VIBRATIONAL TRANSMUTATION AND SOUND ALCHEMY

In advanced work, sound becomes the alchemical fire of
Vishuddha — transforming dense or discordant energies into
coherent frequency.
While Manipura transmutes through heat, Vishuddha
transmutes through tone.

Every breath, hum, and mantra becomes a carrier of intention
— reorganizing energy within and around the practitioner.

Energetic Process of Transmutation:

1. **Perception:** Sense dissonance — constriction, dryness,
   or a vibrational "knot" in the field.
2. **Resonance:** Introduce sound — a hum, mantra, or
   frequency that matches, then gently raises the vibration.
3. **Expansion:** Allow the sound to dissolve tension,
   spreading cool, luminous energy through the aura.
4. **Integration:** Let silence follow — the stillness that
   allows resonance to anchor in every cell.

The key is neutrality — pure tone without judgment.
Sound aligned with compassion becomes medicine; sound
spoken from control becomes noise.
Vishuddha mastery is the art of speaking from the soul, not the
ego.

ADVANCED APPLICATIONS IN PRACTICE

1. Etheric Listening:
Cultivate clairaudient awareness — not only hearing external
sound but perceiving the vibrational field of thought, intention,
and emotion.
As you listen, allow the space between sounds to reveal insight.

2. Resonant Toning:
Use the bija mantra *HAM* or personalized tones to restore
coherence.
Direct sound gently toward areas of restriction in the throat,
jaw, or upper chest.
Visualize cool blue ripples restoring equilibrium throughout the
body.

3. Breath of the Open Sky:

Breath is sound before speech — vibration in its most subtle form.

Practice long, steady exhalations to release static energy and harmonize the nervous system.

Imagine the breath as light flowing through an infinite sky, clearing the pathway for truth.

4. Transmission Through Silence:

In advanced states of resonance, silence itself becomes healing.

Sit with clients in still presence — allowing your field's vibration to recalibrate theirs without words.

This is the highest octave of Vishuddha — transmission through pure being.

ENERGETIC INSIGHT

Vishuddha teaches that mastery is not in how loudly you speak, but in how clearly you resonate.

True expression arises not from effort, but from alignment.

The advanced practitioner learns to hold sound and silence as equal tools — to speak when guided, to listen when called, and to rest in the stillness that contains all vibration.

You are not here merely to use your voice; you are here to become the voice — the living frequency of truth moving through space.

Energetic Assessment: Reading The Resonance

Practitioners assess the **Throat Field (Vishuddha)** by attuning to the quality of vibration, tone, and spaciousness around the neck, shoulders, and upper chest.

Through Reiki scanning, sound resonance, or intuitive listening, you can perceive subtle variations in frequency and flow.

COMMON ENERGETIC PRESENTATIONS

• **Muted Tone:** suppressed truth, difficulty speaking, hesitation to share insight.
• **Fragmented Frequency:** over-talking, scattered focus, inconsistent expression.
• **Constricted Channel:** tightness in the throat or jaw, emotional blockage, withheld grief.
• **Over-Resonant Field:** overstimulation, dominance of intellect over intuition, forced expression.

Each pattern reveals not only the state of energetic flow but also the client's relationship with truth — how they express, conceal, or distort it.

To "read" the Throat is to listen beneath words — to sense where voice and authenticity diverge.

VIBRATIONAL TRANSMUTATION PROTOCOL
From Sound to Silence

In advanced energy work, the goal is not merely to clear the Throat Chakra, but to *refine* its vibration — transmuting emotional dissonance into pure resonance.

This is the alchemy of sound: turning the density of suppressed emotion into the clarity of sacred tone.

Protocol:

1. **Anchor the Heart:**
   Begin by grounding energy through the Heart, creating emotional safety before addressing the voice.
   Visualize soft green light expanding in the chest — calm, compassionate, receptive.

2. **Awaken the Ether Field:**
   Move your hands to the throat area or hover a few inches above.
   Visualize a sphere of sky-blue light rotating clockwise, cool and luminous.
   Inhale gently through the nose, exhale through the mouth — releasing any tension in the jaw or neck.

3. **Invite Awareness:**
   Encourage the client to focus on their throat and ask silently:
   "What truth longs to be spoken?"
   Listen without judgment. The vibration of awareness begins the release.

4. **Channel Reiki or Sound Frequency:**
   Use your hands or voice to channel subtle tone — a hum, mantra (*HAM*), or vowel sound that matches the client's frequency, then slowly elevate it.
   Visualize the sound waves clearing stagnation and harmonizing vibration.

5. **Seal and Integrate:**
   When the energy feels open and flowing, visualize a halo of soft blue light radiating from the throat to the crown and heart.
   Whisper or affirm:
   "All that was silence becomes truth.
   All that was tension becomes song."

TANTRIC RESONANCE AND POLARITY INTEGRATION

The Throat Chakra governs the union of **expression and listening, speaking and receiving, sound and silence.**
It is the sacred polarity between the outer voice and inner hearing — where communication becomes communion.

Within advanced practice, healers harmonize two vibrational polarities:
• **Yang (Active Expression):** vocalization, articulation, outward resonance.
• **Yin (Receptive Silence):** listening, intuition, inward attunement.

When Yang dominates, words overpower wisdom.
When Yin dominates, truth retreats into fear or suppression.
When balanced, the healer speaks through stillness — voice and silence weaving in unison.

INTEGRATION PRACTICE:

Place one hand on the throat (expression) and one on the heart (truth).
Breathe deeply, feeling energy flow between them — a ribbon of pale blue light connecting love and voice.
Repeat silently:
"My words are born of love.
My silence speaks with wisdom."

RESONANCE PRACTICE: THE SOUND WITHIN

For advanced self-practitioners, this alignment technique refines Vishuddha's clarity and restores harmonic balance.

Steps:

1. Sit upright with spine long and shoulders relaxed.
2. Inhale through the nose, drawing breath into the throat and upper chest.
3. Exhale slowly through parted lips, releasing a soft hum or tone.
4. With each breath, feel the tone becoming purer — from murky to clear, from forced to effortless.
5. Visualize a column of silvery-blue light rising from the throat to the crown, vibrating with truth and peace.
6. End by resting both hands over the throat and affirming:
    "I speak with clarity.
    I listen with grace.
    My voice is the sound of harmony."

ADVANCED INSIGHT: THE ALCHEMY OF SOUND

To master Vishuddha is to master vibration itself.
This chakra refines all forms of communication — thought, feeling, sound — into coherent frequency.
Its intelligence lies in discernment: knowing when to speak, when to listen, and when to let silence sing.

At this level, energy healing becomes vibrational artistry.
You no longer merely clear blockages — you *tune consciousness itself.*
Your presence becomes resonance.
Your voice becomes medicine.

When your Throat Chakra vibrates in harmony:
• Truth replaces fear.
• Clarity replaces confusion.
• Resonance replaces reaction.

You become the clear channel — the healer who speaks light, not noise. The teacher whose silence teaches more than words. The vibration that uplifts, never overwhelms.

Hands-On Protocols For The Throat Chakra & Stabilizing Clients

RESTORING EXPRESSION, INNER CLARITY, AND RESONANT INTEGRITY

Working hands-on with the **Throat Chakra (Vishuddha)** calls for sensitivity, silence, and subtle energetic precision.
This is the center of truth — where inner awareness transforms into outer expression, and vibration bridges thought with manifestation.

Here, the healer works not with fire but with **resonance** — the vibration of Ether, the sacred sound current that carries all communication.
To engage this chakra is to enter the realm of the unseen voice — the whispers between words, the stillness between breaths.

When approached skillfully, the hands become tuning instruments — refining vibration, dissolving constriction, and restoring coherence to the frequency of truth and self-expression.
A balanced Throat Chakra radiates cool luminosity, calm focus, and authentic resonance — the clear voice of the soul.

Client Preparation and Energetic Containment

Before working directly with the throat or upper chest, it is essential to create a grounded, trusting, and peaceful container.
Vishuddha governs communication and vulnerability — areas that require gentle permission and energetic safety.

Begin each session by:

1. **Grounding the Space**
    o   Invite the client to take three slow, deep breaths.
    o   Affirm aloud:
        "You are safe to express, safe to release, and safe to be heard."
    o   Allow the space to become quiet and spacious before beginning.
2. **Connecting Heart and Crown Centers**
    o   Place your hands briefly over the heart, then above the crown.
    o   This alignment prepares the energetic pathway between feeling (heart) and expression (throat).
    o   Visualize a luminous bridge of pale blue and white light connecting these centers.
3. **Invoking Permission and Presence**
    o   Explain that you will be working near the neck, jawline, shoulders, and upper chest — sensitive areas associated with speech, breath, and tension.
    o   Ask for consent before beginning, and offer the option for hovering techniques if physical touch feels intrusive.
    o   Maintain warmth, clarity, and professionalism throughout.

Creating this foundation allows the client's voice — literal and energetic — to open safely.
It is not merely a session of clearing; it is an invitation to reclaim one's truth.

Hand Placements for the Throat Chakra

The Throat Chakra is located at the center of the neck, extending through the jaw, ears, vocal cords, and upper chest. It governs breath, sound, self-expression, and the ability to listen deeply.

Primary Positions:

1. **Front Placement (Expression and Clarity)**
   - Place one hand gently over the throat or upper chest, fingers pointing toward the collarbones.
   - Rest the other hand over the heart to link communication with compassion.
   - This connection harmonizes truth with empathy — helping words flow from love, not defense.
   - Encourage slow, rhythmic breathing through the nose.

2. **Back Placement (Releasing Emotional Tension)**
   - Place hands behind the neck at the base of the skull, over the occipital ridge and upper cervical spine.
   - This area often stores suppressed emotion, unshed tears, or "unspoken" truth.
   - Visualize indigo-blue light moving upward through the spine, dissolving resistance into openness.

3. **Side Anchors (Balancing Speaking and Listening)**
   - Rest one hand lightly on each side of the neck, near the ears or jawline.
   - This balances the dual functions of the Throat Chakra: to speak truth and to receive truth.
   - Sense for vibrations, subtle pulses, or asymmetrical flow between sides.

4. **Hovering Position (For Sensitive Clients)**
   - Hold your hands 2–3 inches away from the neck and upper chest.
   - Visualize a glowing sphere of turquoise light expanding gently between your palms and the client's throat.
   - Feel the air and vibration shift as energy harmonizes.

ENERGY MOVEMENT SEQUENCE: "WAVE OF RESONANCE" TECHNIQUE

This advanced sequence clears stagnation and restores fluid communication throughout the throat and upper chakric field.

Steps:

1. **Ground Through Breath:**
   Begin by having both practitioner and client take slow breaths into the belly, exhaling through the mouth with sound (a soft *haaa*).
   This opens the vocal passage without strain and centers the nervous system.
2. **Activate the Etheric Channel:**
   Move your hands to hover over the throat.
   With each exhale, visualize ripples of pale blue light radiating outward — like sound waves expanding through still water.
3. **Synchronize Breath and Tone:**
   Encourage the client to hum softly on the exhale.
   Match their tone with a gentle, sustained hum, allowing your frequencies to merge into harmony.
   This co-resonance stabilizes energy and entrains the vagus nerve for calm expression.
4. **Transmute Tension into Clarity:**
   If tightness, tears, or emotion arise, place one hand on the throat and the other on the heart.
   Channel cool light upward, transforming withheld words or emotion into peaceful expression.
5. **Seal the Field:**
   Visualize a glowing spiral of blue-white light encircling the throat, moving clockwise.
   Whisper or affirm:
   "My truth flows clear. My words serve peace."
   Then sweep energy downward toward the feet to ground the vibration into embodiment.

Signs of Activation and Release

During Throat Chakra work, clients may experience:
• A cooling or tingling sensation around the neck or ears.
• Deep spontaneous sighs or yawns.
• Changes in breathing rhythm or vocal tone.
• Emotional release — laughter, tears, or a sudden urge to speak truth.
• A renewed feeling of openness, calm, and mental clarity.

Practitioner Note: Maintain quiet presence. Do not fill the silence; let it expand. Your role is not to interpret their truth but to hold the resonance in which it can be safely expressed.

ADVANCED INSIGHT: THE ALCHEMY OF RESONANCE

To master Vishuddha is to master vibration itself.
This chakra refines raw emotion and thought into pure frequency — the spoken, sung, or silent word that carries consciousness.

Every whisper becomes a healing note.
Every silence becomes a sacred space.

At this level, you no longer *speak energy* — you *resonate energy*. Your words become instruments of truth; your silence, a chamber of transformation.

When the Throat Chakra radiates harmony:
• Communication becomes communion.
• Truth replaces hesitation.
• Peace replaces noise.

You become the **clear channel** — the healer whose voice restores coherence, whose silence awakens truth, and whose presence vibrates with serenity.

Energetic Ethics and Boundaries for Practitioners Working with the Throat Chakra

HOLDING SAFE SPACE FOR EXPRESSION, TRUTH, AND RESONANCE

The **Throat Chakra — Vishuddha —** governs communication, authenticity, and the sacred bridge between the inner and outer worlds.
It is where thoughts find form through sound, and where silence becomes revelation.

Because this center mediates both truth and perception, it is among the most delicate chakras to approach in healing work. Here, the practitioner is not merely listening to a client's words — but to their *resonance*: the frequency of what is spoken, withheld, and misunderstood.

To work with Vishuddha is to hold space for vulnerability. Clients may touch deep fears of being unheard, judged, or silenced, as well as rediscover the freedom of authentic voice. Practitioners must embody neutrality, compassion, and impeccable energetic integrity.
Healing here is not about giving someone a voice — it is about helping them *remember that their voice was sacred all along.*

The Foundation of Resonant Integrity

Before addressing another's Throat Chakra, the practitioner must examine their own relationship with communication and truth.
Vishuddha reflects the vibrational honesty of both healer and client — any distortion in integrity becomes audible in the field.

Ask yourself before each session:
• Am I listening to understand or to respond?
• Are my words anchored in clarity and kindness?
• Can I hold silence without needing to fill it?

If any of these feel unclear, pause.
Center your breath. Let silence recalibrate your tone.
Your resonance defines the ethics of the healing space.

"The healer's stillness becomes the echo in which truth learns to speak."

Creating Safety Through Communication and Consent

Because the Throat Chakra governs self-expression and emotional truth, how you communicate is as important as the techniques you use.
Every word, glance, and pause carries vibrational influence.

Consent, in this context, is not only about physical boundaries — it is *energetic permission to be heard and seen.*

Best Practices:

1. **Empower Through Dialogue**
   o Clearly explain the session's focus and any areas you may work near (neck, shoulders, jaw, upper chest).
   o Reinforce that the client retains full agency and choice throughout.
   o Use inclusive, invitational language:
   "You are the author of your own healing. My role is to listen and reflect your truth."
2. **Obtain Informed Consent**
   o Invite verbal or written acknowledgment before using hands near the throat.
   o Encourage clients to share if they wish for more space, silence, or sound during the session.
   o Respect all requests to pause, shift, or stop immediately — this restores trust in their own voice.
3. **Observe Energetic Communication**
   o Pay attention to subtle cues — breath holding, throat clearing, gaze shifts, or changes in tone.
   o These may signal emotional resistance or truth emerging.
   o Meet each with patience, not analysis. Allow truth to unfold naturally.

Maintaining Energetic Boundaries

Vishuddha's element is Ether — expansive, subtle, and easily permeable.
Without grounding, practitioners can absorb unspoken energy or become entangled in emotional resonance.
Boundaries are not walls but filters — allowing light to pass while keeping integrity intact.

To maintain energetic clarity:
• Anchor first in your Root and Heart Chakras.
• Visualize a soft blue field around your throat — luminous, cool, and permeable only to truth.
• Set the intention:
"Sound flows through me, not from me. I transmit clarity, not control."
• After sessions, clear residual frequencies through humming, chanting, deep yawning, or silence in nature.

Boundaries are the acoustics of healing — they shape resonance without distortion.

Recognizing Power Dynamics in Communication

The Throat Chakra holds profound power — the ability to shape thought, influence perception, and awaken understanding.
In healing work, an imbalance between speaker and listener can distort this sacred exchange. Both practitioner and client bring patterns around voice and authority — dominance, withdrawal, approval-seeking, or silence.

Practitioner Guidance:

• Speak *with*, not *over*.
• Offer insights as reflections, not proclamations.
• Never assume the role of translator for another's truth.
• If the client idealizes or defers to you, redirect gently:
"Your voice carries the same wisdom. Let's listen for what it wants to say."

Energetic Entanglement and Projection

Vishuddha amplifies resonance — emotional frequencies travel easily through tone and word.
If unobserved, this can create energetic entanglement or projection between healer and client.

Signs of Resonant Entanglement:

• Feeling drained or over-stimulated after sessions.
• Involuntary throat tightness, coughing, or overuse of voice.
• A compulsion to interpret or "speak for" the client.

Response:

• Pause and realign with breath.
• Affirm silently: *"I honor your truth and release all vibrations not aligned with light."*
• Visualize cool blue light purifying the space between your throats.
• Allow silence to reset the field.

Compassion must be balanced by neutrality — clarity is the highest form of respect.

Working with Emotional or Voice-Based Release

As Vishuddha activates, clients may experience involuntary vocal sounds, tears, laughter, or words flowing spontaneously. These are not interruptions but *expressions of resonance clearing itself.*

Practitioner Approach:

• Remain present and quiet.
• Allow vocalization without suppression or interpretation.
• If emotional intensity rises, place your hands on the heart or shoulders to anchor calm.
• Encourage slow exhalations — the breath re-establishes rhythmic balance.

Do not attempt to guide or analyze expression.
Simply hold space for authenticity to sound itself back into coherence.

Transference, Ego, and the Temptation of Voice

Because Vishuddha governs communication, practitioners may unconsciously overidentify with being "the voice of truth." This can manifest as overexplaining, giving advice without invitation, or seeking validation through teaching.

Awareness Practice:

• Before speaking, pause — let stillness filter your words.
• Ask: *"Is this vibration serving truth or my need to be right?"*
• Keep your tone spacious and kind.
• When unsure, return to silence; silence heals distortion faster than speech.

True resonance requires humility.
Powerful words arise naturally from still presence — not from effort or performance.

"When you embody truth, even your silence speaks."

Post-Session Integration and Aftercare

Throat Chakra work can awaken profound realizations about expression, authenticity, and listening.
Clients may feel relief, emotional release, or heightened sensitivity to sound and speech.

Aftercare Recommendations:

• Drink warm water or herbal tea (chamomile, licorice, or peppermint).
• Rest the voice — avoid loud environments or excessive talking.
• Journal or speak affirmations such as:
"I honor my voice and the silence between my words."

• Spend time in nature, listening to the subtle symphony of sound.

Closing Affirmation:
"Your words carry truth.
Your silence carries peace.
You are harmony made visible."

The Sacred Duty of the Practitioner

To work with Vishuddha is to stand at the threshold of vibration itself — where sound becomes creation and silence becomes source.
Your task is not to speak for others but to hold the resonance in which they remember their own song.

True mastery lies in presence — to hear without judgment, to speak without distortion, to rest in the still frequency of truth.

When ethics and awareness unite, the healing space becomes a resonant temple — a place where voice and silence dance as one, and every breath becomes a prayer of authenticity.

"The healer's voice does not command — it harmonizes.
When one tone sounds clear, it teaches all others how to sing."

The Role Of Vishuddha In Remote Healing

CHANNELING RESONANCE, TRUTH, AND
HARMONIC ALIGNMENT ACROSS DISTANCE

While the Heart Chakra carries compassion and unity, the **Throat Chakra (Vishuddha)** governs the transmission of vibration — the subtle sound current that carries consciousness beyond time and space.
It is through Vishuddha that remote healing becomes *resonant*

communication: a dialogue of frequency, where energy travels not by force, but by harmonic attunement.

Where Manipura directs with will, Vishuddha transmits with tone.
Where intention ignites, resonance carries.
In distant healing, this chakra functions as the luminous bridge between energy and expression — transforming inner truth into vibrational light that reaches others through the field of Ether.

The Throat Chakra is the *messenger of energy medicine*: it carries the pure frequency of love and understanding across all dimensions of awareness.

Energy Beyond Physical Sound

In remote healing, the absence of physical proximity heightens the importance of **clarity, tone, and intention.**
The Throat Chakra is the etheric transmitter that converts inner coherence into soundless communication.
Through vibration, not volume, the healer speaks directly to the soul.

When Vishuddha is balanced, your voice — whether silent or spoken — becomes a tuning fork for the unseen.
Energy moves not as light alone, but as *frequency*, reaching the client through resonance.

Practitioners may sense:
• Gentle pulsing or cool vibration around the throat or ears.
• A soft hum or inner sound (nada) during energy transmission.
• Expansion through the jaw, neck, or upper chest as subtle tones arise.
• Awareness of the client's field as an echo, wave, or harmonic alignment rather than as an image or sensation.

This is not imagination. It is **etheric listening** — the healer's capacity to hear beyond hearing and speak beyond words.

"In remote healing, truth becomes tone — traveling not through sound, but through silence."

Establishing Resonant Connection Through Sound and Intention

To engage Vishuddha in distant healing, practitioners cultivate spacious awareness — presence without pressure, sound without speech.
Through this stillness, energy begins to communicate in waves of coherent vibration.

Preparation Practice:

1. **Ground Through the Root and Heart**
   Visualize red roots anchoring into the earth and green light expanding through the chest.
   Stability and compassion prepare the channel for clarity.
2. **Awaken the Voice of Light**
   Bring awareness to the throat.
   Inhale deeply and exhale with a soft hum (*mmm* or *om*).
   Visualize a ring of pale blue light vibrating outward in every direction.
3. **Set the Intention**
   Silently affirm:
   "Through divine resonance, I transmit truth, clarity, and healing sound.
   May this vibration awaken harmony in all who receive it."
4. **Link to the Client**
   Visualize the client surrounded by clear, luminous blue light.
   From your throat center, send a tone — not a word, but a feeling-frequency — gently vibrating toward their field.

The energy connects like matching notes in harmony,
not through force but through alignment.

5. **Sustain the Flow**
   Maintain awareness of your breath and silence.
   Allow vibration to move as subtle waves of presence —
   effortless, continuous, attuned.

Maintaining Energetic Clarity and Neutral Resonance

Because Vishuddha governs communication and subtle sound,
practitioners must remain vigilant about the purity of their
frequency.
In remote work, distortion arises not from distance, but from
personal thought, emotion, or attachment to outcome.

To maintain clear resonance:
• Visualize your words and energy as transparent light, not color
or sound you *make*, but truth you *allow*.
• Affirm silently: *"I transmit clarity, not persuasion. I offer
resonance, not reaction."*
• Stay linked to the Heart Chakra, letting compassion guide
expression and tone.
• After each session, dissolve all energetic echoes with breath or
mantra — returning to inner stillness.

Clarity is your greatest ethical safeguard.
The purer your tone, the farther it travels.

Balancing Sound and Silence in Distance Work

Vishuddha's mastery lies in knowing *when to sound and when
to still*.
Too much vibration creates noise; too little, disconnection.
Balance comes through alternating sound with space —
speaking through silence as much as through tone.

Practitioners can harmonize Vishuddha during remote sessions by:
• Pairing each hum or chant with a moment of quiet listening.
• Alternating between blue (clarity) and white (purity) light.
• Ending with silence — letting energy complete its message without words.

Through this rhythmic conversation between sound and stillness, the healer sustains both receptivity and radiance, transmitting healing through the eternal field of Ether.

The Ethics of Vibrational Communication

The Throat Chakra demands integrity in vibration.
Every tone carries intention, and every intention carries impact.
To communicate energetically is to wield sacred responsibility.

Always remember:
• Sound is sacred; use it consciously.
• Words shape energy — speak only what uplifts.
• Energy does not convince; it invites alignment.
• Your silence is as healing as your sound.

True practitioners know: the power of voice lies not in volume but in vibration. To heal with Vishuddha is to embody the principle that *truth needs no defense — only resonance.*

Closing Reflection

The Throat Chakra in remote healing is the sound that exists before sound — the silent current that connects all beings through the web of resonance.
It teaches that communication transcends language; it is the meeting of frequencies in trust.

When your inner voice rings clear and your heart aligns with compassion, your energy becomes a song that travels beyond sight or distance.

You are no longer sending sound — you are **sounding presence itself.**

"The healer's voice travels not through words, but through wavelength — where one clear tone awakens another across the unseen."

Throat Chakra Techniques For Remote Healing

TRANSMITTING HEALING THROUGH SOUND, VIBRATION, AND RESONANT TRUTH

Each practitioner develops a unique harmonic signature — the subtle voice of their soul.
The **Throat Chakra (Vishuddha)** refines this voice into vibration, transforming thought into resonance that travels effortlessly through the field of Ether.

Where Manipura heals through light and fire, Vishuddha heals through *frequency and silence.*
It does not project force — it emits coherence.
It does not push energy — it attunes it.

Through Vishuddha, the healer learns that healing is not about sending something outward, but about creating a frequency so pure that everything around it naturally harmonizes.

1. Visualization of the Blue Light Resonance

Visualize a luminous sphere of blue-white light spinning gently at the center of your throat.
This is your inner tone — the *Voice of Truth*.
As you breathe, it begins to hum softly, vibrating through every cell of your being.

From this sphere, allow waves of soft blue energy to radiate outward toward the client.
See this vibration as gentle ripples traveling through still water — carrying peace, authenticity, and clarity.

Repeat inwardly:
"I send the sound of harmony and truth.
Our voices meet in resonance, not control."

The blue light expands into a field that envelops both practitioner and client, creating an atmosphere of mutual alignment and serenity — where energy communicates as music beyond sound.

2. Breath Transmission through Sound and Intention

Vishuddha governs both breath and vibration — the sacred union that animates expression.
To transmit healing through the Throat Chakra, use the breath as your carrier wave.

1. **Inhale** slowly through the nose, drawing in pure light from Source into your lungs and throat.
2. **Exhale** gently through the mouth or nose with a whisper or hum — *Om, Ah, or Hu* — whichever tone feels natural.
3. As you exhale, imagine the sound extending outward like a harmonic wave, connecting with the client's field.

4. Visualize the energy aligning with divine intelligence, transmitting truth and calm through vibration.

The sound may be audible or purely internal.
The intent is the same — to let the voice of your soul speak in frequency rather than words.

"Through breath and tone, harmony travels where silence listens."

3. The Ether-to-Light Transmutation

When the client's field feels chaotic, heavy, or filled with conflicting emotions, the Throat Chakra serves as a transmuter — shifting discord into clarity through vibration.

Visualize a stream of radiant blue light flowing from your throat to the client's energy field.
As it meets tension or confusion, see the vibration changing tone — discordant energy softens into melody.
All harshness dissolves into clarity and peace.

Whisper inwardly:
"What was confusion becomes coherence.
What was silence becomes song."

You may feel a gentle hum arise in your own throat — a sign that resonance has aligned and balance is returning.

4. The Mirror of Resonance

Vishuddha teaches that no healer's voice should overshadow another's — all beings possess their own sacred frequency.
In this technique, the practitioner mirrors the client's vibration to remind them of their innate truth.

Visualize yourself and the client surrounded by the same luminous blue light — both voices harmonizing within the same field of resonance.
There is no hierarchy, no superior sound — only shared clarity.

Affirm silently:
"Your voice carries the same light as mine.
Together, we remember the language of truth."

This mirroring restores self-expression, confidence, and trust in one's inner communication with Spirit.

Balancing the Practitioner's Energy After Sessions

Working with Vishuddha amplifies subtle perception — tone, empathy, and energetic communication.
Without closure, practitioners may experience vocal fatigue, overstimulation, or lingering resonance from the client's field.

To restore neutrality and vibrational balance:

1. **Retract the Sound Field**
   Visualize all outgoing tones and frequencies returning softly to Source as pure light.
2. **Seal the Throat Chakra**
   Place both hands over your neck or upper chest and breathe three times deeply.
   With each exhale, feel calm blue light soothing and quieting the energy center.
3. **Affirm:**
   "All sound returns to stillness.
   My energy is clear, calm, and whole."
4. **Return to Silence**
   Sit in quiet for one minute, letting residual vibrations settle into peace.

5. **Ground the Energy**
   Visualize a column of light descending through the heart and spine into the earth, anchoring sound into form.

This closure completes the resonant circuit — leaving the practitioner centered, silent, and refreshed.

THE GIFT OF RESONANT CONNECTION IN REMOTE HEALING

In distant work, the Throat Chakra reveals the sacred truth of healing through sound: that communication exists beyond speech — a dialogue of energy where *resonance replaces distance.*

Through Vishuddha, the practitioner learns:
• To transmit peace through silence, not persuasion.
• To express truth as vibration, not opinion.
• To become the channel through which harmony itself speaks.

When the voice of the healer becomes clear, the universe listens.
And in that stillness, healing unfolds — not by command, but by communion.

"When the healer's tone rings pure, distance disappears — and all hearts remember the one sound beneath all silence."

Clearing Ancestral Fear and Karmic Imprints

RELEASING PATTERNS OF SILENCE, SHAME, AND SUPPRESSION TO RESTORE AUTHENTIC VOICE AND SPIRITUAL CLARITY

Just as the Root Chakra carries the memory of survival and the Sacral holds the memory of emotion, the **Throat Chakra (Vishuddha)** preserves the energetic imprints of *expression, communication, and truth.*
It is the chamber of resonance where generations of unspoken words and withheld truths still echo.

Vishuddha governs how we speak our truth — and how we silence it.
It records the moments when words were forbidden, songs unsung, or authenticity punished.
Where the lower chakras deal with survival and power, the Throat holds the *karma of voice* — the memory of what could not be said.

When this energy center is burdened by ancestral or karmic imprints, one may struggle to communicate freely, fear judgment, or feel unseen and unheard — even when speaking.
Healing Vishuddha means releasing not only your own silence, but the silence of your lineage.

Inherited Patterns of Silence and Expression

Every family carries stories that were never told — truths softened, secrets buried, emotions swallowed.
Across generations, these patterns weave subtle beliefs such as:
• "It's safer to stay quiet than to speak the truth."
• "My voice doesn't matter."
• "Harmony means silence."

• "Saying what I feel will hurt others."
• "If I speak, I'll be rejected or misunderstood."

These inherited programs act like filters over the voice —
creating hesitation, self-censorship, or a chronic feeling of being
unheard.
They are not personal weaknesses, but survival codes passed
down through sound and silence alike.

When these imprints remain unhealed, the voice loses
resonance, and the individual may either over-speak to be heard
or withdraw into wordless frustration.
Releasing them restores the purity of vibration — the freedom
to speak and listen with divine truth.

"The silence you carry was once a shield.
Now it becomes a song — ready to rise again in light."

Karmic Patterns of Truth and Communication

Karma within Vishuddha is not punishment — it is the soul's
ongoing refinement of *truth in action.*
Across many lives, souls experience both distortion and
honesty: speaking to harm, speaking to heal, or withholding
truth in fear.

Through the Throat Chakra, these lessons return for integration.
Recurring karmic themes may include:
• Difficulty expressing needs or emotions.
• Overexplaining, apologizing, or suppressing opinions.
• Attracting relationships with poor communication or
manipulation.
• Speaking truth but feeling ignored or misunderstood.
• Using words to control, defend, or justify rather than to create
harmony.
• Losing one's voice physically or energetically during conflict
or stress.

These experiences are not failures but **vocal initiations** — opportunities to align speech with wisdom and love.
Through each expression, the ego learns to serve truth rather than self-protection. The lesson is not merely to *speak* — but to speak from integrity, compassion, and divine resonance.

Recognizing Signs of Ancestral and Karmic Imprints in Vishuddha

When ancestral silence or karmic distortion resides in the Throat Chakra, it often manifests as:
• Tightness, dryness, or chronic discomfort in the throat or jaw.
• Fear of public speaking or difficulty articulating thoughts.
• Overapologizing or minimizing one's truth to avoid conflict.
• Feeling "talked over," dismissed, or energetically silenced by others.
• Inconsistent voice — either overassertive or withdrawn.
• Emotional constriction in the chest or shoulders when expressing emotion.
• Repeating cycles of being unheard, misunderstood, or misquoted.

These are the echoes of a lineage that learned to protect itself through silence.
Every unsung truth, every withheld cry or sacred word lingers in the energetic memory of Vishuddha — waiting to be purified through breath, tone, and courage.

The Healing Path: Reclaiming the Voice of Truth

Healing the Throat Chakra from ancestral and karmic suppression is an act of liberation — not rebellion.
It requires patience, gentleness, and reverence for those who could not speak before you.

Practices for Release:

1. **Vocal Acknowledgment**
   o Speak aloud words your ancestors could not:
   "It is safe to tell the truth."
   "I honor the voices that were silenced before me."
   "I free my lineage from the vow of silence."
2. **Sound Alchemy**
   o Tone or hum softly, letting sound vibrate through your throat, chest, and skull.
   o Visualize each note clearing the residue of fear or guilt.
3. **Ancestral Listening**
   o In meditation, invite the energy of your ancestors and ask,
   "What truth did you wish to speak?"
   o Listen without judgment; release through breath and sound.
4. **Mantra for Liberation**
   o Chant the bija mantra **HAM** (pronounced *hahm*) to purify Vishuddha.
   o Feel its vibration clear blockages and expand the inner chamber of resonance.

Integration: Speaking as the Soul

As ancestral silence dissolves, truth begins to flow like sacred sound — steady, compassionate, and fearless.
The healed Throat Chakra becomes not just a channel for words, but for wisdom.
Your voice no longer seeks validation; it *vibrates alignment.*

When the karmic imprints of Vishuddha are cleared:
• Honesty becomes effortless.
• Listening becomes sacred.

• The voice becomes an instrument, not a weapon.
• Silence becomes communion, not fear.

You remember that divine truth was never lost — only waiting for permission to sing through you again.

Affirmation of Ancestral Release:
"I honor the voices that came before me.
Their silence becomes my song.
I speak with clarity, compassion, and divine truth.
Through my voice, all generations are set free."

Practices For Clearing Ancestral Fear And Voice Karma

RESTORING TRUTH, EXPRESSION, AND THE
FREEDOM TO SPEAK IN LIGHT

The Throat Chakra (Vishuddha) governs communication, truth, and divine resonance.
Where Manipura refines will through fire, Vishuddha refines consciousness through vibration.
Ancestral and karmic blocks here manifest as silence, shame, or distortion — the inability to express what was once forbidden or misunderstood.

These practices purify the energetic voice, clear the lineage of fear, and restore your ability to speak, listen, and live in truth.

1. Sound Ritual of Release

Since Vishuddha is governed by the element of Ether and the principle of vibration, this ritual uses **sound** to release ancestral silence and restore resonance.

Practice:
• Write down phrases that carry inherited fear, such as "I must stay quiet to be safe," or "My truth causes harm."
• Read each phrase aloud, then hum or tone softly after each one — allowing vibration to dissolve the words into sound.
• When ready, tear or safely burn the paper, releasing both sound and silence into light.
• Whisper or chant:
*"I release the silence of my lineage.
I reclaim the voice of truth and compassion."*

As the sound fades, imagine the air around you shimmering — the echoes of all silenced voices returning to harmony.

2. Reiki or Energetic Vocal Clearing

During energy work, focus on the **throat, jaw, and upper chest.**
Visualize a sphere of blue-white light expanding outward with each breath.
As you channel Reiki or universal life energy, allow the vibration to flow through your throat like a gentle tone, clearing ancestral cords of silence, fear, or judgment.

Affirm:
*"Truth flows through me, not from me.
I speak as love, I listen as light."*

This practice refines the voice as a vessel for higher consciousness — sound aligned with integrity.

3. Breath of Expression (Prana Shabda)

Breath carries sound; sound carries consciousness.
This practice awakens Vishuddha through rhythmic breath and tone, clearing karmic residue from unspoken truth.

Practice:
• Sit tall and place your hands gently at your throat.
• Inhale deeply through your nose.
• On the exhale, softly release a humming tone (*mmm* or *ham*).
• Feel the vibration resonate through your jaw and collarbones.
• Continue for 1–3 minutes, allowing each tone to grow clearer and freer.

Visualize clouds of ancestral silence dissolving with every exhale until your inner voice feels open, calm, and radiant.

4. Lineage Visualization and Vocal Forgiveness Meditation

Close your eyes and imagine your ancestors gathered behind you — not in judgment, but in listening.
You are the voice they once withheld.
As you inhale, draw light into your throat; as you exhale, speak softly to them:

*"I honor your silence.
I understand why you could not speak.
I now give voice to our truth, with love and respect."*

Visualize waves of blue light rippling backward through time, filling every unsung generation with peace.
In their faces, see recognition — their stories finding freedom through you.

5. Creative Expression as Soul Release

Vishuddha transforms energy through **creation and communication.**
Break the cycle of ancestral silence by expressing what was once suppressed — write poetry, sing, paint, journal, or share your truth openly.

Every word, song, or creation becomes an act of redemption for your lineage — proof that truth is no longer dangerous, but divine.

Affirm:
"Each word I speak is sacred.
Each sound I create heals generations before me."

THE VOICE RESTORED

When ancestral fear and karmic silence are cleared, the Throat Chakra shines as a crystalline channel — pure, resonant, and calm.
Communication flows without fear.
Truth becomes compassion, not confrontation.
You no longer fear being misunderstood or unheard, for your vibration speaks beyond words.

You remember that sound is sacred — that every breath, whisper, or silence is part of divine expression.
You become a living instrument of truth — transforming inherited silence into resonance, distortion into clarity, and fear into sacred speech.

"The ancestors once swallowed their words to survive.
You are the one who gives them voice —
not in defiance, but in reverence."

Releasing Voice Cords And Restoring Authentic Expression

RETURNING TO WHOLENESS THROUGH CONSCIOUS COMMUNICATION AND RESONANT PRESENCE

The Throat Chakra is the seat of authentic communication — the energetic bridge between heart and mind.
Through this center, we connect to others through vibration, words, and listening.
Each interaction — with family, teachers, or authority — leaves an energetic imprint.

Where the Sacral bonds through emotion and Manipura through will, **Vishuddha bonds through expression.**
Healthy communication inspires mutual understanding.
But when cords of silence, manipulation, or misunderstanding form, they drain authenticity and cloud clarity.

Healing here is not about withdrawal, but alignment — learning to exchange energy through *truth*, not control.

To restore vocal sovereignty:
• Visualize gentle blue light surrounding your throat and ears.
• Affirm: *"I speak my truth with kindness. I release all voices that are not my own."*
• Imagine cords of misunderstanding, guilt, or fear dissolving into clarity.
• End with silence — listening to the hum of your own true resonance.

Affirmation of Liberation:
"My words are instruments of peace.
My silence is filled with presence.
I speak, listen, and create in harmony with all life."

Understanding Voice Cords

Energetic cords form not only through emotion or will, but also through *sound and speech* — the vibration of thought expressed into the field.
Every word spoken, promise made, or truth withheld leaves an energetic imprint in the Throat Chakra (Vishuddha), the center of communication and resonance.

Some cords uplift — shared understanding, loving dialogue, sacred song.
Others bind — when words are used to manipulate, silence, or dominate, or when one absorbs others' voices and loses their own clarity.

In Vishuddha, these cords often appear as threads of **blue or silvery light** connecting the throat, ears, or upper chest to others.
When balanced, the exchange is harmonious — energy flows as mutual respect and active listening.
When distorted, the current becomes one-sided — overexplaining, withholding, or taking on others' emotional noise — resulting in confusion, fatigue, or loss of authentic voice.

COMMON EXAMPLES OF DRAINING VOICE CORDS

• Feeling responsible for how others react to your truth.
• Withholding expression to keep peace or avoid rejection.
• Taking on others' emotions or expectations when listening.
• Needing to "fix," advise, or defend through words.
• Replaying conversations or arguments long after they've

ended.
• Allowing others' opinions to shape your voice or silence.

These cords anchor themselves in the Throat Chakra because Vishuddha governs *truth, integrity, and communication.*
Releasing them restores **vibrational sovereignty** — the ability to speak, listen, and remain in resonance with your higher self, not the noise of others.

RECOGNIZING SIGNS OF VOCAL ENTANGLEMENT

When Vishuddha becomes enmeshed with others' frequencies, you may experience:
• Tightness, dryness, or pressure in the throat or jaw.
• Fatigue or "buzzing" after long conversations or social media use.
• Anxiety before speaking or guilt after expressing your truth.
• Feeling unheard or constantly interrupted — as if your words don't "land."
• Difficulty discerning your inner voice from external influence.
• Compulsive need to explain or justify your truth.

These are not failures — they are signals inviting you to reclaim your authentic resonance.
Through awareness and vibration, you can return to the purity of your own tone — clear, calm, and aligned.

ENERGETIC ANATOMY OF RESONANT DETACHMENT

True detachment in Vishuddha is not silence — it is *clarity without distortion.*
It means speaking from alignment rather than reaction, listening without absorbing, and maintaining openness without losing your frequency.

Energetic sovereignty of the voice arises not from shutting down communication but from remembering that your truth has its own vibration — distinct, sacred, and whole.
When cords of miscommunication or over-identification dissolve, your voice becomes a tuning fork for divine coherence.

In this state:
• Clarity replaces confusion.
• Peace replaces reaction.
• Expression flows without fear.
• Silence becomes sacred, not suppressed.

THE PRACTICE OF RESONANT PRESENCE

When you stand in the center of your voice, you begin to communicate from being rather than defense.
Words become instruments of light.
Listening becomes prayer.
Truth becomes resonance shared — not argument won.

This is the essence of Vishuddha's mastery: to speak and hear from love, to connect without attachment, and to allow your sound to serve harmony instead of control.

When voice cords dissolve, what remains is communion — the meeting of souls in truth.

Affirmation:
"I release all cords of misunderstanding and distortion.
My voice is clear, kind, and sovereign.
I speak and listen in alignment with divine truth."

Releasing Voice Cords Practice

(To be performed with compassion and neutrality — never judgment or resentment.)

1. Prepare the Space

Sit comfortably and place your hands gently on your throat and upper chest.
Take several slow, mindful breaths.
As you inhale, feel the cool air entering your throat.
As you exhale, release any tension in your neck, jaw, or shoulders.

Visualize a sphere of **soft blue light** glowing at your throat — clear, calm, and luminous.
It hums gently, like the vibration of sacred sound waiting to be spoken.

2. Identify the Connection

Bring to mind a person, conversation, or situation that leaves you feeling silenced, unheard, or energetically "entangled."
Without judgment, notice where you feel this connection — perhaps a **blue-silver thread** extending from your throat to another's.

You may sense pressure, tingling, or an emotional echo.
Do not resist it — simply observe.
This awareness itself begins the clearing.

3. Call in Light and Sound

Visualize a **column of white-blue light** descending from Source above, entering through the crown and gathering in your

throat.
You may feel warmth, resonance, or gentle pulsing.

Whisper or tone softly:
"Only truth and peace remain.
All else returns to the silence of love."

Allow the vibration of these words to ripple through the cord —
dissolving distortion with pure resonance.
Sound becomes the alchemy that restores clarity.

4. Dissolve the Cord with Sound

Rather than cutting or severing, imagine the cord **transmuting
through vibration**.
Hum gently or chant the bija mantra **HAM** (pronounced *hahm*).

With each tone, see the thread shimmer, then dissolve like mist
in sunlight — its energy returning to Source, purified and free.
As it fades, breathe deeply and imagine your throat expanding
with radiant blue light.

Both you and the other are released —
each voice restored to its natural harmony.

5. Seal and Restore Resonance

Visualize your Throat Chakra spinning freely — a clear,
luminous disc of turquoise light.
Breathe through it until you feel calm, open, and balanced.

Whisper or affirm silently:
"My voice is clear and sovereign.
My words serve truth and harmony.
I listen with peace, and I speak with love."

Rest in the quiet hum of your own vibration — the song of freedom returning to your field.

THE RETURN OF VOCAL SOVEREIGNTY

As voice cords dissolve, the energy once tangled in guilt, explanation, or suppression returns to your center.
You feel lighter — clearer — no longer weighed by the need to justify or silence yourself.

The Throat Chakra becomes what it was always meant to be: a temple of truth and resonance, where words are guided by love and silence is filled with wisdom.

You begin to speak from presence rather than reaction.
Your communication becomes a sacred exchange — not performance or defense.
You no longer absorb others' noise or confusion; instead, you hold stillness so pure that it becomes its own language of peace.

This is the true essence of **Vishuddha healing**:
To express without distortion.
To listen without absorption.
To live as the vibration of truth itself.

Affirmation of Freedom:
"When I release others' voices, I remember my own.
When I speak in truth, I free generations of silence.
When I honor my sound, I become harmony in motion."

Cross-Referencing With TCM Meridians: Lung And Large Intestine

THE BREATH OF TRUTH AND THE ALCHEMY OF EXPRESSION

The Throat Chakra (Vishuddha) corresponds energetically with the **Metal element** in Traditional Chinese Medicine (TCM), primarily expressed through the **Lung** and **Large Intestine** meridians.
Both systems recognize this region as the bridge between **inner truth and outward expression** — where energy transforms from inspiration to communication, and from holding to releasing.

Just as Vishuddha refines vibration into voice, the Metal element refines energy into clarity.
Together, they teach the alchemy of *breathing in truth and letting go of what no longer serves*.

When balanced, expression is clear, honest, and compassionate. When imbalanced, one may experience suppression, grief, or the heaviness of unspoken words — a tightening of both the lungs and the throat.

In both yogic and TCM systems, this center governs how we **inhale life and exhale release**, both physically and energetically.

LUNG MERIDIAN — INSPIRATION AND EXPRESSION

In TCM, the Lungs are the *"Delicate Organ"* that governs **Qi and breath**, distributing life force throughout the body.
They are also the seat of **grief and reverence** — the ability to release pain while honoring what has been lost.

Likewise, the Throat Chakra transforms the breath of life into voice and vibration, allowing inner truth to become sound. When this current flows freely, your words carry vitality and authenticity — you speak from your soul, not your shadow.

When Lung Qi Is Balanced:
• Your breath is deep and rhythmic.
• You express emotions with ease and honesty.
• Your tone carries compassion and confidence.
• You feel inspired — able to "breathe in life."

When Lung Qi Is Weak or Stagnant:
• Shallow breathing, chest tightness, or throat constriction.
• Frequent sighing, sadness, or suppressed grief.
• Fear of speaking or expressing needs.
• Voice fatigue, hoarseness, or lack of vocal strength.

Balancing Techniques
• Practice *pranayama* or deep diaphragmatic breathing to expand Lung Qi and open the throat.
• Chant or hum softly, allowing sound vibration to move stagnant energy through the chest and vocal channel.
• Apply gentle Reiki to the upper chest, shoulders, and neck to harmonize Lung and Throat flow.
• Surround yourself with fresh air and nature — especially early morning qi from trees and water.

Affirmation:
"I breathe truth and speak light.
Each breath renews my voice, each word honors life."

LARGE INTESTINE MERIDIAN — RELEASE AND COMMUNICATION

In TCM, the Large Intestine is responsible for **letting go of what no longer nourishes** — physically, emotionally, and spiritually.

Energetically, it works in harmony with the Lungs to create balance between *inspiration and release, intake and expression.*

Just as the Throat Chakra must release unspoken truths and repressed emotion to stay open, the Large Intestine must release waste to keep the body and mind clear.
When energy stagnates here, words become trapped, self-expression feels constrained, and resentment or guilt may accumulate.

When Large Intestine Qi Is Balanced:
• You express yourself honestly and without hesitation.
• You feel mentally clear and emotionally unburdened.
• You can "let go" of old narratives or misunderstandings.

When Imbalanced:
• Constipation or holding patterns (emotionally or physically).
• Difficulty forgiving or releasing grudges.
• Fear of being misunderstood or rejected for speaking up.
• Overprocessing or overexplaining instead of trusting intuition.

Balancing Techniques
• Practice vocal release: sighing, singing, or toning to release tension from the throat and chest.
• Journal or speak aloud what you wish to release — then breathe deeply as if exhaling the past.
• Perform gentle neck and shoulder stretches to support energetic flow along the meridian pathway.
• Include fiber-rich foods, hydration, and mindful exhalation to encourage both physical and energetic release.

Affirmation:
*"I let go with grace.
My words, like my breath, flow in harmony with life."*

THE BREATH AND THE WORD — THE SHARED ELEMENT OF EXPRESSION

Both the Throat Chakra and the Lung–Large Intestine meridian pair represent **refinement and release**.
They teach us that purification is not destruction but transformation — the act of breathing out old energy so that new truth may rise.

In this union of systems, the Throat becomes the *resonant instrument* of the lungs' rhythm.
Each breath becomes a prayer, each word a release.
Through this harmony, expression becomes sacred — not merely sound, but vibration infused with spirit.

Integration Affirmation:
"I inhale inspiration. I exhale truth.
Through breath and sound, I am cleansed and renewed."

The Ether Element: The Essence Of Resonance

TRANSFORMING SILENCE INTO SOUND, THOUGHT INTO TRUTH

The **Ether Element (Ākāśa)** — expressed through the **Throat Chakra (Vishuddha)** and mirrored in Traditional Chinese Medicine through the **Metal Element** — represents the most subtle stage of transformation.
Where Fire ignites change, Ether gives it voice.

It is the vast field through which all sound, vibration, and consciousness travel — the bridge between the inner and outer worlds.
Here, transformation occurs not through action, but through

resonance: the purification of thought into truth, and truth into sound.

When this inner space is balanced, your voice flows naturally — calm yet powerful, expressive yet peaceful.
You communicate with integrity, speak only what serves harmony, and listen beyond words.
When blocked, expression falters — words feel trapped, or silence becomes heavy.
When excessive, speech turns reactive, scattered, or self-focused.

Balance is found in **the sacred pause** — the still point between inhale and exhale, between sound and silence.
It is here that vibration aligns with purpose, and voice becomes an instrument of divine harmony.

THROAT–ETHER INTEGRATION PRACTICE: THE SOUND OF SPACE

1. **Create Stillness**
   Sit comfortably and close your eyes.
   Bring awareness to your throat and the space around it — not the body itself, but the *field of vibration* that surrounds it.
2. **Awaken Inner Resonance**
   Inhale slowly, drawing breath into the base of the throat.
   On the exhale, release a gentle hum — *mmmm* or *ommmm* — feeling it vibrate softly within your neck and chest.
   Sense the sound radiating outward, dissolving tension and clearing unspoken emotion.
3. **Enter the Silence**
   After a few breaths, rest in stillness.
   Feel the subtle hum that remains even after the sound fades — the vibration of Ether itself.
   Here, transformation happens through listening.

4. **Expand the Field**
   Visualize this vibration expanding into a sphere of light-blue radiance around your throat.
   Within it, words, breath, and energy flow effortlessly — clear, kind, and true.

Affirmation:
"I am the sound of truth and the silence between.
Through clarity, I transform vibration into peace.
My words create harmony in the world."

Flow Synchronization: Aligning Practitioner And Client In The Field Of Resonance

ENERGETIC COHERENCE, VIBRATIONAL CLARITY, AND THE HARMONY OF SHARED EXPRESSION

When working with the Throat Chakra (Vishuddha), the practitioner's **clarity of voice, tone, and internal stillness** profoundly influence the energetic quality of the session.
This chakra governs communication, integrity, and vibration — it entrains to the resonance of calm truth.

If the practitioner speaks, breathes, and listens from authenticity, the client's energy naturally begins to mirror that vibration — releasing constriction and reclaiming expression.
However, if the practitioner holds tension, judgment, or inner noise, that dissonance subtly transmits, clouding the field.

Synchronization at the Throat level is therefore a matter of **resonant alignment** — the meeting of two frequencies in truth and peace.
It is the shared sound of integrity — where silence speaks, and words become instruments of healing.

WHY SYNCHRONIZATION MATTERS

• Vibrational Coherence
Vishuddha responds to resonance. When practitioner and client share a unified frequency of calm awareness, sound waves organize energy fields, dissolving resistance and restoring flow.

• Truth Transmission
The Throat Chakra learns through vibration. When a practitioner embodies honesty, serenity, and compassionate listening, that frequency transmits wordlessly — guiding the client toward self-expression and authentic voice.

• Restoration of Harmony
Synchronization allows communication without projection. The practitioner becomes a tuning fork — stabilizing the client's energy through tone, rhythm, and intention, allowing the voice of truth to rise naturally.

PRACTITIONER PREPARATION
1. Attune to Your Inner Resonance

Before beginning, place your hand on your throat and take slow, measured breaths.
Feel the cool air moving through your vocal channel.
Visualize a sphere of **blue light** expanding in your throat —
soft yet vibrant, steady yet spacious.
Silently affirm:
*"I am the resonance of peace.
My words vibrate with truth."*

2. Clarity Check-In

Ask yourself:
• Am I here to listen or to lead?
• Is my voice grounded in authenticity?

• Can I communicate without needing to convince or correct? Exhale any tension, expectation, or attachment to the outcome.

3. Set the Intention

State inwardly:
"May this space echo with honesty, compassion, and harmony. May truth flow freely between us."

SYNCHRONIZATION TECHNIQUES
1. Shared Breath and Tone Alignment

• Invite the client to close their eyes and take slow breaths with you.
• Inhale together through the nose, exhale softly through the mouth — releasing all sound that feels natural: sigh, hum, or whisper.
• Let the tones harmonize gently, aligning the rhythm of your breaths into a shared wave of calm vibration.
• Continue until silence feels resonant and easeful.

2. Resonance Mirroring

• Observe the tone and tempo of the client's energy field — their breath, their subtle sounds, or their silence.
• Without imitation, allow your own frequency to attune — then gradually stabilize to a slower, steadier vibration.
• This entrains their Throat Chakra into coherence, teaching the nervous system to rest in resonance rather than resistance.

3. Harmonic Linking

• Visualize a soft **blue ribbon of sound** — not light this time, but vibration — connecting your Throat Chakra to the client's.
• Sense both fields beginning to hum in unison, like two tuning forks resonating with the same pure note.
• Allow your breath, tone, and heartbeat to align with this

shared vibration. The link is not control, but communion — a shared current of truth and calm frequency.
• Feel the energy between you expand into a **sphere of blue-white light**, steady and luminous, clearing miscommunication and restoring openness in both fields.

4. Closing Resonance

• Toward the end of the session, visualize both throats glowing evenly with soft blue light.
• Gradually allow the sound connection to fade back into silence, leaving a sense of peaceful spaciousness.
• Whisper a closing affirmation inwardly or aloud:
"Truth flows clearly between us.
Each voice stands free in harmony."
• Invite the client to take a deep breath and notice how their neck and jaw feel — relaxed, open, unguarded.

Key Considerations

• **Boundaries with Clarity**
Vishuddha synchronization is about **resonance, not persuasion**. Maintain energetic sovereignty while holding the space of communication. You harmonize through vibration, not influence.

• **Listening as Leadership**
At this level, presence is more powerful than guidance. The practitioner's tone, silence, and pacing create the safety for truth to surface naturally.

• **Integration Practices**
After the session, invite the client to anchor their newfound clarity:
– Journaling or voice recording to articulate insights.
– Singing, toning, or chanting to keep the throat channel open.

– Spending time in open air or near water — nature's echo chamber of sound and stillness.

PRACTITIONER'S AFFIRMATION BEFORE SYNCHRONIZATION

"My words are light, my silence sacred.
I speak from truth and listen from love.
Through resonance, I invite harmony and peace."

PRACTITIONER ENERGY HYGIENE AFTER THROAT WORK

Because the Throat Chakra governs communication and frequency, residual vibration may linger — unspoken emotions, echoes of grief, or traces of tension from the session. Clearing this ensures your own resonance remains pure and expansive.

After each session:
• Stand tall and exhale through the mouth with a soft "haa" sound to release any held vibration.
• Sweep your hands gently around the throat, ears, and chest as though smoothing water.
• Visualize cool blue light washing through your vocal channel, dissolving any lingering resonance.
• Drink warm tea or water to soothe the throat and settle the energy body.
• Conclude with the affirmation:
"All sound returns to silence.
My voice is clear, my spirit calm."

When practitioner and client attune in the field of Vishuddha, healing unfolds through **frequency, not force**. The voice becomes medicine — sound as transmission, silence as integration. Together, you enter the **space where words heal and truth breathes freely**.

"When I speak from stillness, others find their voice.
When I listen from presence, harmony is restored."

WHY ENERGY HYGIENE MATTERS
• **Energetic Boundaries:**

The Throat Chakra governs communication, expression, and
energetic exchange through sound.
Without conscious clearing, practitioners may unconsciously
absorb the vibrations of clients' grief, suppression, or unspoken
emotion — leading to vocal strain, energetic constriction, or
confusion of truth.
Maintaining clarity ensures your voice remains a channel of
truth rather than an echo of others' pain.

• **Vibrational Balance:**

Excess Vishuddha energy can manifest as overtalking, overexplaining, or dominance in communication, while depletion
appears as timidity, self-censorship, or creative block.
Balanced resonance allows your words to flow with peace —
confident but compassionate, expressive yet mindful.

• **Professional Longevity:**

Consistent energetic hygiene keeps your voice and auric field
clear.
It prevents "compassion resonance fatigue," preserving your
ability to listen deeply, speak truthfully, and sustain serenity in
every session.
A pure voice field strengthens not only communication but also
intuitive accuracy.

POST-SESSION RESET PRACTICES
1. Sound Purification Ritual

After each session, gently tone the mantra **"HAM"** (the bija sound of Vishuddha).
Let the vibration travel from the throat into your chest and skull, clearing residual frequency.
You may also rinse your mouth or gargle with warm salt water, symbolizing the cleansing of spoken and absorbed vibrations.
Whisper:
"All sounds return to silence.
My voice is clear, my words are light."

2. Breath of Clarity

Sit or stand with your spine tall.
Place one hand over your throat and one over your heart.
Inhale deeply through the nose, feeling the air cool and purify the throat.
Exhale softly through the mouth with a whispered "haa," releasing tension or emotional residue.
Repeat 3–5 times, sensing your breath, polish the inner channel of communication.

Visualization: imagine pale blue light spiraling through your vocal field, washing it clear and luminous.

3. Resonance Reset Movement

To prevent stagnation, gently roll your neck, stretch your shoulders, and open the jaw with slow, mindful movements. This releases the subtle muscular tension that restricts energetic flow. Visualize blue-white ripples expanding from your throat — like waves across a calm lake — restoring fluid communication within your energy body.

4. Aromatic or Sonic Renewal

Diffuse or apply oils that support clarity and tranquility such as **eucalyptus, chamomile, or frankincense**.
You may also use soft harmonic frequencies (singing bowls or chimes in the key of G) to re-tune the throat's frequency.
Affirm:
"My energy is calm and true.
My words serve harmony and truth."

5. Grounding Through Silence and Breath

After every vocal or energetic exchange, conclude in silence.
Place both hands over your heart and belly; breathe deeply three times.
Visualize the vibration of your words returning to stillness — the silence that births all sound.
This grounds the subtle body, ensuring your voice remains anchored in truth, not tension.

LONG-TERM MAINTENANCE

• **Rest and Reflection:**
Spend time in intentional silence each day — a vocal fast that renews your energetic voice.
Listen more than you speak; in stillness, wisdom gathers.

• **Hydration and Nourishment:**
Drink warm herbal teas (licorice root, marshmallow, or peppermint) to keep the vocal channel supple and energetically hydrated.
Avoid excessive caffeine, shouting, or gossip, which scatter vibration.

• **Breath and Expression Practices:**
Regular humming, toning, or gentle singing strengthens resonance and emotional release.

Movement practices such as yoga's Lion's Breath or Fish Pose can also open the throat center.

• Vocal Baths or Ether Meditation:
Once a week, sit near flowing water or under open sky.
Visualize your words dissolving into the air, transmuting all communication into light.
Let the vastness of space restore humility and expansiveness to your voice.

• Energetic Journaling:
Write about moments you felt silenced or spoke from fear.
Through reflection, you reclaim your right to express truth from compassion rather than defense.

PRACTITIONER'S CLOSING AFFIRMATION

*"I honor my voice as sacred.
I release all vibrations not aligned with truth.
My sound is clear, my silence wise,
and my words echo peace."*

Chapter 10 – Transformation Through Vishuddha

Case Studies: Reclaiming Authentic Voice, Expression, and Truth

The Throat Chakra (Vishuddha) governs communication, self-expression, and the ability to speak truth with compassion. Transformation at this level is about resonance — the alignment of thought, word, and intention into coherent vibration.

When Vishuddha heals, silence becomes sacred rather than fearful, words become medicine rather than weapons, and the individual rediscovers their authentic voice — one that speaks from the soul, not the mask.

The following case studies illustrate how balancing the Throat Chakra restores authenticity, creativity, and harmonious communication.
True healing at Vishuddha is not about speaking louder — it is about speaking clearer, from alignment and peace.

CASE STUDY 1 – FROM SILENCED TO SELF-EXPRESSED

Client Presentation:
A 38-year-old woman presented with chronic throat tightness and recurring sore throats. She described "swallowing words" in

conversations, especially in professional settings. Emotionally, she felt invisible, anxious about confrontation, and prone to apologizing excessively.

Assessment:
Energetic evaluation revealed stagnation in the Throat Chakra with constriction in both flow and resonance.
Her Heart was open, but the channel of expression between heart and voice was blocked by years of self-censorship and fear of judgment.

Therapeutic Process:

- **Reiki & Vocal Resonance:** Hands hovering above the throat with soft toning of the bija mantra *HAM* to open and harmonize the energy center.
- **Truth Journaling:** Daily practice of free writing using the prompt: *"If I spoke my truth without fear, what would I say?"*
- **Breathwork for Voice:** Gentle humming exercises and extended exhalations to strengthen vocal flow and confidence.
- **Communication Awareness:** Guided visualization before meetings — imagining blue light expanding through the throat and radiating calm clarity.

Outcome:
After four sessions, the client reported feeling lighter and more confident in expressing ideas. Throat discomfort subsided, and colleagues noted her speech had become more composed and assertive.

Transformation:
Silence transformed into sound.
She learned that authenticity did not require approval — only presence.

CASE STUDY 2 – HEALING THROUGH SOUND AND TRUTH

Client Presentation:
A 52-year-old musician sought help for creative block and chronic hoarseness. He had recently lost a parent and admitted to "losing his voice" emotionally as well as artistically.

Assessment:
Energetic scanning revealed overextension in the Solar Plexus (excess doing) and depletion in Vishuddha (lack of expression). Grief had constricted both breath and vibration, muting creative flow.

Therapeutic Process:

- **Vocal Toning Therapy:** Guided sound sessions using sustained vowel tones to reopen energetic resonance in the throat and lungs.
- **Energy Alignment:** Reiki over the Throat and Heart chakras to restore connection between feeling and articulation.
- **Water Element Meditation:** Visualizing flowing blue light dissolving emotional tension, symbolizing the throat's purification by the element of ether and water.
- **Creative Affirmation:** "My voice is sacred. My sound is my truth."

Outcome:
By the fifth session, his singing voice returned stronger and clearer. He completed new compositions and described feeling "emotionally fluent again."

Transformation:
Pain became melody.
Through sound, he rediscovered that expression is not performance — it is prayer.

CASE STUDY 3 – RESTORING HARMONY IN RELATIONSHIPS

Client Presentation:
A 44-year-old counselor experienced burnout and conflict in both personal and professional relationships. She described being "the listener for everyone else" but unable to express her own needs.
Symptoms included neck tension, jaw pain, and interrupted sleep.

Assessment:
The Throat Chakra showed energetic congestion with excessive outward flow — giving voice to others but rarely herself. The imbalance between receiving and speaking created emotional fatigue and resentment.

Therapeutic Process:

- **Boundary Communication Coaching:** Practice of "truthful brevity" — expressing needs clearly in a few authentic sentences.
- **Reiki Balancing:** Energy work from Heart to Throat to reintegrate compassion with self-expression.
- **Breath & Stretch:** Neck and shoulder release exercises to restore open energetic flow through the cervical region.
- **Evening Vocal Rest:** Designated time each night for silence, allowing the throat to reset energetically.

Outcome:
Within three sessions, her pain diminished, her sleep improved, and she began delegating more effectively at work. Her partner noticed she was "communicating instead of absorbing."

Transformation:
She learned that listening and speaking are not opposites but

partners in harmony.
By giving her voice the same respect she gave others, balance
was restored.

INSIGHT FOR PRACTITIONERS

Vishuddha healing reminds both client and healer that
communication is sacred exchange — energy transmitted
through sound, silence, and intention.
As the Throat Chakra clears, every word, breath, and vibration
becomes a tool of transformation.

When the voice aligns with the heart,
when speech carries compassion,
and when silence holds wisdom —
the soul itself begins to sing.

Chapter 11 – Reflection & Integration

Daily Self-Care Rituals for Vocal and Energetic Clarity

Healing the Throat Chakra (Vishuddha) is not a single act of speaking truth once — it is a daily devotion to authentic expression, deep listening, and resonance with your higher voice.
Where the Heart teaches compassion, the Throat teaches articulation.
Its strength lies in consistency — the practice of truth without harshness, expression without ego, and silence without suppression.

Daily self-care at the level of Vishuddha means tending to the energetic voice — keeping it open, clear, and balanced.
These rituals cultivate communication that is calm, sincere, and empowered by spiritual integrity.

1. MORNING VOCAL AWAKENING

Begin each day by tuning your voice to truth.

• **Movement:** Before checking devices, stretch your neck and shoulders. Roll your jaw gently and hum softly to awaken resonance in the throat.
• **Breath:** Inhale through the nose, drawing cool air to the back of the throat. Exhale with a gentle sigh, releasing residual

tension or unspoken emotion.
• **Intention:** Whisper,
"Today, I speak with kindness and clarity.
My words align with my heart."

This morning ritual harmonizes breath, mind, and sound —
preparing your voice to express truth throughout the day.

2. VOICE REFLECTION JOURNAL

The Throat Chakra thrives on mindful self-expression and
honest reflection.
Each day, take a few minutes to explore your relationship with
communication.

Write:
• Where did I express myself clearly today?
• Where did I withhold truth or speak in haste?
• What conversation needs compassion or closure?

Over time, these reflections reveal patterns in your
communication — guiding you toward authentic, heart-aligned
dialogue.

3. ETHER ELEMENT RITUALS

Vishuddha corresponds to the element of ether — the vast space
through which sound travels.
Honoring this element restores calmness and clarity.

• **Morning Sound Bath:** Listen to soft music, chanting, or the
sounds of nature. Allow the vibrations to harmonize your field.
• **Aromatic Resonance:** Diffuse or anoint the throat with
calming oils such as lavender, chamomile, or frankincense.
• **Evening Silence Practice:** Spend five minutes in complete
silence, feeling sound dissolve into stillness.

Affirm:
"In silence, I hear truth.
In sound, I share light."

4. EXPRESSION PRACTICE

The Throat Chakra governs creativity, articulation, and communication.
Choose one daily act of authentic expression to strengthen your energetic voice.

• Write a note of gratitude.
• Speak a truth you've delayed expressing.
• Sing, chant, or recite an affirmation aloud.
• Replace one self-critical thought with an empowering statement.

This consistent practice refines integrity in word and vibration — transforming speech into spiritual action.

5. BREATH OF CLARITY

Midday, pause to center your energy through the breath.

• Place a hand lightly on your throat.
• Inhale for four counts, exhale for six through parted lips.
• Visualize soft blue light circulating through your vocal channel.

Feel the breath cool and purify your throat — balancing expression with calm awareness.

Affirm:
"I breathe in truth.
I exhale harmony."

6. EVENING REFLECTION & STILLNESS

At day's end, sit quietly and focus on your breath.
Visualize a gentle blue light spiraling within your throat,
radiating outward like waves across still water.

Ask yourself:
• Did I speak from love or fear today?
• Did I listen with presence?
• What truth do I need to honor tomorrow?

Offer forgiveness for any imbalance, then close with gratitude.

Affirm:
"My voice rests in peace.
My silence holds wisdom."

7. WEEKLY RESONANCE RENEWAL

Once each week, devote sacred time to nurturing your voice and
inner sound.

• Practice vocal toning with the mantra *HAM*.
• Spend time near water — lakes, rain, or baths — to align with
Vishuddha's fluid, purifying nature.
• Declutter your energetic field by journaling or singing
intentions into being.
• Take a vow of mindful silence for a day or an hour —
allowing the voice to rejuvenate through rest.

These practices strengthen your connection between thought,
word, and soul — ensuring your voice remains a vessel for
healing rather than reaction.

INTEGRATION INSIGHT

Vishuddha's clarity is not loudness — it is resonance.
When this chakra is balanced, you speak truth gently yet
powerfully, you listen with grace, and you rest in the calm
knowing that your voice matters.

Through consistent rituals of awareness, honesty, and stillness,
you transform the Throat Chakra into a temple of sacred sound
— where speech becomes blessing, silence becomes prayer, and
communication becomes communion.

"When my voice aligns with truth,
I become an instrument of peace.
When my silence aligns with presence,
I embody the harmony of the soul."

Journaling Prompts For The Throat Chakra

EMBODYING AUTHENTICITY, EXPRESSION, AND
THE POWER OF TRUTH

The Throat Chakra (Vishuddha) thrives on clarity, honesty, and
resonance.
Journaling is one of the most effective ways to balance this
chakra because it transforms silence into voice and confusion
into understanding.
Through writing, you create a sacred dialogue with your inner
truth — aligning thought, feeling, and sound into a single,
harmonious current of self-expression.

These prompts are designed to help you release fear of
judgment, communicate with integrity, and rediscover the
freedom of speaking — and living — your truth.

1. Authentic Voice and Self-Expression

• When do I feel most free to express myself?
• What situations make me silence or soften my truth?
• Whose opinions still influence the way I speak or hold back?
• What would I say if I trusted that my words would be received with love?

2. Communication and Connection

• How do I listen — to others, to myself, to silence?
• What patterns appear in how I speak under stress — overexplaining, retreating, avoiding, pleasing?
• Which recent conversation left me feeling open and connected? Which left me constricted?
• How can I bring more honesty, presence, and compassion to my communication today?

3. Honesty and Alignment

• Where in my life am I not fully telling the truth — to others or myself?
• What truths am I afraid to speak because of possible consequences?
• How does my body feel when I'm being authentic versus when I'm withholding?
• What would it feel like to live in complete alignment with my words and values?

4. Creativity and Expression Through Sound

• What form of expression helps me feel most alive — singing, writing, teaching, storytelling, or silence?
• How can I integrate creative voice into my daily life?
• What have I stopped expressing that once brought me joy?
• How does my creative expression serve as a reflection of my soul's truth?

5. Fear of Judgment and the Courage to Speak

• What is my earliest memory of being silenced, dismissed, or misunderstood?
• How has that moment shaped my current relationship with communication?
• What would I say if fear were not a factor?
• How can I replace the need for approval with the courage to be authentic?

6. Listening, Silence, and Sacred Sound

• When was the last time I truly listened — not just with ears, but with presence?
• What role does silence play in my healing?
• What messages arise when I allow quiet to fill the space between thoughts?
• How can I balance speaking truth with listening deeply to the truth of others?

7. Leadership Through Voice and Presence

• How do my words influence and inspire those around me?
• Where can I use my voice to bring clarity, peace, or healing?
• How can I ensure my communication uplifts rather than dominates?
• What legacy do I wish to leave through my words, stories, and teachings?

8. Sacred Affirmations

After reflecting, close your journaling session with one or more of these Vishuddha affirmations:

- "My voice is clear, calm, and true."
- "I speak with honesty and compassion."
- "My words reflect my soul's wisdom."

- "Silence strengthens my truth."
- "I express myself freely, guided by love and integrity."

INTEGRATION NOTE

Journaling for the Throat Chakra is not about perfect words —
it's about authentic ones.
Let your writing flow as sound does — fluid, unfiltered, alive.
If sadness or anger arises, see it as a vibration seeking release.
If joy or inspiration flows through, let it remind you of your
divine resonance.

Each word is a note in the symphony of your truth.
Through writing, you awaken the courage to speak, the grace to
listen, and the peace that comes from living in harmony with
your voice.

"When I write my truth, I hear my soul.
When I speak from love, I heal the world."

Chapter 12 – Understanding the Journey So Far

How Love Descends into the Body to Become Creation

If you've been following the **Chakra 101 Series** from the beginning, you've already experienced something profound — this journey does not follow the traditional path of ascension from the Root to the Crown.
Instead, it begins at the **Heart**, the divine bridge between spirit and matter, and moves downward — carrying **love into form**, emotion, and power.

This path represents the sacred process of **Involution before Evolution** — the descent of spirit into matter before the ascent of matter back to spirit.
Love must first enter the body before it can rise again as truth.
Just as rain descends before rivers return to the sea, divine energy flows downward before it ascends renewed and illuminated.

In every act of healing, this same rhythm unfolds:
Spirit moves through the physical, love transforms density into light, and energy becomes expression.

The Four Books So Far

Book	Chakra	Element	Primary Lesson
1. Heart Chakra 101 – The Bridge	Air	Love & Compassion	The first initiation — opening to divine love and awareness.
2. Root Chakra 101 – Building Safety, Survival, Foundation	Earth	Grounding & Belonging	Anchoring love into the body and the material world.
3. Sacral Chakra 101 – Creativity, Pleasure, Emotions	Water	Flow & Feeling	Allowing love to move through emotion, creativity, and pleasure.
4. Solar Plexus Chakra 101 – Power, Confidence, Transformation	Fire	Will & Manifestation	Empowering love to act — transforming energy into purpose and creation.

Each step has carried love deeper into embodiment — from spirit into body, from awareness into experience, from feeling into form.

Where the **Heart** awakened love, the **Root** grounded it, the **Sacral** gave it movement, and the **Solar Plexus** gave it power — now, through the **Throat Chakra**, love begins to speak.

Vishuddha – The Voice Of Spirit Through Form

As we reach the **Throat Chakra (Vishuddha)**, the journey shifts direction.
Having descended fully into the fire of action and transformation, energy now begins to rise again — carrying everything it has learned in the physical realms back toward spiritual truth.

Vishuddha is the first point of **refinement**, where power becomes purpose, and purpose becomes expression.
It is the alchemy of sound — where vibration shapes reality and love learns to communicate through words, tone, and silence.

This is the **turning point between descent and ascent**.
The voice becomes the instrument through which divine energy takes form and gives meaning to experience.
Here, creation becomes conscious.

When love has been grounded (Root), felt (Sacral), and empowered (Solar Plexus), it can finally **speak with integrity** through the Throat.
This is why Vishuddha is often called *"The Purification Gateway."*
It filters energy, aligning all that has been learned in the lower chakras with truth, honesty, and resonance.

Through the Throat, love learns to articulate — not just in words, but through vibration, frequency, and authentic presence.
It is where **intention becomes sound**, and **sound becomes creation** once more.

THE MOVEMENT OF ENERGY – FROM FIRE TO ETHER

As the journey moves from Manipura's Fire into Vishuddha's Ether, the energy becomes lighter, subtler, and more expansive.
Fire transforms matter; Ether carries vibration.
The Solar Plexus gives you the courage to act; the Throat gives you the courage to speak.
What was once raw willpower now refines into **wisdom expressed through resonance**.

You may notice your healing experiences shifting here — from physical sensations to emotional releases, from emotion to voice, and from voice to insight.
The Throat marks the beginning of the return journey — **the evolution of consciousness** rising once again toward the higher centers of vision and unity.

REFLECTIVE INSIGHT

Every word you speak carries the memory of your journey so far:

- The compassion of the Heart
- The stability of the Root
- The flow of the Sacral
- The confidence of the Solar Plexus

Together, these layers of embodiment converge in your voice.
Your expression becomes not just sound, but a reflection of everything you have integrated.

Vishuddha teaches that to speak truthfully is to live authentically.
To listen deeply is to honor Spirit.
And to create through sound is to remember that your voice is

divine energy in motion — the very breath of creation moving through you.

THE NEXT STEP

As we move forward, we continue this upward spiral — the **return of love to light.**
Through the Throat, energy refines itself into clarity.
Through the Third Eye, it becomes vision.
Through the Crown, it reunites with Source.

You are now entering the stage where love not only moves through you — it **speaks as you**.
This is the power of Vishuddha: to purify, to communicate, and to create harmony between what you feel and what you express.

"When love finds its voice, the world begins to heal."

Why We Began At The Heart — And Why We Now Rise

THE RETURN OF LOVE AS EXPRESSION

In the first four books of this journey, love descended — gently, powerfully — through the layers of your being.
From the Heart's awakening, it rooted into the Earth, flowed through Water, and ignited the Fire of purpose.
Now, at the Throat Chakra, the direction of energy begins to shift.
The descent is complete.
Love has entered the body.
And now, it seeks to rise — to express, to communicate, to become sound.

Involution has done its sacred work: love has taken form.
Now begins **Evolution** — the upward journey where form
becomes expression, experience becomes wisdom, and
vibration refines into truth.

Just as the Solar Plexus taught you how to act with clarity, the
Throat teaches you how to speak with integrity.
This is where power becomes presence.
Here, love finds its voice.

THE ALCHEMY OF ASCENSION

If Involution is the descent of Spirit into matter, Evolution is the
return of matter to Spirit — the refinement of lived experience
back into light.
Through the Throat Chakra (Vishuddha), all that has been
learned below begins to harmonize and be expressed.
The lower chakras ground and build; the higher chakras refine
and liberate.

You are no longer simply manifesting love into form — you are
translating form back into consciousness.

This movement is not about abandoning the physical; it's about
allowing every embodied truth to resonate with its higher
purpose.
In the Throat, energy begins to hum again — sound bridges the
physical and spiritual worlds.

Love that once became creation now becomes **communication**.
It is here that the journey turns inward to awareness and
outward to connection.

The Voice Of The Five Elements

As the Fire of Manipura rises, it transforms into Ether — the subtle element of space, vibration, and sound.
Ether is not empty; it is full of potential.
It holds the resonance through which all expression takes place.

Each chakra below contributed a note to your energetic symphony:

Chakra	Element	Gift of Love	Expression in the Throat
Heart (Air)	Love & Compassion	The breath of Spirit	Becomes the tone of sincerity
Root (Earth)	Grounding & Safety	The body's trust	Becomes stability in speech
Sacral (Water)	Flow & Emotion	The movement of feeling	Becomes emotional resonance
Solar Plexus (Fire)	Power & Will	The fire of purpose	Becomes passionate conviction
Throat (Ether)	Sound & Truth	The vibration of clarity	Becomes authentic communication

When these elements harmonize, your words no longer come from fear or ego.
They emerge from the Heart's integrity, anchored in Earth, carried by Water, charged by Fire, and elevated through Ether.

Your voice becomes the echo of creation itself.

THE EVOLUTIONARY TRIAD: THROAT – THIRD EYE – CROWN

The next three chakras form the **Triad of Expression and Enlightenment.**
Where the lower triad grounds love into matter, this upper triad releases it back into light.

Chakra	Element	Evolutionary Role	Key Lesson
Throat (Ether)	Sound	Express truth	"I speak what I know to be real."
Third Eye (Light)	Vision	Perceive truth	"I see with clarity and wisdom."
Crown (Consciousness)	Thought	Embody unity	"I am one with all that is."

Together, these chakras lift the frequency of creation — guiding the soul to express, to see, and finally to *become* the vibration of truth itself.

INTEGRATION: THE BRIDGE BETWEEN FIRE AND LIGHT

At the Solar Plexus, love acted through Fire — the will to move forward.
At the Throat, that same fire becomes **light through sound** — the wisdom to communicate what has been learned.

This transformation marks a sacred evolution:

- Fire transforms what is.
- Ether transmits what has been transformed.
- Through sound, experience becomes understanding.

The Throat is therefore not just a chakra of speaking — it is a **portal of purification**, where every frequency you have embodied is refined into expression that uplifts rather than controls, clarifies rather than confuses.

MANIFESTATION BECOMES EXPRESSION

In the previous book, you learned how love manifests through action — grounding, flowing, and igniting into form.
Here, love evolves through expression — clarifying, communicating, and resonating into wisdom.

The Throat Chakra is where **manifestation becomes communication**.
What was created now seeks to be shared.
What was learned now wishes to be spoken.
This is the sacred turning point: where doing becomes being, and being becomes teaching.

You are no longer simply the creator of your life — you are becoming the voice of the life you've created.

THE PATH FORWARD

From this point onward, each chakra will lift love back toward the heavens — not as something lost, but as something refined.

Through Vishuddha, you give your truth sound.
Through Ajna, you give it vision.
Through Sahasrara, you give it silence — the return to pure being.

This is the **upward journey of love's evolution** — where expression becomes illumination, sound becomes light, and communication becomes communion.

"When love speaks through me, truth awakens in all who hear."

REFLECTION

Take a moment to pause and feel how far you've come.
You have journeyed through Earth, Water, and Fire — from stillness to movement, from emotion to will.
You've learned that love isn't just something you feel; it's something you *live.*

Let this next chapter teach you how to direct that love through intention, courage, and manifestation — so that everything you create in the world becomes an echo of your heart made visible.

"With the body now anchored, emotionalized, and empowered, we rise once more to the Heart — not as seekers, but as creators returning home to love, ready to give it voice through the Throat Chakra."

The Cycle Of Manifestation — And Now, Expression

WHEN CREATION SPEAKS THROUGH YOU

Manifestation is not the end of the journey — it is the midpoint.
Once love has descended into matter and taken form, it begins to rise again, seeking to express and refine itself.
This is where the **Throat Chakra (Vishuddha)** enters the cycle — transforming manifestation into communication, and communication into co-creation.

You can think of the **Trinity** and the **DREAM Method** as two sides of the same truth, now evolving into a new phase:

DREAM Step	Chakra Equivalent	Purpose
Unconscious Thought	Root (Earth)	Seed of creation — belief and safety
Conscious Thought	Sacral (Water)	Emotionalization — energy in motion
Action	Solar Plexus (Fire)	Transformation — will made visible
Manifestation	Heart (Air)	Realization — love experienced in form
Expression	Throat (Ether)	Communication — love spoken into the world

Each step builds upon the last, just as each chakra refines the one below it.
Without grounding, emotion drifts.
Without emotion, action lacks vitality.
Without action, creation cannot manifest.
And without expression, the manifestation cannot *expand* — it remains personal rather than universal.

Through Vishuddha, love becomes vibration — shared, transmitted, and echoed in others.
It is the bridge between what you have created and what you are ready to communicate.
This is the **fifth movement of manifestation** — where life begins to speak for itself.

THE FLOW IN SIMPLE TERMS

1. **Root – Unconscious Thought (Earth):**
    Beliefs and fears held in the subconscious set the
    energetic tone.
    → "Do I feel safe to have this?"
2. **Sacral – Conscious Thought (Water):**
    Awareness and emotion give shape and magnetism to
    desire.
    → "Can I imagine and feel this as real?"
3. **Solar Plexus – Action (Fire):**
    Willpower and confidence bring the idea into motion.
    → "Am I willing to act on what I feel?"
4. **Heart – Manifestation (Air):**
    The created reality returns as experience and reflection.
    → "Can I receive with love and gratitude?"
5. **Throat – Expression (Ether):**
    The experience becomes wisdom and is shared through
    communication, teaching, art, or vibration.
    → "How do I give voice to what I have learned and
    created?"

THE PURPOSE OF EXPRESSION

The Throat Chakra marks a shift in how energy moves.
Where the lower chakras **create reality**, the higher chakras
translate reality into meaning.
Expression through Vishuddha transforms manifestation into a
message — turning lived experience into shared truth.

When you express what you've created — whether through
words, art, song, or presence — you give energy permission to
continue evolving.
Expression completes the cycle of manifestation by returning
the energy of creation to the collective.

This is how your life becomes teaching.
This is how love expands.

THE SPIRITUAL PHYSICS OF SOUND

Everything you manifest vibrates at a frequency.
When you speak about it — with gratitude, with authenticity, with joy — that vibration multiplies.
Sound is the transmission of consciousness through Ether.
When your voice carries alignment, it not only strengthens your creation but also harmonizes others with its frequency.

In this way, the Throat is the **voice of manifestation** — it turns reality into resonance.
It says to the universe: *"This is who I have become."*
And in return, the universe replies: *"Then more of this shall be."*

REFLECTION

Take a moment to ask yourself:

• Do I speak truthfully about what I desire — or do I downplay it out of fear? (Throat)
• Am I expressing gratitude and joy for what I've already created? (Heart)
• Are my words aligned with the energy I want to manifest? (Solar)
• Do my emotions fuel my communication with authenticity? (Sacral)
• Do I feel safe being seen and heard in my truth? (Root)

When all five chakras — Root, Sacral, Solar Plexus, Heart, and Throat — work together, manifestation becomes multidimensional.
You not only create with your body, heart, and will — you

broadcast that creation through vibration, influencing reality on an energetic level.

That is the true expansion of manifestation: not just love made visible, but love made **audible**.

THE FIFTH MOVEMENT: LOVE AS FREQUENCY

When love reaches the Throat Chakra, it begins to hum.
Every word, tone, and silence becomes part of the creative current.
Here, manifestation evolves into communication — and communication becomes transmission.

Your life becomes a message of truth, spoken through energy rather than only words.
And the more you express that truth, the more the universe harmonizes with your song.

This is how Spirit continues to create — through you, as you, and beyond you.

"When my words align with my truth, creation listens — and the universe sings along."

Chapter 13 – Quick Reference Toolkit

Throat Chakra (Vishuddha)

The Center of Expression, Truth, and Authentic Communication

CORE OVERVIEW

Location: Throat and neck region, including jaw, mouth, and ears
Element: Ether (Space / Sound)
Color: Sky blue or turquoise
Bija Mantra: HAM
Governing Principle: Purification and truth through vibration
Primary Function: Authentic expression, listening, and energetic resonance
Associated Glands/Organs: Thyroid, parathyroid, throat, larynx, jaw, neck, mouth, ears
Sense: Hearing (listening to self and others)
Astrological Associations: Mercury (communication and clarity)
Symbol: Sixteen-petaled lotus with a white circle representing the purity of sound and truth

KEY THEMES

• Authentic Communication & Self-Expression
• Truth, Integrity & Clarity
• Listening with Presence & Empathy
• Purification of Thought and Speech

• Creativity through Sound, Writing, and Art
• Balance Between Silence and Expression
• Alignment Between Inner Truth and Outer Voice

WHEN BALANCED

• You speak honestly and with compassion.
• You listen deeply without judgment.
• Creative ideas flow freely and clearly.
• You express boundaries and truth with calm confidence.
• You feel heard and understood by others.
• Your words inspire and uplift.

WHEN IMBALANCED

Underactive Throat (Deficient):
• Fear of speaking up or being heard
• Suppressed emotion or creative blockage
• Monotone or weak voice, social withdrawal
• Neck, jaw, or thyroid tension

Overactive Throat (Excessive):
• Talking without listening
• Gossip, criticism, or verbal dominance
• Restlessness in communication
• Difficulty in silence or stillness

BALANCING TECHNIQUES

Physical Practices:
• Neck stretches and shoulder rolls to open the throat channel
• Singing, humming, chanting, or toning HAM
• Breathwork focusing on smooth, steady exhales
• Yoga postures like Fish (Matsyasana), Shoulder Stand (Sarvangasana), and Plow (Halasana)

Energetic Practices:
• Blue-light visualization radiating from the throat
• Sound healing with singing bowls or mantra repetition
• Practicing silence to restore clarity and inner voice

Emotional / Spiritual Practices:
• Journaling to clarify truth and emotional expression
• Speaking affirmations out loud daily
• Practicing active listening and compassionate dialogue
• Forgiveness and truth-telling rituals

AROMATHERAPY & CRYSTALS

Essential Oils:
Lavender – calms and opens communication
Eucalyptus – clears the throat and aids breath flow
Peppermint – stimulates clarity and focus
Chamomile – soothes emotional expression
Blue Chamomile or Sandalwood – promotes truth and peace

Crystals:
Blue Lace Agate – gentle communication and calm
Aquamarine – truth, courage, and clarity
Lapis Lazuli – insight and spiritual speech
Angelite – peaceful expression and connection
Sodalite – honest dialogue and balance

FOODS & NUTRITION

Supportive Foods:
• Blue and purple fruits (blueberries, blackberries, plums)
• Herbal teas for the throat (licorice root, slippery elm, peppermint)
• Light, cooling foods like apples, cucumbers, and raw honey
• Plenty of hydration — water is the medium of sound

Avoid Excess:
• Smoking or overuse of voice
• Caffeine or spicy foods that irritate the throat
• Speaking negatively about self or others

AFFIRMATIONS

"I speak my truth with clarity and grace."
"My voice is a channel for love and wisdom."
"I listen deeply to my inner guidance."
"My words create harmony and healing."
"I am heard, understood, and respected."

MUDRA & MANTRA

Mudra: Granthita Mudra (Gesture of Expression)
– Interlace the fingers with the tips of the thumbs touching each other.
– Hold at the throat center while breathing calmly.
– Activates communication pathways and purifies energy through sound.

Mantra: HAM (pronounced "Hum")
– Chant softly, feeling vibration resonate in the throat.
– Visualize ripples of blue light expanding through the neck and ears.
– Repeat until you feel spacious and clear.

MEDITATION FOCUS

Visualize a brilliant sky-blue sphere spinning gently in your throat.
With each inhale, the sphere glows brighter; with each exhale, it radiates peaceful light.
Imagine this vibration clearing old fears of expression and opening you to truth.

Repeat mentally:
"I speak with love and clarity.
My words carry light.
My voice is the echo of my soul."

INTEGRATION INSIGHT

Vishuddha's mastery is authentic expression — the purity of truth spoken from the Heart and guided by Spirit.
When this chakra is balanced, your words heal rather than harm, your silence nurtures understanding, and your presence resonates with clarity.

You no longer seek to be heard — you become the voice of understanding itself.
Sound is your instrument, truth your melody, and love your resonance.

"When my voice flows from truth, every word becomes a prayer of light."

Conclusion: The Power of Expression and Truth

The Throat Chakra, **Vishuddha**, is the bridge between the heart's wisdom and the mind's understanding — the sacred chamber where truth becomes sound.
It is the voice of the soul and the resonance of divine alignment.

Through this center, love that once descended through Root, Sacral, and Solar now begins to rise — purified by awareness, refined by compassion, and expressed through truth.
Vishuddha is not merely about speaking; it is about becoming the vibration of integrity itself.

When the voice is suppressed, the current of creation becomes trapped — emotions stagnate, inspiration fades, and truth hides behind fear.
When the voice dominates, expression loses its purity — speech becomes noise, and truth is clouded by ego.
But when the voice is balanced — clear, calm, and compassionate — it becomes a channel for Spirit to move through you.
Sound turns into blessing.
Speech becomes prayer.
Silence becomes wisdom.

The Throat teaches that **truth is not what we say — it is what we embody**.
Each word, gesture, and breath carries your frequency into the world.
When aligned with love, that frequency heals.

When colored by fear, it distorts.
Thus, purification — Vishuddha's name itself — means refining the vibration until only clarity remains.

In its mastery, the Throat Chakra is not loud — it is luminous.
It does not argue — it resonates.
It is the poised stillness between inhale and exhale, where presence itself becomes communication.

Through Vishuddha, you learn that expression is not performance — it is devotion.
It is the courage to give voice to your inner truth and to listen deeply to the quiet hum of creation speaking back.
To express from this place is to participate consciously in the music of the universe — a harmony born of both sound and silence.

"I speak truth with love.
My words are light.
My silence is wisdom.
My voice serves the higher harmony."

When this chakra awakens, every act becomes communication — every vibration an offering.
Your voice becomes a vessel of peace, your presence a transmission of grace.
You begin to understand that divine creation continues not through noise, but through resonance — through the soul's alignment with the eternal word.

THROAT CHAKRA BENEDICTION: THE BLESSING OF SOUND

(Vishuddha – The Voice of the Divine)

May your voice be clear and kind,
flowing from the heart of truth.
May your words carry light where silence once hid pain,
and may your silence speak volumes of wisdom.

May you listen to the stillness between breaths
and find the voice of Spirit there.
May your sound uplift and your presence calm,
weaving harmony wherever you go.

May your throat remain open and pure —
a channel through which love may sing itself into the world.
May every tone you utter be born of peace,
and every silence you keep be held in trust.

May your communication become communion —
your speech a prayer, your listening a blessing.
May the air that moves through you carry truth,
and the ether around you remember your name in light.

When fear tempts you to silence,
may courage rise as song.
When anger seeks to speak,
may compassion find the words.

Let every syllable be sacred,
every conversation a chance to bring heaven to earth.

May your voice awaken the sleeping light in others,
reminding them that sound is the first language of the soul.

**"I am the voice of truth.
I am the breath of peace.
I am the vibration of divine clarity."**

Blessed be the Voice of Vishuddha —
the Song of Spirit that never ends.

THE SONG OF TRUTH: ENTERING THE THROAT CHAKRA

The chakra journey is not a climb to enlightenment — it is a conversation between Heaven and Earth.
Each breath of energy you take moves in both directions: love descending to be lived, and wisdom ascending to be shared.
At this point in your journey, you have already brought love deep into the body — you have grounded it (Root), felt it (Sacral), and empowered it (Solar Plexus).

Now, that same love begins to rise again — seeking voice, resonance, and communication.
The current shifts from *doing* to *expressing*, from *manifestation* to *meaning*.
This is the domain of the **Throat Chakra (Vishuddha)** — the sacred bridge where your inner world meets the outer world through vibration.

Here, creation begins to sing.
Energy that once burned as fire now refines into sound — the pure frequency of truth moving through air and ether.
Your words, breath, and presence become instruments of consciousness.

The Throat Chakra is not just about speech; it is about coherence — the alignment between thought, emotion, and will.
When these harmonize, sound becomes power.
When they fragment, speech loses its resonance.

Vishuddha teaches that expression is not about being heard; it is about being *true*.

THE VOICE OF THE SOUL

Through Vishuddha, your soul learns to communicate in its native language — vibration.
Every tone you emit, every silence you hold, carries the frequency of your consciousness.
When you speak from fear, words distort; when you speak from love, they heal.
When your voice flows from an open heart, communication becomes communion — a resonance that awakens understanding beyond words.

To speak your truth does not mean to insist or to prove.
It means to allow the divine sound within you to move freely — the song of authenticity unfiltered by fear or expectation.
This is how Spirit expresses itself through you.
The Throat is where love begins to echo back to the universe.

BEFORE YOU SPEAK

Before the voice awakens, the Heart must remember its stillness.
Pause here and breathe into your chest.
Feel the warmth of your Solar Plexus softening upward into the spaciousness of your throat.
Let the fire of will become the wind of truth — steady, flowing, and kind.

Affirm silently:
**"My voice serves love.
My words carry light.
My silence holds wisdom."**

You are not beginning a new journey — you are entering the next octave of the same song.

The energy that once rooted, flowed, and burned now begins to rise and resound.

Through Vishuddha, you learn that the purpose of power is expression, and the purpose of expression is connection.

As you move through the teachings of the Throat Chakra, may you remember that every sound, every word, every breath is sacred — a vibration shaping reality.

Love now speaks through you.

You are the voice of creation, remembering its source.

Bibliography

CLASSICAL & YOGIC SOURCES

• Feuerstein, Georg. *The Yoga Tradition: Its History, Literature, Philosophy, and Practice.* Hohm Press, 2001.
• Avalon, Arthur (Sir John Woodroffe). *The Serpent Power: The Secrets of Tantric and Shaktic Yoga.* Dover Publications, 1974.
• Swami Sivananda. *The Chakras.* Divine Life Society, 1994.
• Easwaran, Eknath (trans.). *The Upanishads.* Nilgiri Press, 2007.
• Vivekananda, Swami. *Raja Yoga.* Advaita Ashrama, 1896. (Foundational for understanding prana, will, and concentration — key aspects of Manipura energy.)
• Satyananda Saraswati, Swami. *Kundalini Tantra.* Bihar School of Yoga, 1984. (One of the most detailed modern explanations of chakra dynamics and pranic awakening.)
• Paramahansa Yogananda. *Autobiography of a Yogi.* Self-Realization Fellowship, 1946. (Classic narrative on inner power, pranic transformation, and divine will.)

CHAKRA & ENERGY HEALING WORKS

• Judith, Anodea. *Wheels of Life: A User's Guide to the Chakra System.* Llewellyn Publications, 1987.
• Myss, Caroline. *Anatomy of the Spirit.* Harmony Books, 1996.
• Brennan, Barbara Ann. *Hands of Light: A Guide to Healing Through the Human Energy Field.* Bantam, 1988.
• Sills, Franklyn. *Foundations in Craniosacral Biodynamics: The Breath of Life and Fundamental Skills.* North Atlantic Books, 2012.
• Leadbeater, C. W. *The Chakras.* Quest Books, 1972.

(Influential in shaping early Western models of chakra color and function.)
• Judith, Anodea. *Eastern Body, Western Mind: Psychology and the Chakra System as a Path to the Self.* Celestial Arts, 1996. (Bridges Manipura psychology — self-worth, ego, and transformation — with modern therapeutic insight.)

REIKI & SPIRITUAL HEALING

• Takata, Hawayo. *Reiki: Hawayo Takata's Story.* Reiki Alliance, 1998.
• Petter, Frank Arjava. *This Is Reiki: Transformation of Body, Mind and Soul from the Origins to the Practice.* Lotus Press, 2012.
• Rand, William Lee. *Reiki: The Healing Touch.* Vision Publications, 1991.
• **Santego, Constance.** *Reiki Wisdom Series.* Maximillian Enterprises, 2024–. (Especially relevant to energy harmonization and practitioner ethics.)
• Stein, Diane. *Essential Reiki.* Crossing Press, 1995. (Emphasizes personal empowerment and the ethical foundations of energy work.)

PSYCHOLOGY, PERSONAL POWER & SELF-TRANSFORMATION

• Assagioli, Roberto. *Psychosynthesis: A Manual of Principles and Techniques.* Hobbs, Dorman & Co., 1965. (Explores will and integration of personality — core Solar Plexus themes.)
• Jung, Carl G. *The Archetypes and the Collective Unconscious.* Princeton University Press, 1969.
• Csikszentmihalyi, Mihaly. *Flow: The Psychology of Optimal Experience.* Harper Perennial, 1990. (Modern psychological parallel to balanced Manipura energy.)
• Hillman, James. *The Soul's Code: In Search of Character and Calling.* Random House, 1996.
• Tolle, Eckhart. *A New Earth: Awakening to Your Life's*

Purpose. Penguin, 2005.
• Viktor Frankl. *Man's Search for Meaning.* Beacon Press, 1959. (The psychology of will and purpose under adversity — a profound Solar Plexus insight.)
• Borysenko, Joan. *Minding the Body, Mending the Mind.* Bantam, 1993. (Mind-body alignment through awareness and self-mastery.)

CROSS-CULTURAL & MYSTICAL REFERENCES

• Halevi, Z'ev ben Shimon. *Kabbalah: Tradition of Hidden Knowledge.* Thames & Hudson, 1991.
• Hanh, Thich Nhat. *Peace Is Every Step.* Bantam, 1992.
• Ibn Arabi. *Journey to the Lord of Power.* Inner Traditions, 1981.
• Underhill, Evelyn. *Mysticism: A Study in the Nature and Development of Spiritual Consciousness.* Dover Publications, 2002.
• Campbell, Joseph. *The Hero with a Thousand Faces.* Princeton University Press, 1949. (The archetypal journey of empowerment mirrors the Solar Plexus path of transformation.)
• Rumi, Jalal al-Din. *The Essential Rumi.* Trans. Coleman Barks. HarperOne, 1995. (Poetic voice of surrender and divine purpose.)
• Sri Aurobindo. *The Synthesis of Yoga.* Sri Aurobindo Ashram Press, 1999. (Integrates will, consciousness, and transformation — key Solar and Throat Chakra themes.)

MODERN SCIENCE & RESEARCH

• Pert, Candace B. *Molecules of Emotion: The Science Behind Mind-Body Medicine.* Scribner, 1997.
• Lipton, Bruce H. *The Biology of Belief.* Hay House, 2005.
• McCraty, Rollin, et al. *Science of the Heart: Exploring the Role of the Heart in Human Performance.* HeartMath Institute, 2015.
• Dispenza, Joe. *Becoming Supernatural: How Common People*

Are Doing the Uncommon. Hay House, 2017.
• Kauffman, Stuart. *At Home in the Universe: The Search for Laws of Self-Organization and Complexity.* Oxford University Press, 1995. (Explores transformation and self-organization — metaphors for Solar Plexus empowerment.)
• Pert, Candace & Chopra, Deepak. *Everything You Need to Know to Feel Go(o)d.* Hay House, 2006.
• Emoto, Masaru. *The Hidden Messages in Water.* Beyond Words, 2004. (Demonstrates vibrational resonance — relevant to Throat Chakra studies on sound and frequency.)

ADDITIONAL RESOURCES

• Eden, Donna. *Energy Medicine.* TarcherPerigee, 2008.
• Osho. *The Book of Secrets: 112 Meditations to Discover the Mystery Within.* St. Martin's Griffin, 1998.
• Chopra, Deepak. *Quantum Healing.* Bantam, 1989.
• Hay, Louise. *You Can Heal Your Life.* Hay House, 1984. (Affirmations and the psychosomatic link to the digestive system and self-worth.)
• Judith Blackstone. *Belonging Here: A Guide for the Spiritually Sensitive Person.* Sounds True, 2012.
• Sadhguru. *Inner Engineering: A Yogi's Guide to Joy.* Spiegel & Grau, 2016. (Practical approach to self-mastery and willful awareness.)
• Wilber, Ken. *The Spectrum of Consciousness.* Quest Books, 1977.
• Paramahansa Yogananda. *The Divine Romance.* Self-Realization Fellowship, 1944.
• Sivananda Radha, Swami. *Kundalini Yoga for the West.* Timeless Books, 1978.
• Sri Nisargadatta Maharaj. *I Am That.* Acorn Press, 1973. (Essential for understanding the pure consciousness that guides personal will and expression.)

Message From The Author

By the time you've reached this fifth book in the *Chakra 101 Series*, you've already awakened the foundations of your inner world.
You have opened the Heart — discovering the source of unconditional love and compassion.
You have grounded that love through the Root — creating safety and belonging in the world.
You have let it flow through the Sacral — expressing emotion, pleasure, and creativity.
You have ignited it within the Solar Plexus — transforming intention into confident action.

Now you arrive at the **Throat Chakra — the Voice of Truth and Expression.**
Here, energy becomes sound, and sound becomes creation.
This is the moment when love begins to speak, where purpose finds its voice, and where your inner light learns to resonate in the outer world.

The Throat Chakra invites you to refine the art of expression — to speak not from ego, but from essence.
It reminds you that words are not merely communication; they are vibration, carrying the power to heal or to harm, to connect or to divide.
When guided by the Heart, your voice becomes medicine.
When anchored in truth, it becomes liberation.

In this sacred space of Vishuddha, the soul remembers that silence can be as powerful as speech — that listening is a form of love, and that authentic expression is born from presence, not performance.

As you explore these teachings, may you learn to speak with integrity, listen with compassion, and express with courage. May your words align with your heart, your truth with your purpose, and your voice with the wisdom of Spirit moving through you.

And above all, may you remember that you are not finding your voice — you are remembering it.

With love, clarity, and resonance,
Dr. Constance Santego

About the Author

Dr. Constance Santego, Ph.D., DNM, is a bestselling author, teacher, and natural medicine doctor with over twenty-five years of experience in energy healing and holistic wellness. A Grand Reiki Master and founder of multiple wellness and educational programs, she has trained thousands of students worldwide in Reiki, holistic therapies, and intuitive development.

Her passion is to translate ancient wisdom into practical, modern tools for healing and self-discovery. Dr. Santego has authored more than forty books — including the *Reiki Wisdom* series, *Secrets of a Healer* guides, and the *Nine Spiritual Gifts*

novels — each uniting spirituality, science, and story to awaken the soul's potential.

Blending Eastern philosophy, Western natural medicine, and modern energy science, her teachings emphasize compassion, awareness, and self-empowerment as the foundation of all true healing.

Dr. Santego's mission is to help others connect with their inner wisdom, awaken their intuitive gifts, and live with balance, joy, and love. She lives in beautiful British Columbia, where the natural world continues to inspire her writing and her work as a lifelong student of Spirit.

ALSO AVAILABLE

For additional information on

Constance Santego's

wide range of Motivational Products, Coaching Sessions,
Spiritual Retreats,
Live Events and Educational Programs

Go to

www.ConstanceSantego.ca

Follow on Instagram - Constance_Santego and
Facebook - constancesantegoo

Subscribe and receive Free Information and Meditations on her
YouTube Channel - Constance Santego

Secrets of a Healer, Magic of Reiki

ISBN: 978-1-7772220-0-0

Secrets of a Healer, The Reiki Master's Manual

ISBN: 978-1-990062-34-6

www.ingramcontent.com/pod-product-compliance
Lightning Source LLC
Chambersburg PA
CBHW071702120626
46550CB00001B/80